D1733366

Dag Österberg

Metasociology

Dag Österberg

Metasociology
An Inquiry into the Origins and Validity of Social Thought

Norwegian
University Press

Norwegian University Press (Universitetsforlaget AS), 0608 Oslo 6
Distributed world-wide excluding Scandinavia by
Oxford University Press, Walton Street, Oxford OX2 6DP

London   New York   Toronto
Delhi   Bombay   Calcutta   Madras   Karachi
Kuala Lumpur   Singapore   Hong Kong Tokyo
Nairobi   Dar es Salaam   Cape Town
Melbourne   Auckland

and associated companies in
Beirut   Berlin   Ibadan   Mexico City   Nicosia

Published with a grant from the Norwegian Research Council for Science and the Humanities.

British Library Cataloguing in Publication Data

Österberg, Dag
    Metasociology: an inquiry into the origins and validity of social thought.
    1. Sociology, – Philosophical perspectives I. Title
    301'.01

    ISBN 82-00-02723-6
    ISBN 82-00-02722-8 Pbk

Printed in Denmark
by P.J.Schmidt A/S, Vojens

Contents

Introduction

1. The concern with the social

The importance of the *social* feature of human life, as distinct from the *political*, was asserted with increasing force from the end of the eighteenth century. The realm of social relationships was claimed to be a possible topic for a new branch of knowledge. Social thought was opposed to political thought, and the notion of Society to that of the State. This was the beginning of a specifically social science: It came as a riposte to doctrines relating to those power units which arose in the sixteenth and seventeenth centuries under the designation 'State'.

This thinking of and about the State had, in turn, two sharply distinct strands. The first was part and parcel of the State's endeavours to get control over those living on its territory. its 'subjects', and consisted in doctrines justifying absolute princely power, and in the use of 'statistics'. The aim of the second was to provide protection against the State's possible abuse of its power, to transform 'subjects' into 'citizens' by procuring for them some independence and some inalienable rights, a realm of freedom on which the State could not trespass, but had to respect and even guarantee. This is the Liberal doctrine of politics and market economics.

Social thought challenged both strands of thought, the justification and implementation of Absolute State power, and its Liberal opposition as well. The thinkers whose attention was caught by the social, groped for concepts to replace those of the State, the market and individual freedom. Bonald appears to be the first to have made a plea for a social science to fulfil this quest. He was followed by Comte, who coined the term 'sociology' and worked out the first sociological doctrine.

Sociology, in the sense here outlined, had from the very first a rival in the 'materialistic conception of history' introduced by Marx and Engels and developed by their followers. They regarded sociology disdainfully as a bourgeois enterprise designed to bolster the dominant social classes against Socialist and Communist movements. Nevertheless, both Sociology and the Marxian conception emerged to act as a substitute for, or at least as correction and supplement to, the prevailing statistico-politico-economic thinking.

To discuss these partly interlaced chains of thought and assess their validity is the main purpose of this book.

Clearly, speaking of the social as something neatly distinct from or even opposed to the State is against current usage. For in Western countries, it has come to be one of the State's main preoccupations to cope with what are called 'social problems', through the elaboration and carrying out of a 'social policy'. Above all, the 'social security system' consumes a considerable share of the State's resources. Moreover, in party politics the word 'social' denotes the will to increase the State's commitment to help solve 'social problems', as when Social Democrats are opposed to Liberal Democrats. But this widespread usage, conflating the State and the Social, is harmful in the present context. For the vernacular of everyday politics is the outcome of all sorts of compromises; it is not designed to understand essential differences, nor is it conducive to such understanding, and should be resisted for the purposes of this book.

Also, to designate by the term 'sociology' highly discrepant kinds of inquiries into human beings' mutual relationships, or to speak indifferently of 'sociology' and 'social research', while expedient for many administrative purposes, obfuscates the different realms of being and knowledge which the present work endeavours to describe.

2. Two essential conceptual distinctions
Throughout, the exposition will employ two conceptual distinctions which, even if by no means home-made, may be new to many readers, and therefore may with advantage be set forth and explained at once.

The *first* is that between *external and internal relations*. An external relation exists between two entities (things, objects, people, etc.) each of which remains the same irrespective of the other's existence. The constitution of the one does not entail any reference to that of the other. This means that their relation is *contingent* in the sense that it may or may not obtain, and that one cannot from the existence and knowledge of the one infer the existence of the other.[1] The external relation is accidental; it happens to be what it is.

Without doubt, the most famous proponent of the conception that all relations between existing things are external, was the young David Hume, with his interpretation of the causal bond. From the state of affairs at one point of time, he asserted, we can infer nothing about the state of affairs at the next. They are entirely independent of each other, and if we think or feel that the one engenders the other through a kind of necessity, this is just a habit we have acquired after having experienced that externally related events and sequences repeat themselves. The necessary or causal relation, he contended, is nothing but a repeated external relation.[2]

Hume was countered some one hundred and fifty years later by another English thinker, Francis Herbert Bradley, who, with great zeal and even vehemence, sustained that all relations in the world are internal, externality being mere appearance. This doctrine he had (as Russell said) 'distilled out of Hegel's system',[3] without for that reason being an unreserved follower, an Hegelian.

Two entities stand in an internal relation to each other if each of them is what it is through the other. We understand the one by seeing it in relation to the other and conversely. They refer mutually to each other and make a unity without being identical.

What we call a piece of art is a whole of internal relations; each part of it (each colour, tune, word, etc.) conveys meaning to and obtains meaning from the other parts. The same holds for all that is called 'organic'. The terms of the organic relations

1. 'In its broader philosophical usage a state of affairs is said to be contingent if it may and may not be. A certain event for example, is contingent if, and only if, it may come to pass and also may not come to pass' D. Runes (ed.) *Dictionary of Philosophy* p. 66 (1942)
2. Hume's *Treatise of Human Nature* (1734) and Sartre's *Nausea* (1936) resemble each other both as regards content and the circumstances of their production. They describe desperately the experience of contingency, and were written under conditions of isolation and solitude, in Northern France.
3. Bertrand Russell: *My Philosophical Development*, p. 54 (1959). Cf. A. Manser: *Bradley's Logic*, chap. 7 'Internal relations' (1983).

are altered essentially or even destroyed when detached from the whole to which they belong.

The organic whole is an expressive totality, each part expressing the sense of the whole and getting its meaning from the other parts.[4]

These two examples refer not to movement, but to states, to the perfect in the grammatical sense of what is done, finished. But processes, too, may consist of internally related events, where the present, past and future refer mutually to each other.[5]

To avoid the misinterpretation that processual internality just means a causal necessity, the instance of chord progression within Western major/minor music may be referred to: A chord progression is said to be logical if it follows certain rules, but this logic is different from that of causal necessity or mathematical deduction or mere analytical statements.

Kant takes an intermediate position in the struggle over externality and internality. What he called 'synthetic judgements *a posteriori*' are equivalent to statements about external relations, while 'synthetic judgements *a priori*' are about internally related entities or events. Among these Kant considered not only mathematical propositions, but also statements within his 'transcendental logic'. The transcendental deduction is expressly offered as a reasoning different from both the establishing of external relations, from the analytical statements, and from mathematics. The regularity of experience is internally related to the unity of the experiencing I (the synthetic unity of apperception).

By his doctrine of knowledge Kant strengthened the already current usage to speak indifferently of external relations and 'empirical relations', since to Kant, all assertions about what is purely empirical are synthetic *a priori*. But this usage is misleading and prejudges the questions about experience—*empeiria*. Especially, the expression 'empirical social research' signifies both a concern with the contingent and external, and a conviction that all knowledge of the social domain is perforce of this contingent kind. But one should be careful not to slide from the preoccupation with that which is contingent in social life to

4. The Romantic movement was generally concerned with internal relations, and their favourite topics (besides Love) were Art and Biology.
5. I have elaborated this thought in *Metasociological Essay* (1976).

the affirmation that all that is social can be described as external and contingent relations.

A vivid discussion about internal and external relations took place in England in the first decades of our century (as part of the young neo-Realists' challenge of neo-Idealism).

Moore,[6] in his habitual cautious way, confined himself to affirming that not all relations were internal, but at least some were of the external kind. He was followed by Russell[7] and others. The New Realists in the USA were more boisterous. In their manifesto, all relations were declared to be external. The old distinction almost fell into oblivion. However, in other quarters, the distinction between internal and external relations has been considered important all the time; for instance, it sustains the great works of Merleau-Ponty and Sartre, which appeared in the middle of the century. Recently, it has been taken up anew within an Anglo-Saxon context.[8]

The *second* distinction concerns *facticity* as opposed to *project* and *form*. The notions of facticity and project may be traced back to Fichte's *Doctrine of Science*, but in recent times they have been taken up by Heidegger and Sartre, and I shall follow the latter's interpretation.[9]

The human being's intentions, acts and, more generally, projects transcend everything that is given to his consciousness. But they are strictly conditioned by what is given. Every project is specific, a response to and a transcendence of specific data. Now these data are ineffable as such; they are experienced only through a project. Thus a rock reveals itself as steep if I try to surmount it, but as solid if used as a shelter. At the same time, it is not a product of my imagination; it is there as something other than my consciousness. This being-there is the facticity of the rock.

On the side of the projecting human being himself there is also facticity. Everything I intend or project is strictly conditioned by what I am—my past, my place, my language, my stature, my

---

6. G. E. Moore: *Philosophical Studies* (1922).
7. Russell: 'I could not make myself believe that knowledge changes what is known'. This made him break with the dialectic thinking he had been introduced to as a young man.
8. Cf. Bhaskar's new Naturalist thought.
9. Sartre: *Being and Nothingness* (1943).

capacities—and at the same time transcends everything that I am. What I am is my facticity. When I act I forget my facticity, but it is indicated to me in experiences such as nausea, or being worn out. For instance, when overworked I become aware of my brain as the facticity of my mental activity, or of my skeleton as that bodily facticity which is continually transcended as I move around. The facticity of my body indicates the non-human of the human being and reaches its extreme in the corpse.[10]

The (internal) relation between project and facticity may also be supplemented by that between facticity and (symbolic) form, in the vein of Cassirer.[11] Facticity then becomes that 'thing in itself', that unknown and unknowable which is given only in experience mediated by the forming activity of the human being. Thus, what is usually called culture is the designation of symbolic forms—the French culture, the Chinese culture, etc.--through which human beings experience the world, and the mediation of these forms is necessary for the world to be experienced at all. And corresponding to the nausea experience, there are the destructions of culture (by colonialism or otherwise) and the ensuing misery of perception, which is the opposite of finally having access to the world as it truly is. The opposite of cultural form is not nature, nor reality, but damaged form.

3. Structure of the book

The order of the exposition is chosen to bring out the oppositions between the various ways of conceiving inter-human relationships, and to show how these differing conceptions emerged historically as objections and rejoinders.

That is why the first chapter outlines the emergence of the State and the science of statistics in the seventeenth century as a point of departure. Statistics in the form of moral statistics, social statistics, etc. has always had a strong affinity to public administration, and so have the main forms of Social research or Sociography which evolved somewhat later. The purpose of the chapter is twofold: First it intends to show that Social statistics and Sociography express and apply a specific mode of thinking, specific concepts and relations between concepts.[12]

10. For this reason, Sartre designates fatigue as inhuman. Cf. Chapter 8.
11. Cassirer: *Philosophie der symbolischen Formen* (1921–27).
12. In fashionable terms, one might say they delimit or constitute a specific 'paradigm' or 'problematic', as described by Kuhn and Althusser.

Next, it intends to describe the limitations of their mode of thinking, and how it explicitly or tacitly presupposes and indicates other modes of conceiving human relationships, especially Sociology as the science of the social as such.

The next two chapters (which purely for the sake of convenience are not combined into one large one) deal with Liberal thought as another specifically distinct way of conceiving human beings and their inter-relationships based on the notion of the single human being—the individual and his freedom, that is, his capacity to act in the world, to carry out his own intentions and mould his own conditions of living.[13]

The individual's activities are considered in two respects, with respect to the State, and with respect to the Market, that is, politically and economically.

Chapter 2 presents in its first section the basic tenets of Liberal politics and law, understood as a desirable framework for the living together of free human beings. After this presentation essential ripostes to this political thought are restated in a second section: serious objections which were raised long ago, and—as in the case of Social statistics—point out the shortcoming of this mode of thinking, and how it should be substituted or supplemented by another mode of thinking concerned with the *social* level of human existence.

Chapter 3 expounds the corresponding assumptions which underly Liberal economics, as a desirable order of economic life, permitting free exchange between free human beings. And just as in the preceding chapter, the presentation is followed by a restatement of the essential objections levelled against this mode of thought, objections which make it apparent that Liberal economics is either false, or, at the very least, cannot stand alone.

But since a shift in Liberal economics took place a century ago, leading to the conventional distinction between 'classical' and 'neo-classical' doctrines, Chapter 3 is tripartite: the first section describes classical, the second neo-classical Liberal economics, while the third section contains the ripostes, old and new, to these doctrines.

---

13. The human being is conceived of, not as an 'object' or 'passive subject', but as an 'active subject', an 'agent'.

In Chapter 4, it is time to expound Sociology as the one great riposte to both Social statistics and Liberal thought. This doctrine of social integration in the strict sense got its rudiments through the work of Comte, and has been elaborated in manifold ways since then. The main conceptions are interpreted, including the synthetic efforts of Sorokin and Parsons; two great examples are recalled, and, lastly, the fears and hopes attached to sociological thought as strict doctrines of social integration.

Chapter 5 gives an account of another great response and rejoinder to Liberal thought, the historical, dialectical teachings inaugurated by Marx and Engels and widely known as 'historical materialism'. The chapter has two parts. The first attempts a succinct rendering of Marx's and Engels' contributions, where pains are taken to show a point-to-point opposition between their assertions and those of Liberal politics and economics. The second part surveys some salient contributions to renew and amplify the original conceptions of Marx and Engels, as an up-to-date interpretation of history in this century, at least in the Western hemisphere. As a whole, this chapter endeavours to make clear in which sense this kind of historico-dialectical thought poses as a specific, distinct riposte to Liberal thought.

The three first chapters constitute one whole, with an internal opposition; the next two also belong together in the sense that the doctrines set forth in both were provoked by the existence and prevalence of Statistics and Liberal thought.

Chapter 6 considers some attempts to encompass the distinct and mutually opposed conceptions dealt with in the foregoing chapters.

Chapter 7 contains a general discussion of the claims to validity of Social statistics and Sociography, of Liberal politics and economics, of Sociology and Historico-dialectical thought, and of the synthetic attempts.

*

These chapters constitute the essential bulk of the book. However, there exists some impressive work on human inter-relationships which cannot be discussed appropriately within the conceptual framework of the topics referred to above. The work in question partly challenges it overtly, partly tacitly implies a break. For this reason, the first seven chapters are presented as Part One, followed by a second, smaller part, consisting of four chapters.

The title *Metasociology* should, therefore, be understood in the double sense of the word *meta*; it refers both to a reflection *on* sociology, and to ways of thought that have arisen *after* it.

Whether or not the work should be read as a small contribution to the 'history of ideas' depends on what one means by that expression. It may be so understood if that does not exclude the intention to discuss the ontological and epistemological validity of the 'ideas' presented; for my concern is first and foremost ontico-epistemological. If books published long ago are referred to and cited, that is as a rule because they set forth the first and usually unsurpassed statement of the conceptions at stake. Nor should use of the expression 'history of ideas' imply the conviction that 'ideas' are not 'real', or externally related to 'reality', or kindred conceptions.

*

While Part Two mostly surveys recent contributions, some of them from the last decade, Part One contains what I should have wished to have found in a book when I came to sociology thirty years ago. In fact, that book might have existed, since the main thoughts expounded in Part One were by then already expressed, if not by one single author. Later, many books anticipate to some extent and degree, but not so much and so clearly that I could have spared myself the work of writing.

Part One

1

Social Statistics and Social Research (Sociography)

A. Social Statistics

1. The origin of statistics

The mode of thinking long designated by the name 'statistics' emerged in the seventeenth century, and dealt with the concerns of the States and their statesmen, such as the number of inhabitants living on each State's territory. Thus, Petty's *Political Aritmetick* discussed the magnitude of London and Paris, trying to demonstrate that the former was the more populous. When, therefore, the proponents of 'political arithmetics' took over the term 'statistics' from the German school of Conring and his follower Achenwall (who used it synonymously with *Staatswissenschaft*), they had good reasons for doing so. For the questions they raised and attempted to answer were closely connected to and part of the formation of that power concentration which we call the (absolutist) State.[1] The State exerts authority and other forms of power over its subjects, and is for several reasons eager to gain insight into their number and living conditions. The subjects, for their part, sometimes feared that such insight might be used to their disadvantage, and were reluctant to be shown up by the State. In a general way, the State sought to transform the more or less amorphous and diffuse clusterings of people into a 'population', that is an aggregate of distinct citizens, 'individuals', and to collect and store knowledge about them in registers and archives. As Foucault pointed out in his excellent exposition,[2] the State's 'statistical' activities did not merely aim at a description of properties and objects (subjects)

---

1. For instance, the statesman John de Witt, the friend of Spinoza, was concerned with 'social mathematics'.
2. *Surveiller et punir* (1975).

already given, but contributed to their very making. Character-istically, the police was originally a most important collector and producer of statistical facts. The State fabricated its individuals through a series of controlling measures to which Foucault, here following Max Weber,[3] gives the general name 'discipline'. Thus the disciplinary individual is subject to, the subject-matter of, and the product of statistical descriptions.[4]

The new construction of cities was another way of making the inhabitants less recalcitrant to being controlled and sur-veyed. The muddle of the feudal city with its nooks and corners was replaced by the order of straight lines and squares. The same holds for the construction of houses. They became easier to survey. Thus the architectural conditions for treating inhabi-tants as discrete entities were improved.

Statistics, then, was not just a new way of acquiring knowl-edge about a human multitude, but also part of an endeavour to constitute a specific kind of human multitude, one which had not existed before (save in monasteries and similar select circles). The rise of statistics was both an epistemological and an onto-logical (or at least an ontic) event, since its object (or subject-matter) was both discovered and produced.

2. The extension of statistical thinking

As time went on, statistics came to be conceived of, not as the understanding of this specific region of being, but as a mode of understanding valid beyond the realm of the State. It was ap-plied to topics within agriculture, meteorology and other physi-cal domains. This extension finally made statistics a branch of mathematics, that is a *mathesis*, a way of thinking with no particular subject-matter, and for that reason called a *formal* science. Statistics was divided into descriptive and inductive, and derived from more basic mathematical structures. Descrip-tive statistics is now seen as founded upon general measure theory, while inductive statistics rests on the probability calcu-lus, which in turn has been given an axiomatic treatment and derived from still more general mathematical propositions.

3. 'Thus, discipline inexorably takes over ever larger areas as the satisfaction of political and economic needs are increasingly rationalized.' Weber: *Economy and Society* (1924).
4. For further details see Chapter 9, the section on Foucault.

As the word 'statistics' had now acquired a new meaning, one had to speak of 'population statistics', 'moral statistics', 'social statistics', etc. when the topic dealt with was relations between human beings.

3. General features of statistics

Statistical relations are external relations. The introductory books are fond of pointing out how the facts dealt with are given as a flickering multitude, which is subsequently brought into order through the concepts and operations of statistics. The presupposition is that everything is contingent, that is, may well have been otherwise. Thus, a given rate of child mortality happens to be low, or the correlation between income and political voting happens to be strong, or the interest in sporting competitions happens to be uneven in the different social strata and so on. Whether there are any members at all in a defined set is a matter of contingent fact. A man happens to be member of the set A, and also of B and C, while another man happens to be member of A, B and D, and this similarity and difference are once more contingent.

Descriptive statistics is the science of describing the distribution of externally related units (items) relative to some property or properties, by measures of dispersion and centrality. Inductive statistics is the science of inferrring from the properties of a sample to the universe from which the sample is drawn, an inference stated with a numerical probability.

The language of statistics offers more precise and refined accounts than ordinary language in many cases. Its importance to the study of mankind—anthropology in the widest sense— seems beyond doubt. But social statistics does not encompass the whole realm of human relationships. An unlimited application of statistics to relationships between human beings will in many cases entail a distortion. To show this some essential examples will be discussed.

4. Statistics and the organic or organized individual

If we think of a multitude of human beings as united by a common task so as to form a group or organization, then we are outside the proper domain of descriptive statistics. For we cannot without distortion represent the individual member of such a group as an element of a set, with external relations to the others. For each member is internally related to the others and the group as a whole, since his or her actions, thoughts and feelings are constituted by their reference to those of the others. If one single member of the organization is asked by an outsider to declare his (or her) attitude to a question vital to the organization, the answer may be: 'I cannot say anything before I have discussed the matter with the others, since my own opinion depends upon the others', that is, upon what we as a community are capable of and want to do. As organized individuals we do not have our own attitude. Of course, the organized individual may also reply: 'Well, as for my part ...' But this merely shows that to ask an organized individual about his (her) own attitude is to confront him with the choice of remaining a full member or not. This is why statistical public opinion polls and surveys are ambiguous, as many writers have pointed out. The opinions collected are taken out of their context and given a new one. If the former context was one of compulsory silence or collectivity, the statistical inquiry may have a liberating effect. But if the context is one of organization, it may act, even if slightly, in a disorganizing way.

5. Correlation analysis and socio-cultural synthesis

To be intelligible, statistical interpretations of human relationships overtly or tacitly presuppose a different understanding.

As an example of this I choose one of Blalock's investigations, which he presents in his *Social Statistics* as a piece of 'partial correlation', that is, calculation of the interrelation between three entities or 'variables'. The topic is racial discrimination in the USA, and its relation to the degree of urbanization and the percentage of negroes in the various areas. On the basis of previous experience Blalock assumes (1) that the greater the percentage of negroes in the area, the more discrimination against them, and (2) the more urbanized the area is, the lesser the percentage of negroes in the area. This implies that if there is less racial discrimination in urbanized areas, this may be because they have relatively fewer negroes. To find out whether this is the case may seem impossible, since one cannot give all districts, urban and rural, the same percentage of negroes and thus keep this 'factor' constant. But partial correlation can give a good approximation:[5] The residuals of the two regression equations are correlated. Applying this device, Blalock finds that racial discrimination—taken as 'economic discrimination'—is negatively correlated with the degree of urbanization and positively correlated with the percentage of negroes in the area.

Even if this may be impeccable as statistics, it appeals tacitly to an understanding of human relations that is not itself statistical and contingent. The notion of discrimination obtains its significance within a socio-cultural context prescribing that human beings be dealt with according to *universal* criteria. Now, industrialization is a process requiring and expressing the use of universal criteria, as Marx, Weber and many others have shown. (For instance, in a society based upon wage labour, the citizens must be equal before the law.) Urbanization, as the word is used in the West, in its turn has connotations of industrialization, since most cities in the West are industrial centres. Therefore, the notion of urbanization involves that of norms prescribing universal criteria, and Blalock's findings accord well with this conceptual connection. This is not to say that Blalock's investigation merely documented what we might have known beforehand *(a priori)*. On the contrary, his findings could have been the opposite. But then they would have been most upsetting, provoking us to rethink our notion of and experience with urbanization. His research would have been epoch-making in the strict sense of forcing us to suspend (perform an *époché* regarding) our notion of urbanity. Clearly, it rather confirmed our previous understanding. However, the essential thing is that what makes research of this kind intelligible is some structure[6] of internally related notions such as those of universality, industrialization, urbanization—a cultural form. Without doubt, Blalock's research springs from his commitment towards norms prescribing universal criteria, and more generally, towards a specific socio-cultural structure, which is made of internally related notions. This internality does not imply logical necessity,

5. Blalock is careful to point out that partial correlation is not a strictly valid ('scientific') procedure since 'in a sense we pretend that the control variables are kept constant' while in reality they are not.
6. Such a structure is termed 'connexion of meaning', *Sinnzusammenhang*, by Rickert and Weber.

but nor is it reducible to mere externality. It is the tension between internal and external relations, between what Sorokin termed the 'logico-meaningful' wholes and the contingent 'congeries' of data that make Blalock's investigation meaningful. To discriminate is to deviate from a socio-cultural norm, and this deviance is what makes the statistical measures of deviance meaningful.

Correlations of this kind therefore refer to another mode of understanding and a corresponding other realm of human relationships—to 'sociology' as the science of social (or socio-cultural) integration—as its presupposition or complement.

The causal concept of statistics, it seems, is moulded on (classical) mechanics or statistics, which conceives of all forces acting independently of each other, as, for instance, in the construction of a parallelogram of forces. But even if such ingenious causal reasoning is suitable in one realm of the social, it is apt to divert the attention from another realm where it would distort or misinterpret the relationships.

Consider the impact of acquiring a car on the buyer's situation. Through the devices of statistico-causal reasoning one can compute how much the aquisition alters the former pedestrian's expected life span, his (her) chances of getting a heart disease, or augmenting his income, the time spent on transport and so on. The (nominal) variable 'means of transport' is given (say) the two values 'own car' and 'walking or collective transport', and the impact of scoring on the one or the other can be assessed by causal thinking.

But this reasoning does not exhaust the experience of buying a car. For becoming a car-driver changes the quality of nearly everything in my situation. It does not simply enable me to travel faster from one place to another (under favourable conditions). Driving means *not* taking the bus or walking; it means polluting the air; it involves worries about parking facilities; it signifies spending every fourth or fifth crown or dollar on car expenses; it signifies increased abstract possibilities of locomotion (I can suddenly set out for a journey in the night) and so on. In short, the cultural form of car-driving is different from that of not having a car at one's disposal.

One might say, that these two descriptions of car-driving are not at all incompatible, and therefore the difficulty does not exist. But it does exist in so far as we are led to consider our own situation not as analogous to a chemical synthesis, but to a mechanical parallelogram of forces. The causal-statistical reasoning must always be integrated into a synthetic conception, just as all facticity is to be transcended by a project. The 'facts' about automobilism will never in themselves make anybody convert to or refrain from car-driving. The significance of this activity within one's whole situation as cultural form will be decisive.

6. Numerical and non-numerical sociality

To count human beings is not always adequate. This insight was present already in the Bronze age, as testified by the legend of King David. Because he ordered his captain Joab to carry out a census, he was severely punished by Jehova's judgment.[7]

The statisticians Yule and Kendall wondered (with slight irony) why David was punished when he counted the living, but not when he counted the dead (on the battle-field).[8] However, the reason is easy to discern. David, as it were, overlooked the distinction between project and facticity on the one hand, and brute facts on the other. Human corpses can be counted like other objects. But as long as a human group is alive and active, it strictly speaking does not have any definite number, but is non-numerical.

When a group is about to enter a lift, it must sometimes take into consideration the number of individual bodies and their weight. This feature of a human group is non-human, since it cannot be transcended by the group's project. It is extreme facticity, bordering upon mere fact. Or one may put it differently, and say that this situation is bordering on the non-situational. Precisely because the group cannot act as a group

7. Second Book of Samuel, chap. 24.
8. Yule & Kendall: *An Introduction to the Theory of Statistics* (1937). In the novel *Dr. Faustus* (1946), Thomas Mann lets the ultra-conservative Dr. Breisacher interpret the story as follows: 'David, indeed, was quite as ignorant of origins and quite as besotted, not to say, brutalized, as Solomon his son. He was too ignorant, for instance, to realize the dynamic dangers of a general census of the population; and by instituting one had brought about a serious biological misfortune, an epidemic with high mortality; a reaction of the metaphysical powers of the people, which might have been foreseen. For a genuine folk simply could not stand such a mechanizing registration, the dissolution by enumeration of the dynamic whole into similar individuals ...' (chap. 28).

while being transported in the lift, its number and weight imposes itself on the group's attention.[9]

But these are marginal situations, where the non-human predominate over the human aspects. In the vast majority of situations, it is the other way around: the facts are transcended by the projects, and this is experienced as a facticity which is essentially indeterminate and ambiguous.

To present an important case, the mode of existence of social classes can only partly be rendered by descriptive statistics, since a social class is both a facticity and a project. In its facticity aspects, a class is constituted by a certain number of people having similar characteristics and properties (position in the process of production etc.), organization buildings, newspapers and other mass-media, archives and other structures of *matériel*. But a social class is never merely this inertial aggregate of people, since every class is involved in conflicts and alliances with other social classes, and to that extent determined by its activity. True, a social class is scarcely ever an entirely integrated whole; it perpetually fights against its tendency to fall apart and become sheer facticity. But most often, it is a totality in movement, interpreting the environment and itself in the light of its, often contradictory and vague, prospects of the future. In so far as it is an acting totality, a social class does not have a determinate number of members or adherents. This is why so many statistical investigations of the class structure of our society throw so little light upon the actual economico-political class conflicts that do go on.[10]

Generally speaking, every action group transcends its number through its activity. But when its activity fails or stops short, the group members notice their number. Some of the disgust many people feel toward social statistics may have the same significance as the nausea many feel at the sight of blood: in both cases facticity as such is laid bare, facticity untranscended by any project or cultural form. Numerical descriptions of human beings therefore refer to a different interpretation—a

9. The same goes, *mutatis mutandis*, for the calculation of the necessary minimum of calories required by human beings to sustain life under conditions of starvation.
10. See chapter 5 for further comments on social classes.

'theory of (social) action'—as their presupposition or complement.

7. Probability and sociality

Inductive statistics is based upon the calculus of probability. The question must therefore be raised whether there are limitations to the application of probability concepts to social interaction and social relationships. The discussion presupposes that a description in terms of probability is more precise than other descriptions when it is valid: It makes the described better understood, but does not alter it essentially.

Let us first consider a case where a probability approach seems appropriate; security on the streets of big cities. Here it may be asked whether it is dangerous for the elderly to walk alone, and to this question one may want an answer that specifies the numerical probability that an elderly person will be harmed. The situation referred to is an anonymous one, the pedestrians are strangers to each other, and their relations, consequently, fortuitous and contingent.

The contrary social situation is that of mutual trust, and of sharing a common world. Here the notion of probability will not make the situation more precise, but will transform it into a different kind (perform a *metabasis eis allo genos*). Thus, a relation of friendship will cease when the two friends begin to reckon with the probability of each other's behaviour. For friendship is a relationship in which two human beings experience the world in the same way; the other is like myself in some very important respects, and I trust the other.[11] Especially those trained in inductive statistics may take this to mean that trust is the limit of increasing certainty or security (in parallel to the conception that truth is the limit of increased probability). But such an interpretation would be erroneous. The probable and the certain are both modes in which an object may be given, and this means that the object is presupposed as given in what Husserl called 'originary experience'. Thus, the Other may be experienced as probably my friend or as certainly my friend, in both cases an understanding of what friendship is, is presup-

11. Cf. C. S. Lewis on friendship in *The Four Loves* (1960).

posed. More generally, trust in the fundamental sense is not constituted by probability.

To take a still wider perspective, the very thought that other people probably experience the world in much the same way as myself involves a distance or distancing which may border on the terrifying if this probability is estimated as very small. For the thought of being completely alone in the world among strangers each of whom is also alone, is deeply horrifying. (Hell is sometimes interpreted as total exclusion or solitude).

The world is mostly given to us as a shared world, an experience the truth of which we may be more or less certain of. But to interpret this sharing with the others in terms of probability is to alter and distort the sharing experience.

In a similar way, a moral expectation cannot be identified as a mathematical expectation. Nelson's famous *dictum* 'England expects every man to do his duty' does not simply mean that the nation or the government puts the probability high that every man is going to do his duty. A moral attitude is invoked, appeal is made to authority, and this constitutes the situation as solemn. Through this 'performative utterance' Nelson endeavours to integrate the mariners into a larger social whole, and make the pending battle an experience shared with millions of English men and women, past as well as present. To interpret his saying as a probability statement may very well signify an attempt to reduce it to derision.

Conversely, many situations are constituted by the mostly tacit agreement of the participants to consider them as determined by sheer luck or equiprobability.[12] Assignment of tasks through allotment is one of many examples, or throwing dice. Here to insist on a more accurate calculation of the probability means to misunderstand the social situation, or trying to change it deliberately.[13]

8. Weber's probabilistic concepts of social interaction

To Weber, social life is essentially dependent on chance, and his basic sociological concepts are entirely couched in terms of

12. Cf. Vilhelm Aubert: *The Hidden Society* (1966), chap. 5, 'Change in social affairs', where an array of examples is discussed.
13. Keynes asserted that not all probabilities could be assigned a number, a conception which has received very little attention on the part of social statisticians.

probability. The social relationship, he states firmly, 'consists entirely and exclusively in the existence of a chance that there will be, in some meaningfully understandable sense, a course of social action.'[14]

This definition is meant as a demarcation in relation to a 'substantialist' conception, according to which such entities as a church or a State exist as such and by virtue of some kind of necessity (as 'ideal', 'eternal truth' or the like). To ensure that his opposition is clearly perceived, Weber repeatedly asserts that any State exists on the mode of probability, and so do intimate relationships such as friendships.[15] Also, the well-known definitions of power and domination are framed in terms of chance.

In the light of the above discussion it is clear that Weber's procedure is wrong and leads to a picture of social life where the reckoning with the probabilities of Other's actions and activities constitutes the relationship between human beings. Now there is apparently one way to defend Weber's position—to admit that the participants in the social relationship do not themselves experience it solely in terms of the chance-like, but that the observing sociologist should do so. But this will imply an untenable distinction between the point of view of the participant and that of the observer, one which I think was definitely refuted by Winch,[16] who took Weber to task precisely on this point.

Weber's account, while erroneous as a general description, is valid for a more restricted domain, i.e. that of mutual *indifference*. In the mode of indifference other human beings may appear to me as objects whose activities may be more or less probable, useful or harmful. This comes out in a forceful passage of an earlier work in which Weber attacked Knies' contention that human beings are free and for this reason not subject to scientific laws in the way nature is. Against this, Weber affirmed that a military man calculates on soldiers' obedience in a way that differs not in the least from the probabilist calcu-

14. Weber: *Op.cit.,* Basic concepts.
15. 'Thus that a "friendship" or a "state" exists or has existed means this and only this: that we, the observers, judge that there is or has been a probability that on the basis of certain kinds of known subjective attitude of certain individuals there will result in the average sense a specific type of action'. *Ibid.*
16. Peter Winch: The *Idea of a Social Science* (1958), p. 24.

lations of a bridge-builder or an agriculturist. In all three cases, he contends, one is satisfied with probable knowledge and probable outcomes.[17]

Anyone who has refused to obey a military order may have experienced a tension that goes far beyond the failing of probabilities. Much more is at stake, both on the soldier's and the officer's side. The situation may become grave if the refusal is seen as a challenge to the whole structure of legitimate power, or even of national solidarity. There is a 'shaking of the foundations', a questioning of one's identity, which is the opposite of indifference. True, an indifferent attitude is also possible, for instance on the part of an officer who has experienced such recalcitrant behaviour several times before. He may say to himself: 'Well, here is another troublesome young man; that was only to be expected, since the recruits have all toed the line for a long time now.' Likewise, the disobedient soldier may reassure himself by trying to adopt a probabilist attitude: 'After all, it is not the first time in history this has happened; the military are surely used to such aberrations from time to time.' When such an indifferent attitude is carried to the extreme, it is called cynicism. The whole general sociology of Weber is kept in a cynical tone, mostly due to this probabilist approach, but also due to the frequent recourse to the 'as if' clause. But the probable and the apparent both refer to something not probable and apparent, but originally given and real.

This means, once more, that social statistics presupposes other modes of understanding human relationships.

9. *Probability and novelty*
Probability is conceptually related to repetition. An event is more or less probable if it is more or less likely to happen again. One may object that we also foretell with greater or less probability events that, if actually occurring, will do so for the first time. But such events can always be reduced to (combinations or variations of) past events. The probability calculus assumes, therefore, that the future will be basically the same as the past and the present.

17. Weber: 'Roscher und Knies und die logischen Probleme der historischen Nationalökonomie', in *Gesammelte Aufsätze zur Wissenschaftslehre,* p. 64.

However, essentially new events take place continuously in our world, that is, events the novelty of which defies prediction by virtue of the probability calculus. These are events that were inconceivable before they happened, and that require a transcendence of our conceptions in order to be understood. Bergson is the thinker who in a lucid and forceful way showed the importance of the irreducible new as a property of the world.[18]

Such novelty may also be described by making a distinction between determinate and indeterminate possibility. The determinate possible event is one that has already happened and which can therefore happen again. Probability calculus deals with such possibles. The indeterminate possible, on the other hand, is a possible of which we can at most have images or phantasies which strictly speaking are impossible in terms of the concepts through which we now understand the world. But experience and the past have taught us that what is impossible in the sense of inconceivable today, may be actuality later through a transcendence (a 'revolution') of our concepts. Experience, in other words, has taught us that there is an indeterminate possibility of something irreducibly and hitherto inconceivably new arriving.[19]

This structure of irreducible, transcending novelty constitutes the *historic* or historicity in the strict sense. Hegel's *Phenomenology of Spirit* narrates such a history, a succession of figures or conceptions, each of which is new in relation to the foregoing. It is dialectic, since each figure emerges only as the outcome of the Spirit's internal struggles. Non-dialectical conceptions there are, but the dialectical seems to be more important.

Anyway, novelty and historicity mark the limitation of inductive probability thought within the domain of relationships between human beings.

10. Concluding remarks
As a region of being, the domain of human relationships partly displays external relations to be understood by the (epistemo-

---

18. For further discussion of the new and the repetitious, cf. my *Metasociological Essay,* chap. 3.
19. I first elaborated this distinction more than 20 years ago, in *Forståelsesformer* (Forms of understanding), a work not translated outside Scandinavia.

logical) mode of understanding called statistics; partly internal relations to be understood by modes of understanding such as 'sociology' and historico-dialectical conceptions, Liberal politics and economics, to be dealt with in ensuing chapters.

B. Social Research (Sociography)

1. Social research and State administration

Administration has been the paramount form of domination since the rise of the (Absolutist) State some hundred years ago, and is intertwined with the use of statistics. At the beginning of this century Max Weber described how it works, and his description is still valid in its main points: 'bureaucracy' works through written rules and regulations, through appointments according to examination certificates and other attested merits, and through promotion by seniority; decisions are made on the basis of documents and archives; the whole process should be anonymous and impersonal, and the bureaucrat himself should behave *sine ira et studio*, the bent of mind being impartial, neutral, and detached. The corrections of this general picture undertaken by March & Simon bear mainly on the alleged 'rationality' of the bureaucratic machine: The optimal decisions searched for by the 'rational' bureaucrat should rather be described as decisions which are satisfying, given the inherent 'limited rationality' of every decision-maker. But regardless of whether total or limited rationality is pursued, administrative decisions need a certain kind of data as a support, which are provided through committee reports and similar investigations. These data must be such as to be recognized as data by competent people – whether they are experts with an authority accepted by the administrative apparatus, or ordinary citizens endowed with common sense and 'normality', that is, a capacity for judgment which is at least average. In particular, facts are such statements as participants in a conflict must accept as true, whether these statements weaken or strengthen their own case. These facts are said to be 'inter-subjectively' or 'objectively' true.

It follows that the administrative appeal to the facts is circular, since only objections from respectable people will be respected: Administrative decisions are based on administrative facts, that is, statements to which the administrative apparatus grants the status of facts. Nevertheless, the legitimation by appeal to facts clearly marks off administration from more arbitrary, harsh forms of domination, since the reference group is largely extended to include the normal, well-informed member of society.

The facts which support and are produced by administrative processes are marked or constituted by a certain conformity or even conformism (i.e. compulsive conformity with norms and expectations).[20]

Administrative discourse (or rhetoric) will apply concepts and formulas with which the administrators and their reference group are familiar, and avoid those words and expressions which will interrupt the tacit consensus of the administrative context. Thus, the language of administration, especially political administration, is strongly marked by compromises. The skilful administrator knows how to describe a given case or situation in a way that blurs conflicts, and tacitly invites the conflicting parties to accept a compromising exposition, and, next, a decision that amounts to a compromise. The allegedly neutral discourse is one that calls on the conflicting parties to settle on a compromise. Thus, instead of social classes, one speaks of social groups being more or less under-privileged, to avoid every controversial formulation. But even this vague term can only be accepted by those who endorse political opinions which are 'central' and shared by the political mass parties. The place of administrative discourse is the common place, the *trivium;* the triviality of its reports is both a consequence and a guarantee of its respectability. This does not exclude 'sensational' and 'shocking' administrative reports, since these may very well presuppose an understanding of the social world which is based on, expresses, and reinforces conformity with prevalent values and norms.

That social facts are constituted by reference to a mostly tacit agreement among those concerned is shown by the following conflict: Two social researchers published a book on police violence in Norway, reporting that a host of citizens had claimed

---

20. The notion of compulsive conformity comes from Parsons' interpretation of deviance and conflict, cf. chapter 4.

to have suffered bodily injury at the hands of the police. When some of those who had complained had to confront the police, they withdrew their testimonies on the violence suffered. But then the social researchers pointed out that data collected during social research are not supposed to stand the test of police inquiry or a court.

Parts of social research have emerged at the request of the administrative apparatus, demanding (more) data to underpin its decisions. The questions asked, the concepts and conceptions expressed, will therefore be those of the administration. It will be research *ad hoc*, that is an attempt to provide more data about some issue or domain which, from a general point of view, is arbitrarily delimited. Administration is never concerned with the understanding of the whole, but with segments of the social field. Administrative social research will therefore strongly tend to be segmental, piecemeal, and contribute very little if anything to the formation of a general knowledge of the social: It will not cumulate, since the research tasks as a rule have no connection with each other. It is not likely to contribute to social science, in the traditional sense of universal and coherent knowledge, neither is it in most cases intended to do so.

The term *sociography*—coined by Tönnies, and Jahoda, Lazarsfeld & Zeisel, apparently independently of each other[21]—may with advantage be reintroduced, in order to designate social research that neither does nor pretends to go beyond description of social life couched in administrative or common sense language. *Sociography* would then stand for different activities or writings than, for instance, *sociology*, even if there would be no clear line of demarcation between the two.

2. Social research and the Realist movement

The Realist movement in science, art and philosophy reacted against the Romantics' *Schwärmerei*, their depicting of the world as it ought to be or possibly might have been—permeated by love, and, consequently, a beautiful totality, where all that is petty, dull, unpleasant or bad is endowed with significance

21. Cf. Tönnies: *Einleitung in die Soziologie* (1932), and Jahoda, Lazarsfeld & Zeisel: *Die Arbeitslosen von Marienbad*, Soziographie einer unbeschäftigen Gemeinde (1933) and the Afterword by Hans Zeisel: *Zur Geschichte der Soziographie* (Towards a history of Sociography).

by virtue, so to speak, of the totality thus conquered. The Romantics give idealized descriptions of things and people, not as they are in their brute giveness, but as vehicles of ideality. For instance, Goethe remarked that his knowledge of women stemmed from his inner image of them, his *Urbild*, not from those he had actually met in his life. This image or *Urbild* is the 'ideal womanhood', the eternally feminine (*ewig-weibliche*). In a similar way, his science of biological forms, the Morphology, springs from his intuition of 'ideals' such as the originary plant, *die Urpflanze*. Generally, nature is conceived of as a totality which expresses its meaning in innumerable ways, shading from the latent, dormant to the manifest. Even anorganic matter is thought of as animated, and thus endowed with a certain 'form' or 'ideality'. The Romantic conception of nature opposed that of the Rationalists and Rational mechanics of the eighteenth century, asserting that Love, not domination of nature is the proper attitude. The elf, the fairy should be accepted as natural entities, the Romantics contend, while the Realists consider them just to be creations of unreal imagination and phantasy. But the 'phantastic' is important to the Romantic, since phantasy is understood as a source of knowledge of its own. As a consequence, social life is understood as something great and heroic, like the masterpieces of dramatic art. And society is seen as a totality, based on a unity of the hearts, a *concordia*.[22]

To the Realists, ideality properly belongs to the domain of the imaginary, and the Romantics' error is to confound the real and the imaginary. In science, the reaction to this alleged error mainly takes the form of an appeal to what is given, to experiment and sense observation; in art it manifests itself as the intention to substitute for the idealistic presentation the harsh and rude facts of the world, and especially of human reality. Thus, from *Madame Bovary* to *Buddenbrooks*, or from Balzac to Hemingway and Morante, the will to dissolve illusions, to show the untruth of ideals underlies Realist literature, as does also the urge to show the fragrance, the tastes, the colours of the real world. In legal thinking, the Realists emphasize what

22. On the different meanings of the term 'Romantic', cf. C. S. Lewis, *Pilgrim's Regress,* Preface (1941).

really goes on in the legal institutions, in contrast to what ought to go on according to ideal law. In philosophy the reaction to idealist thinking came partly as declared Realism (Moore, Russell)[23] or New Realism (Perry and others), or as Pragmatism (James, Schiller, Pierce) and somewhat later, Logical Positivism and Existentialism.

The rise of social research can partly be understood as an aspect of this Realist movement—to the extent that its basic conceptual opposition is that between ideals and reality, and that the profound intention is to correct those who more or less deliberately, more or less in good faith, present the ideals' beautiful appearance as reality itself. To uncover, unmask, shock, scandalize, ridicule, mock or tease are modes of this kind of social research.

As early examples may be mentioned Engels' book on the English working class (1844) or Sundt's book on the moral level in Norway (1857).[24] Sundt's investigation is particularly illustrative.

After having completed his theological studies and entered on a university career, he changed his mind, obtained a grant from the State, and travelled in the countryside to observe the population's sexual and family morals. This meeting with 'reality' was literally a shock, which kept him confined to his bed for several days. ('God help us all!' he wrote to his wife). Moral conditions were far below what he had been able to imagine. The Romantic movement's image of the 'people', with their mores and customs, had to be replaced by the Realist notion of the 'population' and its disorderly, immoral and ugly way of life. Sundt's research consisted in participant observation, ordinary observation, and the compilation and interpretation of a huge statistical material.

When Realist social research confronts ideals with realities, it may sometimes be on behalf of the very same ideals. Such was the case with Sundt. The remedies he proposed to fill the gap he discovered between ideal and actual morality take for

---

23. Cf. Russell's account of his early conversion from Idealism and his Realist delight in thinking that the grass really was green (*My Philosophical Development*, pp. 61–62).

24. Cf. Otnes: 'Social Change and Social Science in Norway', in *Current Sociology* 1977, No. 1.

granted a Christian-bourgeois morality and do not entail far-reaching changes of the basic social structure of the country. More often, perhaps, the intention is to replace the ideals that were confronted with reality, with other ideals, for instance, to replace one conception of justice by another. This was the case with Engels' social research.[25]

More generally, the Realist approach in social research opposes not only 'ideals' by submitting them to confrontation with reality, but also 'ideas' as such. That is, this kind of social research finds highly important the distinction between what we think is the case, and what really is the case, that is between 'thought' or 'ideas', and 'reality'.

The so-called 'operationalization of concepts' is important in Realist social research, because this is a way to make clear the hiatus between thought and reality. For instance, one may have an image (or 'representation' or 'idea') of the family in our society, and perhaps visualize a married couple with children, living for themselves. But if one were to investigate family life as it really is, the concept of family would have to be 'operationalized', and then one would be confronted with all kinds of exceptions to this image or preconception. There will be incomplete families, families joined by one or more relatives or friends, several incomplete families living under the same roof, and so on. The preconceived notion of 'the family' will then undergo a change, and be regarded as a more or less suitable label for a series of human relationships which resemble each other, but have no intrinsic unity. One may even reach the conclusion that the label 'family' should be discarded because it diverts one's attention from social life as it really is. Thus, operationalization helps one to see the difference between day-dreaming and imaginary attitudes towards social life, on the one hand, and real experience, on the other.

Distrusting all kind of 'a priori' knowledge, the proponents of Realist social research share the British empiricists' concep-

---

25. In the present context, the statistical and 'sociographical' parts of Marx's *Capital* may be seen as a Realist riposte to Hugo's Romantic novel *Les Misérables* (published five years before), even if the two wrote without taking notice of each other. Both works have the same topic, 'la dégradation de l'homme par le prolétariat, la déchéance de la femme par la faim, l'atrophie de l'enfant par la nuit' (cf. the preface to *Les Misérables*).

tion that knowledge is solely obtained through (sense) experience, but they are much less prone to delimit sharply what shall count as research experience, and also less concerned with the project of a social science as a coherent whole of verified hypotheses and generalizations. Thus, such a work as *The Polish Peasant* by Znaniecky & Thomas, exemplifies social research of this brand. It uses all sorts of information, letters and interviews. But it does not aim at exploding some social prejudice or illusion, or put to the test some sociological theory. It is rather descriptive; it reports what was unknown hitherto. Thus, such social research may present trivial results. But even triviality is defendable in social research, as pointed out by Halbwachs long ago. For often two states of affair may seem equally probable, and therefore the only way to find out which of them actually exists, is by research. The outcome of the research may seem trivial in the sense of not being unexpected, but not in the sense that one could have known it just by thinking through our concepts.

An example of Realist social research that lacks bite, without for that reason being trivial, is Katz & Lazarsfeld's discovery of the opinion leader[26] mediating between the mass media and the particular member of society (the so-called 'two-steps' hypothesis). Although this finding seems to present a brute *datum*, something wholly contingent, it is one which one tends to remember.

A considerable body of social research undertaken in Britain has had a Realist intention, often combined with movements for social reform. Often the aim has been to arouse public opinion, by demonstrating that the state of affairs was not what most citizens thought it was, but, as a rule, much worse, in contrast with officially professed morals, and consequently something that should be amended through some political enactment, by legislation or otherwise.

The same goes for the USA. One might for instance consider the plethora of investigations into social mobility, which purport to show how far from social reality is the ideal of 'equality of opportunity' so important to the dominant value pattern. The real probability of realizing this 'American dream' is small

26. Katz & Lazarsfeld: *Personal influence* (1960).

within most social strata. Or one might take as an example all the studies of racial differences demonstrating how badly prejudice about foreign ethnic groups corresponds with reality[27] – though in that case it is rather the ideals of universalistic humanism (*Alle Menschen werden Brüder*) which are vindicated, while the pretended realism is proven wrong.

Again, the 'Kinsey report', which created such a stir in the 1950s all over the Western world, presented a sexual reality that differed strongly from dominant norms or ideals.[28]

Still another example could be Lazersfeld & Merton's research on mass media propaganda. This result confronts democratic ideals of freedom and expression with an undemocratic reality, but should not be taken as a contribution to the Marxian doctrine of class struggle, since they make no attempt to fit the concept of 'psychological exploitation' into their conceptual network. It is a piece of Realist social research.[29]

In Scandinavia, there has since 1945 been published an impressive body of Realist social research. In particular, Vilhelm Aubert's work on the legal institution's place in social life carries out the Realist intention in an excellent manner. One may consider, for instance, how he interprets the enactments of laws, by examining the case of the Norwegian Housemaid Law from 1947, a law of which Aubert and two colleagues made a thorough investigation (including questionnaires, tests etc.)[30]

The law's professed purpose was to protect and better the lot of housemaids. But for several reasons, the law could not be expected to achieve this aim. In the first place, the majority of housemaids (and housewives) were ignorant of the law after its enactment, because of their alienation from the legislative apparatus. In the second place, the text of the law, couched in the usual language of jurisprudence, was to a great extent unintelligible to the housemaids. In the third place—and this is decisive—the law made the following most 'unrealistic' or farfetched presupposition: It assumed that in the case of trans-

---

27. Cf. Klineberg's presentation of his own and others' investigations on prejudice in *Social Psychology* (1950).
28. Alfred Kinsey et al.: *Sexual Behavior in the Human Male* (1948).
29. Lazarsfeld & Merton: 'Mass communication etc.', in Rosenberg & White (eds.): *Mass Culture* (1957).
30. Cf. Aubert: 'Some functions of legislation' (1966), in Aubert (ed.): *Sociology of Law* (1969).

gression on the part of the housewife, the offended housemaid would take legal action and in the meanwhile continue to live in the defendant's house keeping her job as a housemaid. While this is legally (or 'ideally') possible, it borders on the socially absurd, and it is obvious that most housemaids will not invoke the law in such a situation, but leave the job. What, then, is the significance of passing such an impracticable law? Aubert's answer is that in this case, and also generally, legislation often serves as a compromise that settles conflicts in the legislative assembly between groups which in turn represent larger organizations. The legislation is a gesture, a pretence, a half-hearted effort to strengthen the position of one group of people without weakening that of other groups. This subtle interpretation of the ambivalence of legislation is strictly parallel to the ironic narrations of much Realist literature.

3. Social research and induction based on sense experience

The doctrine that knowledge is acquired through generalizing our experience, which is ultimately sense experience, is usually termed Empiricism. Introduced in a common-sense fashion by Locke, carried to its extreme, self-dissolving, consequences by Hume, it received a balanced statement through the epistemological works of John Stuart Mill, who elaborated induction as a way of thinking. Mill, as is known, besides his contributions to economics, was also attracted to the project of Sociology, and corresponded for some time with Comte on this topic. Their ways, however, soon parted, Comte being oriented towards the understanding of social wholes, while Mill maintained the Empiricist orientation towards the particular *datum*. Mill outlined a prospect for sociology as a science of social facts, basically similar to the sciences of physical facts, but with smaller claims to exactness and predictive power. Social science, according to Mill, would consist of broad generalizations that would be more or less probable; it would be a stochastic form of knowledge.

The basic notions of British Empiricism, as already stated, are contingency and externality of all relations between things. Everything that is the case happens to be the case. What is the case, can, therefore, never be deduced from certain and necessary thinking about the world, but must be discovered by observation and other forms of experience where the relation between the knower and the known is external. The term '*empirical research*' came into circulation to designate the preoccupation with the contingent, with the 'facts', as distinct from the 'theoretical', conceived, not as insight stemming from the eye (according to the etymology),[31] but as assumptions and conjectures about contingent states and relationships between such states, being confirmed or weakened through some kind of confrontation with the facts, through what is termed 'empirical tests'. 'Theory' is subordinated to 'empirical data' in the process of acquiring knowledge. To make a science of the social one should start in a piecemeal way, investigate a small area of the social field, venture some tentative generalizations on the basis of the collected empirical data, proceed to other small areas in the same way, thus accumulating factual knowledge of social relations and structures, with the justified hope that some day this knowledge and these generalizations would converge towards a larger unity of empirically founded theory, on a par with the sciences of nature.

This is the program usually professed in the text-books on so-called method in social research. The introductory chapters as a rule present considerations on such matters as the relation between ethics and science, politics and science, and an empiricist interpretation of science as a research process.

The proportion of social scientists who have adhered to this program has always been small. Nearly all work that could be labelled social research during the last centuries has been undertaken for purposes of administration or social reform, and not for the sake of theory-building.[32] A change of orientation did not take place in the USA until ca. 1930, as testified by Ogburn's

---

31. *theoreo:* to look at, view, observe, etc.
32. 'It is necessary to distinguish between empirical work done for specific purposes and similar endeavours motivated by the desire to discover general laws.' Paul F. Lazarsfeld in his Foreword to Oberschall (ed.) *The Establishment of Empirical Sociology,* 1973 (p.xii) Even if Lazarsfeld made important contributions to quantitative social research, one should not think of him as a scientist who only valued quantifications. Indeed, he himself points out a case of what Sorokin named 'quantophrenia' in the following passage: 'When Booth quantified the concept of poverty, he intended to settle an argument with socialist friends. When quantification had become part of American sociological training the tables were temporarily turned: Doctoral candidates looked for problems to quantify rather than for the burning issues of the day.' (*Ibid.,* p.xiv).

presidential address, advocating 'the accumulation of bits and pieces of new knowledge' obtained through the spending of most of the time on 'hard, dull, tedious, and routine tasks.' Combined with the conviction that 'sociology as a science is not interested in making the world a better place to live in',[33] this conception amounted to a heroism of triviality that recurs off and on in social science publications: To abstain from sweeping generalizations about social wholes, founded on mere impressions and one's own limited life experience, and to confine one's attention to the petty facts of a carefully circumscribed topic.[34]

However, notwithstanding the spread of this conception of what social research should be, it still remains true that only a few social researchers devote themselves to the discovery of law-like propositions about the social world. The above-mentioned program is only paid lip-service to; it has decayed into a cliché or a legitimating declaration without obligation.

Disregarding the reasons, there has been little cumulative growth of the knowledge obtained through research processes conducted according to the rules of Empiricist methods (whether inductive or hypothetico-deductive). This fact may have discouraged many social scientists and made them choose research topics that were at least important from the viewpoint of administration or reform, even if their relevance to social science as such should turn out to be negligible. The reluctance, noted by Lazarsfeld, to replicate previous social research—so important from the viewpoint of inductive generalization—may also stem from the apprehension that the replication will be tedious and in vain. This apprehension in turn may have been called forth by the awareness that there has been little cumulative growth in social research.

Introductory books on sociology used, at least in the 1950s and 1960s, to state that social research was a relatively recent undertaking, and for this reason lagged behind the 'empirical research' which was supposed to have led to the brilliant achievements of physics. This seems odd, since leading pro-

33. Quoted in Oberschall's chapter 'The institutionalization of American sociology' in Oberschall: *op.cit.,* p. 243.
34. A case in point is Homans' *The Human Group,* (1950), ironically admired for the iron self-constraint of its author, who, incidently, is not without self-irony.

ponents of social research like Lazarsfeld were well aware that social statistics and social research commenced in the seventeenth century. Rather the striking difference between these two branches is this, that after 300 years of sociography no progress had been made in the direction hoped for: No laws have been discovered, no store of knowledge accumulated, just an immense heap of collected, contingent facts or data.

To this very day, it is not the hopefulness of Lazarsfeld on behalf of inductive social research that has been confirmed by history, but the resignation of Keynes.[35]

The reasons for this have already been touched upon in the preceding section (on social statistics) and will be considered again later in the book.

The British epistemology called Empiricism considered itself the proper interpretation of the knowledge obtained within medicine, physics, astronomy and affined realms; but so did the epistemology termed Rationalism, and the dispute has never been settled.

Far more easy to defend is the statement that Empiricism is the most suitable interpretation of social statistics and sociography.

Therefore, even after the Empiricist epistemologies have lost much of their importance in the physical sciences, Empiricism will continue to be paid homage to. Nor is training in inductive social research ('methods') likely to fade away, since its exercises are suitable practice for much future administrative or Realist social research.

4. Social research and the Modernist movement

What is called Modernism in poetry and novels is a break with the traditional use of language, both of everyday life and of *belles lettres*. This use of language no longer satisfied many writers, who felt that its expressions and patterns had become worn-out and inapt for descriptions of the contemporary world.

---

35. 'The hope, which sustained many investigators in the course of the nineteenth century, of gradually bringing the moral sciences under the sway of mathematical reasoning, steadily recedes – if we mean, as they meant, by mathematics the introduction of precise numerical methods. ... I, at any rate, have not the same lively hope as Condorcet, or even as Edgeworth, 'éclairer les Sciences morales et politiques par le flambeau de l'Algèbre'. *A Treatise on Probability* (1920), p. 349.

They therefore began to use language in what at first glance may seem to be a meaningless or absurd way. Syntax and metaphor, metre and form, were altered so as to make the literary texts incomprehensible to the majority of minds moulded by the education of official and quasi-official schools. Modernism is a way of experiencing the world as fragmented, as a whole gone to pieces. In a fragmented world, things will not constitute a web of meaning nor an expressive totality where all parts are internally related. On the contrary, what we encounter in our lives are very often accidental happenings, contingent facts, disorder, all of which is concealed by traditional art. To expose and render intelligible in a new way the world of 'modern' human beings is the task of the Modernists.

Social research, especially that brand devoted to the discovery of scientific laws, sometimes resembles literary Modernism both in its distaste for totality concepts and its insistence upon the isolated, detached fact or case, whose relation to other facts or cases are considered a purely 'empirical question', in other words, as contingent. Thus, even the best-documented findings are interpreted as contingent bits of knowledge: The rich happen to vote in favour of non-socialist political parties; the social classes happen to raise their children each in its own way; criminal behaviour happens to correlate strongly with low socio-economic status, and so on. Essentially, every set of social facts may hypothetically be related to any other set. This assumption of Empiricist social research is equivalent to the fragmentation conception.

One may surmise that the widespread dislike (or even abhorrence) of social research is partly affined to the equally widespread dislike of Modernism in art. However, there is a difference: The social scientists in question will as a rule be Modernists against their will, without intending to be so and not aware that they are. If one wants to discuss the Modernist approach to social research, one had therefore better turn one's attention towards a different intellectual movement, the so-called Frankfurter School or the adherents of Critical Theory.[36]

5. Concluding remarks

While not equally strong, the affinity between social research and social statistics persists in all for four kinds envisaged:

36. Cf. chapter 6.

As part of State administration social research will very often deal with quantitative relations between the state apparatus and the citizens, and think statistically. Also, the piecemeal character of most such research makes its topics statistical, in the sense that they do not constitute a totality, but an aggregate of externally related topics, eventually to be interpreted by statistics.

As a feature of the Realist movement, social research will often resort to statistical interpretations, either in order to challenge the State's own statistical reports or for other reasons, or in order to tear asunder illusory misconceptions of social totalities. The isolated, disconnected or unconnected *datum* of social life is sometimes important to Realist social research, and, consequently, the external relation between seemingly internally related human beings.

As a feature of the Inductivist movement in science, the bond between social research and statistics is very strong, since the findings of this kind of social research can hardly be other than statistical.

Finally, as part of the Modernist movement, the bond to social statistics may be weak or non-existent, since such social research may not be about quantities at all. However, as far as externality prevails in these accounts of social life, an affinity to social statistics obtains.

*

The underlying assumption of social statistics and social research (as here reviewed) is that singular human beings can be treated as externally related individuals. The State and its individuals are the notions from which both social statistics and social research derive. And both obtain their full significance by being set in relation to, and sometimes in opposition to, essentially different conceptions, the sociological and the historico-dialectical.

2

Liberal Politics

A. Main Tenets

The rise of Liberal thought is another aspect of the formation of States in the seventeenth and eighteenth centuries. While Statistics deals with the mass of human beings as something to be surveyed and controlled, Liberal politics is concerned with them as citizens that seek to safeguard and defend themselves against the State's possible abuse of its power. The main tenets of the Liberal doctrine will now be presented.

1. Individuals' natural rights

Gradually, the Aristotelic-Thomistic justification and glorification of monarchy as emanating from God was replaced by a doctrine that derived political authority from every human being's natural right. The notion that human beings exist by virtue of being a member of a whole (such as a Church or a kinship group) is discarded. Instead it is asserted that each singular human being is or has a distinct being (a substance in the sense of the Schoolmen), that is, has an independent existence. Every human being is an 'individual', who by essence or 'nature' is endowed with certain rights. These concern the protection and preservation of life and property, and in this respect all human beings are equal, in so far as they have the same liberty to seek their own well-being. Temporally or conceptually prior to government there is a *status naturalis* where the natural rights are enjoyed.

2. Social contract and the State

In order to show how government can be reconcilable with the freedom and equality of human beings (in so far as they partake of the same natural rights), several versions of an initial contract were set forth. A certain number of human beings come together and renounce their natural right to punish infractions upon their life, freedom and property. This is the transition from the natural state into the (civil) State. Natural rights are handed over to a special body, the government, and this brings into existence the State or civil or political society. To enter into civil society is an act of freedom, and the pact one of mutual advantage. The state exists for the sake of the individuals, its purpose is to augment their security and well-being. The basic Liberal tenet is that the human being is ontologically prior to the State.

The State is constituted by individuals, and in so far as it is holy, it gets its holiness from the singular human beings, all of whom are (even if imperfect) emanations of the Godhead as creatures. These teachings were first put into practice in two Protestant states, England and Holland, where political liberties for a part of the population were introduced in the seventeenth century.

3. Representation, majority rule, voting

In this way government is derived from the power of independent and free individuals, who have joined into a 'body politic' in order to secure life and property. Those who are in governmental power, act on behalf of the other citizens as if they were present. All governmental power must be representative in order to be acceptable and justifiable, lest it should encroach upon freedom, which is essentially individual. Monarchy too is compatible with this Liberal frame, provided the monarch's power can somehow be shown to have been delegated from his (her) subjects.

Such delegation is conceived of as a real or imagined decision of the citizens, where every citizen is entitled to express his or her will on an equal footing with all the others. When there is disagreement as to who shall govern as representatives, the majority shall decide.[1]

Majority rule, in turn, is connected to elections and voting. A Liberal state is therefore conceived of as encompassing a determinate number of citizens, essentially countable, part of whom have a right to vote and choose among delegates, representatives and their various prospects and possibilities. Thus, the Marquis de Condorcet (1743–1793)—philosopher, mathematician, Girondist and an unreserved follower of Locke—claimed that the right to vote was a prolongation of the human being's Natural Rights, and from this standpoint projected his *mathématique sociale*, dealing with voting and election contexts.

The first Liberal thinkers accorded the franchise and other political rights only to the propertied classes. But this is no ineluctable consequence of Liberal thought, and in our time suffrage is nearly universal in most States throughout the world. Hence, Liberal democracy has long been one of the leading and dominating forms of politics, even if *élite* democracy is considered its paramount mode. The citizens (the people, 'demos') only govern through its *élites*, as shown by Realist political thinkers such as Schumpeter and his followers.

4. The doctrine of utility
Having demolished the notion of government by Divine Right, the doctrine of Natural Right was itself attached and partly vanquished by the doctrine of Utility. Hume, Bentham and others in England, Constant and the Ideologues in France led this movement of thought, which ramified into divergent directions. Utilitarian thought in England developed into an attempt at a calculus of universal happiness, while the version particularly prevalent in France emphasized the importance of the individual and the private vis-à-vis the collective and public.

Founded upon the notion of utility, Liberal thought was still mainly concerned with the freedom of the individual, since the individual's balance of pleasure and pain was the unit of calculation, and since the individual was assumed to act in a way conducive to his or her well-being, at least as a rule. Any limitation of the individual's liberty to carry out his intention was therefore seen as an infringement. Such infringements are necessary, since a multitude of human beings are active within the same area at the same time and therefore may harm each

---

1. Rousseau's version of the social contract is an exception, and precisely for this reason his doctrine is ambiguous, lending itself to both a Liberal and an authoritarian interpretation. The pivotal point is the distinction between *volonté de tous* and *volonté générale*. If this last notion is to mean neither the sum of individual wills nor the will of the majority, a third entity, not derivable from individual citizens, seems to be denoted, which implies a break with Liberal politics.

other so as to lower the sum of happiness below what is attainable. Government is therefore useful, there must be legislation and enactment of laws, there must exist courts of justice and prisons, and also public educational institutions, means of payment guaranteed by the State, and so on.

But a utilitarian interpretation of human co-existence may also endanger the individual's position. This becomes particularly visible when it comes to punishment. If the well-being of society as the aggregate of human beings is solely taken into consideration, the offender may be subject to the gravest inflictions, provided the estimated effects upon society are favourable. To find a viable solution to this difficulty was one of the main tasks of the Utility doctrine.

Likewise, considerations of general utility and well-being may lead away from Liberal economy of competition and *laissez faire* and recommend institutions associated with the term 'socialism', as shown by the famous example of John Stuart Mill, and, somewhat later, Hobson. The Welfare State of our century is widely justified by reasonings about utility.

5. Vindication of natural rights and social contract by transcendental logic

Convinced that happiness is not the ultimate end of moral conduct, and that it is morally bad to treat other human beings merely as means, Kant attempted to renew the doctrine of natural right and social contract. He did not justify it by having recourse to Stoic-Christian conceptions, nor by appealing to the evidence of all men's inborn equality, but by deducing it from what he held to be universally valid obligations and rights, as he himself had stated them in his *Critique of Practical Reason*. The task he set himself was to derive law and constitution from his concepts of free will and the categorical imperative. The human being, he says, is his own legislator and should not accept any commands other than those which can be apprehended by reason. Now, human reason seeks and deals with the universally true and valid. In order to be morally right, an act must therefore stand the test of universality. What is morally valid for me must also be so for other human beings. Restating the Golden Rule, our basic (categorical) duty is to act with due regard for others, and to submit our conduct to an impartial, universal judgment. In this way, Kant attempts to make the reciprocity between human beings constitutive of morality. We should always respect others as members of 'the kingdom of ends', as endowed with practical reason. These assertions have from the very first been charged with emptiness, but Kant himself went on to show their application in social life, on both the legal and moral level.[2] He undertakes a cumbersome 'deduction' of the possibility of the right to possess something, connecting it to its public enforcement and consequently to a civil constitution. He wishes to show how everybody's (moral) freedom can be compatible with legal institutions of his own society, always trying to make them at least reconcilable with his conception of the individual as a being whose 'natural rights' are identical with his 'practical reason'.

A fervent admirer of the French revolution, Kant interprets its achievements as the establishment of the individual as a moral and rational being, and of a legal constitution the truth of which is essentially related to the individual's understanding. To him, the liberal movement is ultimately connected to 'practical reason' and the Enlightenment that put an end to 'man's self-inflicted tutelage'.

6. Relation to selfishness

Societies with a Liberal political constitution have always been accused of calling forth egotism and selfishness. Thus, to Balzac, the Royalist and Catholic novelist, the France of his time, and especially the new dominant class—the merchants, industrialists, and speculators designated as the *bourgeosie*—appeared as selfish, greedy, shameless or hypocritical, in any case immoral or amoral. And to Marx (the revolutionary Communist), the Liberal doctrines were superficial and deceptive. The talk about Liberty concealed the oppression by capital.[3]

In our century the Fascist movement has often been regarded as the truth of Liberalism: when seriously threatened, the domi-

---

2. *Metaphysik der Sitten* (1794).
3. Cf. the caustic remarks in *Capital;* 'Freedom, equality, Bentham!' and 'Had I the courage of my friend, Heinrich Heine, I should call Mr. Jeremy a genius in the way of bourgeois stupidity.' (*Capital* I, chap. 22,5). Marx found Balzac's glaring descriptions most valuable, notwithstanding their diverging political commitments.

nant classes cast off their Liberal cloak and assert that might is right.

It appears, however, that the greatest Liberal thinkers were always concerned with justice and reason, that is, with what every impartial individual should acknowledge as the best way to regulate relations between human beings. Therefore, Liberal politics should not be confounded with conceptions which take as their point of departure the human being's essential selfishness and leave out of account any reference to universal goals. Nevertheless, such conceptions have always accompanied Liberal thought proper. Thus, in the beginning of the Liberal era, Hobbes and Spinoza wrote political treatises based upon the conviction that human beings are essentially selfish and enemies of each other. According to Hobbes' *Leviathan*, when human beings leave the state of nature and unite into a state, they do so from mutual fear and from the urge for peace. He does not impute to them any mutual benevolence, any *appetitus socialis* (as did Grotius and Pufendorf). Civilian life is chosen only because it gives security; compliance with laws is nothing but expediency to the citizens.[4] For this reason, Hobbes would make the State omnipotent.

This interpretation of social life may be traced back to the anthropology and politics of Luther, who, like Hobbes, wrote in the midst of uprisings and cruel civil wars. He taught that human beings are depraved and wicked (by virtue of Orginal sin), and hence that a governor with the harshest means available was required to castigate them.

During the eighteenth century, notions like that of self-interest and *interêt personnel* were current within political discourse. The very concept of interest had a ring of selfishness, as in the saying 'Everybody follows his own interest'.

Still later, partly under the sway of Darwin's doctrine of evolution, thinkers came to the fore who rejected outright the traditional justifications of government and liberties, advocating the individual's unlimited expansion and self-assertion (Stirner,

4. Tönnies is considered to be the first to interpret Hobbes as the originator of the doctrine of natural right, basing his interpretation above all on *De cive* (1642). (Cf. *Hobbes' Leben und Lehre,* 1899). Experts hold there is a shift from *De cive* to *Leviathan* (1679), and a similar change in Spinoza's thinking from *Tractatus theologicopoliticus* (1670) to the posthumous *Tractatus politicus.*

Nietzsche and the Social Darwinists). Max Weber's political writings express a similar conception: power relations determine political life; there exists no moral truth in terms of which the struggle and competition between groups and fractions can be judged. Each has his *daimon* and ultimate values which cannot be reduced to a common denominator. Morality is a value on a par with eroticism, art, religion, science and so on. The diversity of values and the lack of a universal value order make life 'demonic'. Nothing really limits the struggle for power.

This way of thinking—whose last avatar hitherto is the 'theory of strategic games'—is aptly characterized by M. Prélot's term 'exasperated liberalism', since it issues from Liberal thought, and implies a break with it. Prevalent political science as it is taught at Western universities is based upon this 'exasperated liberalism', through the insistence upon and training in 'value free' or 'value neutral' descriptions of 'interest groups', 'legitimation processes' and the like.

7. *Rule of law and limits to government*

An important strand of Liberal thought emphasizes the importance of a (written) constitution to prevent arbitrary exercise of governmental power. This is the Liberal notion of *Rechtstaat* or the rule of law.[5]

To have a body of laws serving as the State's foundation or constitution and a corpus of legal specialists who improve upon, interpret and enact these laws is felt to be most assuring. It binds those in government and prevents abuse of power, in so far as Right cannot be immediately identified with Might. True, in a state of emergency the constitution may be set aside, but that does not imply that the individual citizens could do as well without it in everyday life. On the contrary, the citizen can appeal to the law when in conflict with the State, and even take legal action against the State. For the State is obliged to obey its own laws.

This notion of the rule of law was at first connected to that of a very limited State, as in the writings of some French thinkers. Here, the individual's wish to stand apart and live

5. Later, Max Weber's typology of domination designated this as *formal-legale Herrschaft*, as distinct from traditional (despotic, capricious etc.) and charismatic domination.

independently of others, prevails.[6] This branch of Liberal thought renews the original discussions of the relationship between the citizens and the State, but this time without any conception ressembling *ius naturae*. Instead it is simply asserted 'la liberté comme l'isolement salutaire et fécond de l'homme' (Mme de Staël). From this standpoint Constant works out his conception of a minimum of government, whose task it is to protect the individual's freedom. This government, he claims, must have as its object liberty itself, and must be constitutional. The constitutional rights, protect the individuals against their protector, the State.

History has shown that this notion of a minimal State is no necessary part of the Liberal doctrine. The expanding, intervening governments of the last century (the *Sozialstaat*, the Welfare State, and other forms) have retained their Liberal constitution and creed.

Equality before the law is part of Liberal politics, in the sense that the nobility's privileges are condemned as unjust. To abolish the estates, and constitute a State consisting of individual citizens determined by the relatively universal equal rights as political and legal subjects or agents was the endeavour of the Liberal movement in the preceding centuries.[7]

Not birth, but talent and merit shall see to it that the citizens may co-operate and compete in a peaceful, non-violent way, on an equal footing.

This again entails the statement that men and women should be equal in legal respects. To treat women as minors is contrary to reason; they must be accorded the franchise, the right to dispose of their property, and equal status in relation to their husbands. Liberal thought—as in John Stuart Mill's example—is therefore led to reconstitute or reform marriage as a contract between two juridically independent and free agents. Women's access to all sorts of formal education must also be granted.

However, equality between the two sexes reaches a limit when

6. 'Par liberté, j'entends le triomphe de l'individualité tant sur l'autorité qui voudrait gouverner par le despotisme que sur les masses qui réclament le droit d'asservir la minorité à la majorité'. B. Constant, quoted in M. Prélot: *Histoire des idées politiques,* 3rd edition, p. 446 (1966).
7. Machiavelli (1469–1527) is now considered one of the very first to have advocated the equality of all citizens before the law.

it comes to the question of military conscription. The obligation to fight and eventually die for one's state (or 'country') is imposed upon men only (though it remains to be seen whether this last discrepancy can also be overcome). Besides, the duty to risk one's life is hard to interpret within a Liberal conception, at least in its utilitarian versions. For life and death are beyond utility and disutility, advantage and disadvantage.

Punishment is an important subject for Liberal thought, since it was one of the main activities of the governmental apparatus at the beginning of the Liberal era. In order to ensure that the laws regulating conduct are obeyed, a penal code should be drawn up which is intended to be superior to the penal practices of the Feudal and the Absolutist regimes. The Liberals' proposals for penal reform have a double aim: to make punishment at the same time more mild ('humane') and effective.[8] (There was also a third objective: to deprive monarchs of the power of arbitrary punishments and pardons.) The mildness had to do with respect for the individual, which the Liberals sought to heighten. The maiming of an offender does violence to his dignity as a human being, and also debases the executors and the general public. Moreover, the consequences of gruesome and harsh penalties may be the opposite of deterrence. In order to gain fuller knowledge of these consequences, they had to be investigated by a special science, 'criminology' or 'penology'. Knowledge of what constitutes proper punishment presupposes knowledge of causes and effects, that is, how an offender will react to the inflictment of bodily or mental pain. The line between penology and medicine, the criminal and the sick is blurred,[9] since the notion of cure and treatment of the offender is near at hand. This involves a dominance of the intellect in relation to affectivity, or better, a differentiation of a cognizing activity—'the intellect'—where affectivity is left out. For punishment should not be an outburst of anger, a furious revenge or the expression of hatred. It should be a controlled reaction on behalf of society, striking the balance between consideration for

8. Not all Liberals were in favour of the penal reforms. For instance, Kant disagreed with Beccaria on the topic of the death penalty, characterizing the latter's attitude as one of 'affected humanity' (Kant, op.cit.).
9. For a more recent discussion of this distinction, cf. Aubert & Messinger: 'The criminal and the sick', reprinted in Aubert: op.cit.

the offender and the public weal. The liberal thinker who perhaps went farthest in this direction was Bentham, with his nearly realized project of the correctionary machine 'Panopticon'.

Moreover, all guilt is strictly individual—a citizen's parents, siblings, friend or allies cannot be punished for his (or her) infractions. The Liberal legal institution in itself contributes to the making of the individual as an entity.

8. Tolerance and public opinion

While the preceding political doctrine presupposed a *consensus* as to a Christian legitimation of government, Liberal politics takes as a point of departure *dissensio* between citizens with regard to church adherence. The ferocious struggles over diverging creeds that raged in Europe in the sixteenth and the seventeenth centuries fostered the conviction that the most reasonable thing to do was not to fight over such matters. The notion of forbearance or *tolerance* is introduced. Thus Locke contends that it cannot be the task of the civil magistrate to force a certain creed and ritual upon the citizens. The salvation of the soul must be each individual's own concern. The citizens of a political state need not be united by common basic beliefs. One should learn to respect the creed of others. Freedom of thought and (though somewhat restricted) freedom of speech should be granted to the citizens.

This reinforces the distinction between the public and the private already touched upon. The human being's ultimate convictions may be his (or her) private concern, (a *privatio*) that is, something the others are deprived of. Private property and private beliefs are constitutive of the Liberal citizen. The private sphere permits the formation of private opinions, the confrontation of which leads to discussions. Public discussions of differing opinions develops into a Liberal political institution, generating a public opinion. Coffee houses, clubs and newspapers are the media of such political discussions, which mediate between the masses of citizens and the government.[10]

10. Cf. Tönnies: *Kritik der öffentlichen Meinung,* (1922), and Habermas: *Strukturwandel der Öffentlichkeit,* (1961).

9. Education, intellect and will

Liberal education differs from the transmitting of traditions. Its aim is to mould young people in such a way as to make them independent, tolerant, and imbued with a love of liberty. They should not accept propositions as true merely out of reverence, but trust their own reason, and, as far as possible, their own experience. The young, however, are, dependent upon others. The Liberals want to ensure that they are not bullied either by the goverment or by their parents. Childrens' work should be limited, and some education compulsory, since capacities such as the ability to read are judged to be necessary for the future adult citizen, if he (or she) is to enjoy and fulfil his political rights and obligations. But fathers' unrestricted dominion over their progeny is contested, and so is the State's unlimited right to order children to attend schools and similar institutions.

To strengthen and train the intellect is more important within a Liberal education. One should learn to think unaffected by all kinds of emotions or feelings. This implies strengthening the will. When one is inclined to give up a line of reasoning or action deemed right by the intellect, an effort of the will should be made. To the outward political liberties there ought to correspond an inner freedom from unreasonable cravings and desires. The essential liberty of the human being is associated with freedom of the will. The human being, it is asserted, is free in so far as his conduct is determined by his own will, and not by involuntary motives. Now, a strong will is a product of the will, and therefore those who have a weak will are responsible for their own weakness. We must will to will, and in so far as we succeed in acquiring a strong will, we are free, that is, self-determined, under all conditions and circumstances.

*

The Liberal doctrine outlines a framework within which human beings can co-exist in a peaceful and just way. It is designed first and foremost to secure the independence and freedom of each and all, and make the amount of coercion as little as feasible. But will this design, if carried out in real life, produce the results wished for? Is Liberal politics viable or consistent with itself? Strong reasons to deny or doubt that were set forth, especially after the French Revolution.

B. Ripostes

Among the early objections raised against the Liberal doctrines, the following three will be considered:

1. Primacy of community vs. primacy of the individual

Since the State is treated by the Liberals as a means, and not as an end in itself, its character of *communio* is disregarded. More generally, human beings do not and cannot stand exclusively in an instrumental relationship to each other. If one insists on treating government as something useful and nothing but useful, then one must admit that something other than government makes citizens constitute a whole, in other words, that one must distinguish between the *State*, on the one hand, and the nation or *society*, on the other.

Romanticism was above all concerned with love as the most important human attitude: love of God, love of Nature, of the Nation or the beloved Other. It is conceived in the mode of a fusion, a union of opposites where duality is transcended. Medieval, feudal Europe was seen by Romantics not as an age of darkness, but as one of unity, where every human was part of a larger whole, the guild, the village, the community, the church. Looking not only backwards, but also forwards, the conception of the nation or the people (as different from the population) evolved. A nation is an expressive totality where every singular participant expresses the whole in his or her specific way, and at the same time cannot be understood unless in relation to this totality.

Fichte's (1762–1814) doctrine of the nation belongs to this movement. Building on Kants' thinking he nevertheless strives towards a clear conceptual understanding of a human multitude as a real whole, not a mere *compositum*, but a *totum*.[11] To arrive at this conception, one of the examples he gives is the difference between a tree and a heap of sand. The branches are parts of the tree and belong to it in a different way than the grains

11. *Grundlage des Naturrechts* (1796).

belong to the heap; the relation between the citizen and State can be likened to that between branches and tree. The contract refers to a unity beyond utility, a protecting whole. But Fichte does not stop here. In later works he describes the state as a skeleton or a rigid form compared to the entity called the nation.[12]

Nationality mediates between humankind and the singular human being, and is constituted above all by a specific language, and by a specific history, a past and a future. The existence of language as such shows the insufficiency of Liberal thought, since language transcends the individual. A nation or a people (Volk) is not simply a general denominator of a number of individuals, but an ontological realm.

Savigny's (1779–1861) teachings on law also involve the notion of a people or a nation. He likens law to language, considering both as expressions or part of each singular people. Law is not primarily nor essentially written law, but common law, which springs from customs and *mores*, which is never the work of an arbitrary legislator, but of the people. He therefore denies that legal codes like the *Code Napoléon* can be made by individuals or groups of individuals through a break with the past. Such codes must always build upon already existing collective notions of what is lawful and just.[13]

Hegel (1770–1831), too, throughout his work attempts to show that the individual depends for his existence upon the collective, both historically and ontologically.

For instance, he describes the adventures of a consciousness that strives for individuality in the sense of developing one's own singular and limited ability (one's 'natural talent' or the like). Immediately, this promises the easy existence of an animal. All human beings have their unique talent (or 'nature'), which they should develop and express through their works, and these works could not be judged superior or inferior to each other, since they all are just expressions of unique individualities.

12. The *Reden an die deutsche Nation* (1806) and other writings.
13. He states that 'the true basis of law is the common consciousness of the people' (chap. 2). And: 'Generally, everyone who undertakes a thorough historical study of the literature will convince himself how little of its manifestations can be imputed to single individuals, independently of the powers and endeavours of the epoch and the nation.' (chap. 8). Savigny: *Von Beruf unsrer Zeit für Gezetzgebung und Rechtswissenschaft* (1814), p. 249 (My translation).

Nobody bothers about the others, but concentrates upon his (her) own self-expression, as for instance the painter who claims to paint solely for his own sake, without regard to fame and wealth, or to be devoted exclusively to the cause of art, without caring for what other artists do. In turns out, however, that the encounter with other individualities and their works makes one aware that one's activity implied a claim to universal validity. The only satisfactory thing is to express an individuality that is also universal and is acknowledged as such by others. since 'the whole is the spontaneous interfusion of individuality and the universal'.[14] The notion of an individuality that cares only for its own development contradicts itself and leads to the concept of *collectivity*, 'an I that is a We and a We that is an I'.

Bonald (1754–1840) asserted against the Liberals that the human being is essentially social.[15] To develop the capacity of speech and thought, one must grow up in society. Language suffices to show the sociality of individuals. Further, the family is said to be the basic social unit, not the individual.[16] Finally, he claims that Christianity is profoundly social in character. For these reasons, he states that the *science of society* is 'the first of all the sciences'.

2. Primacy of tradition vs. primacy of decision

To construct a State's constitution through deliberate decision and action is a frail and superficial enterprise. Such an undertaking is doomed to fail unless the constitution decided upon happens to express the customs and *mores* of the land in question.

Burke eloquently opposed the French revolution on these grounds. He rejected the notion of rights derived or deduced from universal reasons independent of time and place. He defended rights by appeal to inheritance, thus, by referring to the

---

14. *Phenomenology of Spirit* (1806), section on 'The Spiritual Animal Kingdom' (Miller's translation).
15. 'La société est la vraie et même la seule nature de l'homme.' *Recherches philosophiques,* (1818) chap. 11.
16. This is echoed in Balzac: 'Aussi regardé-je la famille, et non l'individu, comme le véritable élément social. Sous ce rapport, au risque d'être regardé comme un esprit rétrograde, je me range du côté du Bossuet et de Bonald, au lieu d'aller avec des novateurs modernes.' *La comédie humaine,* Avant-propos (1842).

forefathers, the past, history. Distrustful of 'naked reason', he pleads in favour of habits and prejudice resting on the past experience of the nation. 'No rational man did ever govern himself by abstractions and universals.' Society, he states, is too complex to be grasped by the intellect of single individuals, therefore it is better to confide in the wisdom of bygone generations. If a society is to improve, it must build upon that which is already achieved, that is, it must continue, and not throw away, tradition. The spokesmen of the French revolution adhered to recent versions of the doctrine of Natural Right, founded on thinking ('principles') with a claim to universal validity, abstracted from any concrete, traditional setting. Likewise, the transition from the natural to the civil state was interpreted by a contract that was presupposed by thought, and not as an event that ever took place. Burke's own conception of contract differed widely from this rational construction: 'a partnership in all science; a partnership in all art; a partnership in every virtue and in all perfection'. This cannot be achieved by one generation alone, and therefore the contract engages 'those who are living, those who are dead and those who are to be born.'[17] This extends the meaning of social contract so as to turn it into a different, non-Liberal, concept: an obligation, an 'inviolable oath', a commitment to ends so general and imprecise that they can arouse affections, but defy the delimitations of ordinary contracts between individuals. Burke's conception of social contract comes to this, that every individual belongs to a whole whose ends by far transcend his own, and that every individual is under obligations to this larger whole.

Albeit not a believer in tradition, Hegel, too, objects to the abstractness of Liberal politics. In the first place, the legal order of personal property, contract, and their protection is determined as 'abstract right'; this means that this order is not intelligible in itself, but as part (or 'moment') of a larger whole, first internalized morality, and then the ethical (*Sittlichkeit*), the institutions of family, economy, government and religion. In the second place, he charges Liberal thought with neglect of history. Legal rights and obligations must correspond to the stage of historical development reached by a people. One cannot

17. Edmund Burke: *Reflections on the Revolution in France* (1790).

arbitrarily impose a constitution upon a people, since 'a certain people's constitution depends upon the mode and culture of its self-consciousness'. Moreover, one should not think of a constitution as something (man) made, but rather as that which exists in and for itself, as something divine. As a consequence, he considers nonsensical the question of who has the right to make a constitution. For it is impossible, he asserts, to make a constitution, since, in order to do so, it must already exist.[18] What can be done, is to make explicit in a legal code that which existed *implicitly* as the spirit of the people at this determinate historical stage.[19] In other words, politics and law presuppose an ontological level of ethical spirit, which later by some thinkers came to be determined as *the social level*.

The Terror following the French revolution is interpreted by Hegel as a consequence of conceiving society as a heap of individuals (or atoms). After the estates were dissolved, everybody became an abstract universal will, a citizen. But the citizens as such were disorganized and incapable of any constructive collective action. The only action possible for the political leaders was that of destruction. The universal and the particular had fallen apart.[20]

3. Primacy of economy vs. primacy of politics

Another group of adversaries of Liberal politics referred, not to language, *mores*, history, but to the level of the economic. Political rights and liberties, even if they were granted, are of no avail to the propertyless masses. Political discussions and struggles are superficial and shallow, since they have little impact upon what is more important, the production and distribution of economic goods. Thus, Saint-Simon and his followers urged the replacement of politicians in the government by the

18. *Philosophy of Right* (1821), §§ 273–4 (My translation). Bonald and de Maistre had already developed this thought. Consider for instance this passage: 'Une de(s) folies (de la philosophie moderne) est de croire qu'une assemblée peut former une nation: qu'une *constitution* ... est un ouvrage comme un autre ... et que des hommes peuvent un jour dire à d'autres hommes: *Faites-nous un governement* comme on dit à un ouvrier: *Faites-nous une pompe à feu ou un métier à bas* ... *Nulle grande institution ne résulte d'une délibération* ... ' de Maistre: *Considérations sur la France* (1796), chap. 7.
19. Hegel: *Encyclopedia,* (1830) § 540.
20. *Phenomenology of Spirit,* section on 'Absolute Freedom and Terror'.

leaders of production. According to his famous parable, the loss of all the leading civil servants, clergymen, police officers, ministers and proprietors would not cause serious damage, while the loss of all the leading physicians, engineers, architects, carpenters, masons etc. would be disastrous to a country. A rational organization of the industrial order seemed important, not reforms on the political level. Again, Fourrier and his movement emphasize their indifference towards political action. 'We are social engineers', they declare, presenting 'a new social mechanism.' This consists in the invention of a new form of economic organization, the *phalanstère* where *l'attraction sociale*—Fourrier's discovery—will be active. Likewise, Proudhon considers the science of the economy to be the clue to the question of human freedom, and not Liberal politics. Every form of politics which aims at governmental power stems from and in its turn spreads illusion.[21] Society does not need to be governed. It exists by virtue of the functions of economic life. Once more, Owen and other forerunners of the syndical movement do not share the Liberals' concern with government, but locate the centre of society at the place of economic production.

Marx, strongly influenced by writers like the above-mentioned, elaborated his doctrine of human praxis, showing how the human being, through the making of tools and their application in work, changes the environment and himself in a never-ending process which is history. Through this material activity the human being affirms himself and develops his capacities, and also affirms those of other human beings through co-operation and mutual exchange of activities and products. On this level of primordial economic activity the human being discovers himself as a generic being (*Gattungswesen*), as essentially related to all other human beings. The emergence of specifically political relationships is an aspect of the more fundamental alienation of the economic, through the division of labour, the split into propertied and propertyless, class struggle etc. Later, government and other political institutions are described as belonging to the superstructure, while the economic mode of production is seen as the basis. While political struggle is by no means

---

21. 'Le plus sûr moyen de faire mentir un peuple est l'institution du suffrage universel'.

considered unimportant, what goes on at the economic level—-
development of the forces of production, contradiction between
relations of production and forces of production—is 'in the last
instance' decisive.

4. Conclusion

These three objections bear on the insufficency of Liberal politics: it cannot stand alone as a science that covers all relations
between human beings, even if supplemented with social statistics. Not only *auctoritas*, but also *communitas* is contrary to
libertas. When liberty is conceived of as the right to do as one
pleases, in so far as one does not harm others, the concept is
defined as a privation. But being and living with others is also
an enjoyment, an experience making one's being more complete,
and in some respects even a condition governing the possibility
of one's private existence. Liberal thought and politics call forth
an awareness of this truth, and an urge to elaborate it into a
doctrine or a science—the science of the social.

Second, Liberal thought, aiming at upheaval and revolution,
was internally related to the conviction that a civil state can be
constituted entirely afresh, after a complete break with the past
order of things. This specification of the *tabula rasa* epistemology expresses a fallacious conception of time as a sucession
of externally related points or instants (an 'instantanéisme'),
thereby misjudging the impact of tradition. This leads to an
overestimation of abstract throught in relation to concrete
thought rooted in feeling. The radical way of uprooting or
cutting the root (*radix*), instead of furthering what grows already, overlooks the significance of conserving and improving
customs and folkways. The attempt at rational constructions of
politics should not blind one to the affective web of relationships
which supports them (as a *substratum.*) These relationship
should also be investigated by a science different from (Liberal)
politics, as part of or a feature of the social as different from
the political. These two objections both point to a supplement—sociology as a source of social integration.

Third, Liberal politics occupies itself with the understanding
of relationships of power, that is, of command and obedience,

of submission and independence, and with the struggle for power. But power relations do not exhaust the realm of human relationships, and if they are unduly emphasized, they may divert the attention from what is equally or even more important, that is, economic relations in the widest sense. Thus, liberty in the sense of Liberal politics is quite compatible with economic subjection and oppression. Hence, socialists of all varieties agree in accusing Liberal politics of superficiality or even hypocrisy. Keeping the metaphor, one must pierce Liberal politics and investigate its basis, the domains of work, its tools and products, a project carried out most daringly through Marx's and his collaborator Engels' 'materialistic concept of history.'

3

Liberal Economics

A. Classical Liberal Economics

1. Emergence of an economic domain proper and of 'political economy'

Agriculture, the crafts, manufactures and trade became less controlled by the Church and the Crown in the seventeenth and eighteenth centuries. Christian exhortations concerning generosity and alms and warnings against greed and usury lost some of their sway over people's minds. The restrictions and regulations through corporations, guilds, tariffs and privileges were partly abolished, partly weakened. Money circulated more freely and abundantly. The end of adscription increased the number of wage labourers. Production of goods for sale as commodities prevailed over production for one's own consumption. Market relationships—sale and purchase of commodities—became paramount, as well as *exchange* in an extended sense (exchange of work and money-wage, of money and merchandise). The inventions and implementation of machinery and the building of factories contributed to the emergence of *the economy* as a relatively independent sector of human existence. To this new (ontic) object corresponded a new kind of knowledge, that of 'political economy'.

2. Market and State

The prices of goods and services are determined through the market, which is the totality of the multitude of mutually independent and mostly unknown buyers and sellers. Through the market operates 'the law of supply and demand': the prices are fixed when demand and supply equal each other, when nobody will buy at a higher price, nor anybody sell at a lower.

Through each market participant's endeavour to obtain an

advantage, the economy as a whole is best served. This is the 'invisible hand' which makes everybody work for the public weal while striving for selfish gain. This famous notion of an 'invisible hand' is a specification of Divine Providence. A. Smith was convinced of a pre-established harmony, as expounded earlier by Leibniz. For this 'mechanism' to operate it is essential that the participants do not try to co-operate, nor have power to command the prices. No single participant decides what the prices shall be; the anonymous mass decide *en bloc*. Everybody is free to participate or withdraw; the market is therefore an instance of free competition.

The conviction that a Liberal economy works smoothly was also expressed in the general statement (or 'law'), associated with the name of J. B. Say, that supply creates its demand: The very moment a product appears it offers a new possibility for other products to be sold, and, therefore, overproduction is impossible.

Since the market allocates commodities in the economically (and morally) best way, it should be left to itself. It is incumbent on the State to protect the market from enchroachments. Its legal apparatus must punish theft and fraud, and settle disputes over agreements and contracts. It is also the task of the State to keep armed forces as a defence against foreign enemies. In addition, the State also has some constructive obligations, such as to build roads and bridges, or provide some basic education in public schools. Above all, most Liberal economists assigned to the State the task of managing the money institution through a central (national) bank, which issues the currency and decides its relation to that of other States. Relief of the poor may also be a concern of the State, though on this point Liberals have never been unanimous. The conception of a *natural order* in the economic domain was common to both Physiocrats and the founders of Liberal economics. The experience of the market 'mechanism' as something marvellous recurs over and over again in the history of Liberal economics.[1]

---

1. Here is a relatively recent testimony: 'The problem that gave rise to economics, "the mystery" that fascinated Adam Smith as much as it does a modern economist, is that of market exchange: there is a sense of order in the economic universe ...' (p. 6); and 'In the process of studying economics, every student is

3. The labour doctrine of value and the productivity of labour division

The activity designated *work* or labour was asserted to be the source (or cause) of wealth of a State and not the fertility of the soil (as the Physiocrats claimed), nor a favourable balance of exchange with other States and a large stock of gold (as the Mercantilists maintained). When goods are bartered, the amount of work required for their production determines the ratio of exchange, or, in other words, the labour-time determines the exchange value of goods. This is generalized to cover the relation between wage labourer and the owner of the means of production ('capital'): the wage covers the means of subsistence which the wage labourer needs. The value of wage labour is determined by the work time required to produce these means. The economic value of tools and all other kinds of *matériel* can be traced back to work activity. The notion of a subsistence wage was often associated with that of 'natural price', a Thomist notion.

The differentiation of economic activities into a plethora of occupations, termed division of labour, is considered a source of wealth in itself, since it augments tremendously the productivity of work. The emerging economic order called industry indefinitely carries on the division of labour and thereby the accumulation of wealth.

The existence of profit and rent is interpreted in several ways: partly as deductions from the wage, due to the capitalists' advances of the means of subsistence before the work is done, partly as the value of the services provided by the capital-owners as organizers and entrepreneurs.

4. Utility doctrine of value

Beside the labour doctrine of value it was posited that human desire was the origin of economic value, (l'abbé de Condillac and others), more generally, that economic value was ultimately

sooner or later made aware of the fact that the price system is a mechanism that imposes orderly rules of behavior on economic agents, and imposes them automatically, without central direction or collective design. ... it is the kind of mechanism that is capable of harmonizing the pursuit of private interest with the achievement of social goals. This insight comes to each of us in its own good time with all the thrill of a personal revelation'. Marc Blaug: *Economic Theory in Retrospect,* 2nd. ed., p. 61 (1968).

reducible to utility. (The co-existence of natural right and utility within liberal politics is paralleled by the co-existence of labour and utility doctrines of value.) J. B. Say and Bastiat in France, and Carey in the USA represent this strand of thought. One pays for the effort one has spared oneself. This is the beginning of the consumer's sovereignty: the economy offers services among which the consumer chooses in his (her) endeavour to make life pleasant. This expresses the 'optimism' of most of liberal economics (in contrast to the 'pessimism' of Malthus and Ricardo): the market economy, based upon private property, produces even more utilities, making life better every day.

Human needs and wants make things appear as more or less scarce, useful and valuable. In the market transactions, the exchange creates value, since what is useless to the seller is transferred to the buyer, for whom it is of value. What goes on within a Liberal economy—on this interpretation—is the production, distribution and consumption of utilities, and, hence, the optimal satisfaction of the citizens' needs, desires and wants.

5. The belief in the truth and superiority of a Liberal economy
Even if it would be wrong to say of Smith, Malthus and Ricardo that they lacked a sense of history (since their works are evidence of the opposite), many other Liberal economists were prone to present this kind of market economy as the perfect solution of mankind's millenian economic troubles. The 'spontaneous' market mechanism was compared to the (presumed) unshakeable truths of classical mechanics. The 'law of supply and demand' was conceived of as on a par with the 'natural laws' of mathematical physics. Once the laws of a Liberal economy were discovered, they ought to be obeyed or adapted to, just as it is reasonable to adapt to the laws of the physical environment. The alleged truths of a Liberal economy were considered to be valid for all economic activities and transactions in the past. This implied the elaboration of the conception of *homo oeconomicus*. In certain respects, the human being has always been the same: he seeks to satisfy his bodily needs, seeks pleasure and avoids pain, pursues his own advantage (his 'interest'.) The economic order which secures each human being's unhampered ('free') pursuit of satisfaction and wealth

while at the same time respecting others' pursuit of the same, is the just order, since it allows human beings to express their essential economic properties.

According to this interpretation, Liberal economy appears as the end towards which human history has been striving or progressing. As regards the essential traits, there will be no more progress of the Liberal economy, but it will itself contribute to progress through producing and accumulating ever more wealth, or utilities. What is needed for progress to continue, is the Liberal State's protection of the Liberal economy.

6. An overview

To resume, what is termed classical Liberal economics consists of several inter-related propositions concerning the economic order that has prevailed in North-Western Europe since the eighteenth century. They tried to interpret the existence and distribution of rent, profit and wages as reasonable and just; to show the productivity of division of labour as a source of wealth (thus combating tariffs between countries, pleading the superiority of Free Trade as a case of division of labour between countries); to show how the institution of the market allocates goods in the best way through the 'law' or 'mechanism' of demand and supply, which makes prices oscillate about the natural price or the value of commodities, and hence that the government should not intervene in market transactions, but protect and secure its unhampered functioning. In its 'optimistic mode', Liberal economics interprets this economic order as the institution of Progress, producing ever more wealth for all nations, provided its liberty is respected. In its 'pessimistic mode' (Malthus, Ricardo, J. St. Mill), population increase, especially caused by the working class's lack of self-restaint, threatens the economy with increased poverty (which shows that it is highly dangerous to help the poor, since that will make them proliferate and cause still more poverty.)

This doctrine is partly descriptive, partly prescriptive; it states that if this economic order were perfected, it would be the best economic order conceivable, since it is based upon individual freedom, property, and leads to justice and wealth. But it also describes how this order is not left completely to itself in actual life, and explains deplorable traits by imputing them to this fact. It attacks previous regulations of the market, and defends the Liberal order against proponents of forms of 'socialist' and 'communist' order.

B. Neo-Classical Liberal Economics

Neo-classical economics, like the classical version contends that an economic order based upon private property and market competition is the one that will lead to the best and most just social life. It, too, endeavours to demonstrate how the products become allocated in the most 'economic' way through market competition, how Liberal economy really is a 'system', in the sense that the domain of production, distribution, consumption and investment (accumulation) are interrelated and constitute an *order*. It, too, adopts Say's law, according to which over-production is impossible in a market which is allowed to func tion without interference from outside.

What is novel, is above all the *marginal calculus* of consumption and production, the treatment of three *factors of* production,[2] and the concept of *general equilibrium*.

1. The marginal calculus
a) Marginal utility—The labour theory of value was relegated at the end of the nineteenth century by the doctrine of utility, which had undergone an important reformulation: The price of a commodity—it was now said—was determined by its use value, but by its *marginal* utility, not its total utility. Presuppos-ing that the utility of a unit of a commodity decreases the more units we consume, there is an (imaginary) final or marginal utility for which we are willing to pay, and which settles the price. This holds for the isolated consumer, and also for the market, since the purchasing consumers are substitutable, in the sense that each is conceived of as buying his or her marginal unit.

In order to illustrate this reasoning, one often presents ab-stracted examples (*Gedankenexperimente*) like the following: A hungry customer is willing to pay (say) 10 shillings for a loaf of bread, which is consumed immediately, 5 shillings for another

2. This notion, it is true, goes back to J. B. Say.

loaf, 3 shillings for the third loaf, and so on. At some moment the consumer will be replete, and will therefore pay nothing for an additional loaf of bread. The sum of money paid for the last unit of bread he (or she) was willing to buy will partly determine the market price for the bread. The marginal unit purchased partly determines the price of all units.

This explains why useful things like water are cheap, and diamonds expensive.

b) Marginal productivity—After having been applied to interpret consumption, the use of the marginal calculus was generalized to the domain of production, too. The reasoning was parallel: one visualizes a production process where the productivity of labour diminishes continuously the more units of labour power are employed. By derivation of this production function one can determine the point at which the market value of the goods or services produced by an additional unit of labour power is equal to the wage paid for this unit. The owner and director of the means of production will stop hiring wage labourers at this point, and the productivity of the last worker that could be hired before this point was reached—the marginal productivity—will determine the wage level for all the workers. The difference between the wage and the market value of the product (which is greatest for the first worker and decreases towards zero) accrues to the owner of the means of production (the 'capital owner').

2. The factors of production

While the classics of Liberal economics conceived of rent, interest and profit as deductions from the economic value created by (wage) labour, neo-classical economists treat land and capital on a par with wage labour as factors of production. Each factor is thought of as being 'rewarded' according to its productivity or cost. Thus, a marginal productivity is reckoned with as regards both land and capital owners and propertyless wage labourers; it may be demonstrated that each factor of production in a competitive market gets what is its due. In particular, wage labourers are paid according to the market value of the product of the marginal worker hired, and therefore the only reasonable way wages can rise, seems to be by increased efforts, improved means of production or both.

3. General equilibrium

By means of the marginal calculus it became feasible to abandon such metaphors as that of the 'invisible hand' or 'economic harmonies' and describe the inter-relations of the Liberal economic order as a set of mathematical functions, illustrated by the curves of analytical geometry. It was shown how a Liberal economy can be in a state of general equilibrium, in the sense that the market prices clear the market and all the goods and services offered are purchased.[3] This implies that the conception of a class society is replaced by that of a mass society of producers and consumers participating in various markets (the labour market, the market of means of production, of consumption goods etc.).[4] The producers set up their production functions, the households their consumption functions and, if the aggregate consumption and production functions intersect, there is an equilibrium point.

Owing to its highly general formulation, the demonstration of a general equilibrium does not pertain to any determinate, existing economy. It rather serves as a Kantian regulative idea, which orients thought in a certain direction, inducing economists to think of economic life as something that tends toward equilibrium, as a desirable state of affairs.

The State and the government's relation to this kind of economic order is the classical one, but since government has taken charge of more economic activities than it did in the *laisser-faire* period, it must be given more attention. The possibility of a governmental 'welfare economy' within the frame of Liberal economics, was therefore investigated.

4. Mathematics and economics

With few exceptions,[5] neo-classical economists increasingly expressed their thoughts by means of mathematics. Through the

3. 'It is the mutual dependence of economic phenomena which makes the use of mathematics indispensable for studying these phenomena.' Pareto: *Manual of Political Economy* III (1906), § 228.
4. Pareto's optimum presupposes a mass society without solidarity. In a solidary group it is not necessarily true that the group as a whole is better off when one member has bettered his lot, while the others are not worse off than before.

concept of diminishing utility, economic reasoning was linked with the differential calculus: the last or marginal unit could be interpreted as a differential quotient of a mathematical function, and this opened up a vast field where mathematic analysis could be applied, followed subsequently by other forms of mathematics. This usage was connected to the conception of knowledge as somehow a simplified thought model of that sector of reality of which one sought knowledge: to know something is to have an adequate model of what is known. In order to know something, one should set up a tentative model and put it to the test of reality. If the test was passed satisfactorily, the model could be considered correct and the knowledge it conveyed valid. However, an economic model may be correct even if its derived propositions were disconfirmed by observed reality, since counteracting contingent factors may have been operative. Thus, a Liberal economic order never functions undisturbed by force and fraud by labour unions, monopoly, governmental intervention or relations to non-liberal economic orders, and therefore observed economic reality can never decide whether the neo-classical doctrines are true. The economists are thrown upon their power of judgement, and make a reasonable estimate of the correctness of their thought models.

For this reason, the tendency has been strong within neo-classical economics to make extended use of the *ceteris paribus* clause: other things being equal, a relationship is said to obtain between entities. If not observed, one maintains that it holds, referring to more or less specified disturbances.

C. Ripostes

The emergence of the economic *sui generis*—both as an ontic and an epistemologic object—was always resisted, and thus there were always at least two opposing 'schools' dealing with matters economic—such as the British school of Liberal economics and the German Historical school, or somewhat later the neo-classical Liberal school and the American institutionalist school.

5. The most prominent, perhaps, was Ludwig von Mises, who repeatedly rejected the use of mathematical analysis and statistics in economic science. Cf. *Human Action* (1949).

1. Productive force of culture

Adam Müller—the founder of the Romantic school of national economics—discussed the spiritual capital embodied in language and the other cultural institutions. Friederich List followed up: While praising Adam Smith for his doctrine of the division of labour, he at the same time thought that this great discovery prevented Smith from elaborating his second profound insight, that labour is a source of wealth. Smith rather distorted this insight, List thought, especially through the distinction between productive and unproductive labour. For it is wrong to say that it is productive to raise pigs, unproductive to raise children. Culture—the institutions of family law, of religion and science—is a most important productive force.[6]

This led to the conception of economics as a moral science. To Knies, morality is inherent in all human action, and this cannot be ignored by economists.[7] To support this statement he draws on Kant's moral philosophy; in addition to 'the causal laws of natural processes' he invokes 'the causality of the morally free human being'.[8]

Still later investigations, like that of Max Weber's on Protestant ethics and the rise of the Capitalist mode of production, bear on the same topic. To Weber, the urge (the 'motive') to save and invest cannot be taken for granted at the beginning of the Capitalist era. This bent of mind should be accounted for, and a possible interpretation is to consider it a derivation of an initial Protestant attitude towards life. In other words, ethics can be a productive force.[9]

6. Friederich List: *Das nationale System der politischen Oekonomie,* 1842.
7. Karl Knies: *Die politische Oekonomie vom geschichtlichen Standpunkte,* pp. 24–5, (1874) (The first edition was published 20 years earlier). Knies also approvingly quotes Schmoller, who (with Thornton) denies the abstract 'law' of supply and demand', since the medium of customs and mores intervenes: 'The total demand is nothing but a piece of concrete history of morals of a particular period and a particular people ...' He also approvingly cites and refers to Le Play: 'Le Play is a firm adversary of modern economic life, of the system of free competition etc. The centre and cornerstone of his considerations are not the free individual, not religion or the State, but the *family* ...' *Op.cit.,* p. 137). (My translation).
8. *Ibid.* p. 440.
9. Max Weber was trained within the Historical school of jurisprudence and economics *(Nationalökonomie),* which was part of the Romantic movement. When he was in in his thirties he collapsed mentally and physically, and slowly recovered. When he began to publish again, he must have been regarded by

Veblen's interpretation of the economic conditions of his time also brings in moral considerations. First, the 'instinct of workmanship' is dominated by the opposed 'predatory instinct' searching to 'get something for nothing', which expresses itself as the rule of bankers and other owners of huge pecuniary assets over industrial activity. Next, the moral of craftmanship and its concomitant respect or even worship of individual property has survived in an economy where industrial work has become essentially collective and calls for public forms of ownership. This moral therefore impedes an economic development in accord with reason and justice.

2. Historicity

The historic objection was put forward especially succinctly by Knies. What he termed 'absolutist' economics—that of Ricardo, and later of Jevons and Walras—made the claim 'through the scientific treatment of the tasks of political economy, to offer unconditional thruths, valid in the same way for all times, countries, and nationalities'. To this erroneous conception he opposed the historical conception of political economy, the fundamental theorem of which was that 'the economic conditions of life, and hence also the theory of political economics ... is a result of historical development ...' The egoistically minded people A. Smith wrote about, are not transhistorical characters, Knies states, but a historical specification of nationality.[10]

3. Oppression and alienation

The labour doctrine of value (especially in Ricardo's version) could easily be used to repudiate the claim that a Liberal economy is a unity of differences, an affirmative whole, a 'harmony' of 'interests'. If Labour creates all economic value, the existence

many as a renegade. For he attacked collective and 'organic' conceptions, accepted much of marginalist economics, thus siding with Menger rather than with Roscher, Knies and Schmoller in the *Methodenstreit*. True, his neo-Kantian doctrine of 'objectivity' in the social sciences and, in particular, the notion of the *Ideal-type*, is meant to offer a position different from both Emanatist and Empiricist empistemology, but this doctrine brought him closer to the latter than to the former.

10. Knies, *op.cit.,* p. 24.

of rent, profit and interest is due to the propertied classes' oppression and exploitation. The relation between the three great classes of society is one of conflict.[11] This conception was fully developed later by Marx's doctrine of surplus value.

In addition to the asserted unjust distribution of the economic product, the Liberal economic order was accused of debasing the human being, especially the unpropertied, both during the production process and in social life in general. This accusation was raised within different quarters. Thus Kant, the Liberal, worries over whether selling one's labour is compatible with human dignity. Hegel, taking a mediate position, accepts wage labour and the 'atomism' of the market, provided it is mitigated by corporate institutions. Comte deplores the homeless situation of the *prolétaires;* they have to be integrated into society.[12] Adam Müller launches his attack from the standpoint of an admirer of feudal, medieval society, deploring the dissolution of guilds, and the masses' enslavement under the money owners.[13] Adam Smith, too, worries over the debasing effect upon the workers.

Comte writes that the division of labour should not be evaluated solely according to the gain it gives in productivity—'in the infinitely narrow sense of the economists'—but in relation to the unity of society. It makes everybody work for others, but pushed to the extreme, it is a threat to community, and is in need of a moral ascendant of a spiritual kind.[14]

4. Abstractness of political economy

To Comte, political economy is an essential part of the 'critical philosophy' of the Enlightenment, and as such it contributed to the victory over the outdated social order of *l'ancien régime.* It promoted the development of 'modern industry', but has become in its turn harmful, owing to its 'grave political inconveniences'. In an age of social disintegration (decomposition) it

---

11. Cf. Halévy: *Histoire du socialisme* (1937), which comments on Owen, Hodskin, Thompson and other early socialists; and Engels' foreword to the 2nd volume of Marx's *Capital.*
12. 'Le prolétariat campe au milieu de la société sans y être encore casé.'
13. Cf. Roscher: *Geschichte der Volkswirtschaft* (1874).
14. This anticipates Durkheim on division of labour.

is indispensable to reinforce the movement of *re*composition and integration. Therefore, political economy becomes dangerous, since it erroneously states ('as a universal dogma') that every regulating intervention in the economic process is useless or harmful. Having observed a few, unimportant cases of 'spontaneous' readjustment and re-establishing of an order, political economy draws the obnoxious conclusion that a regulating institution is always superfluous. Thus, when the labouring classes protest against the perturbations of their existence provoked by the introduction of machines in their production process, the political economists merely repeat 'their sterile aphorism about absolute industrial freedom'. They answer that these perturbations are transitory and that in the long run even the working class will obtain a real and permanent bettering of their lot. But this answer is really ridiculous, Comte affirms, pretending as it does to forget that human life does not last indefinitely.[15]

He flatly rejects political economy's separation of utility and selfishness from the total situation, 'it remains certain that man's conduct is guided neither uniquely, nor even chiefly by calculations'.[16]

The increasing use of mathematics in Liberal economics during the last fifty years has made stronger the charge of abstractness. One obvious reason why mathematics so easily pervades Liberal economics (apart from the prestige it gives in some quarters to engage in something resembling mathematical physics) is that in a commodity and money economy, the economic seems to consist of mathematical orders and magnitudes. As Simmel remarked, in no other previous society have so many been occupied with counting and computing. At the same time, everybody knows that money in itself is not an economic good, and that the topic of economics is 'use values'—i.e. means of subsistence, houses, equipment, tools, natural resources etc.—which the prices somehow represent or reflect. These use values are 'qualities' which ultimately constitute a life style or a Culture. The 'critique' of a country's 'gross national product' that points out how wrong it is that everything we pay for

15. Comte: *Cours de philosophie positive,* 47th lecture (1840).
16. Comte: *Système de politique positive,* Appendix V, Considérations sur le pouvoir spirituel (1826). (My translation).

is considered an economic good or a service, is cheap, but nevertheless correct. Taking a step further, one can see that all economic calculations are no more than indicators of something not itself liable to be treated by the *mathesis*.

For this reason, the very elaborate mathematical propositions of much neo-classical economics do not lead to more precision, but, on the contrary, move away from economic realities. When carried to the extreme, mathematical economics becomes an exercise in mathematics only.[17]

This is the danger of constructing 'models' which, as one knows beforehand, make unrealistic assumptions about economic life: they become so to speak immune against reality tests.[18] This can be exemplified by the neo-classical doctrine of consumption. This branch is often little else than an exercise in mathematical analysis. One starts by assuming the existence of a utility level, U, which is a (mathematical) function u of the vector of goods x, and one assumes further that the consumer maximizes the function $U = u(x)$: *not* in the sense that the consumer in fact applies such an equation, but that he (she) behaves *as if* he did. For the sake of simplicity one also assumed that all goods are *infinitely dividable* (like flour). Defining the concept of utility ordinally through reflexivity, transivity, and continuity of preferences, one proceeds to prove mathematically the existence of one best element within the set of possible consumption functions.[19] Mathematically, this may be impeccable or even brilliant. But the very concept of preferences that are ordered in a continuous series is misleading when we consider human life in general. In particular, one may point out that consumption is

17. 'By their intention to cut off the *économie politique appliquée* from the *économie politique pure*, in order to make a stringent science of the latter, they will not arrive at an *économie politique pure*, but at a *mathématique appliquée*. Here one tries to solve a mathematical problem through labouring a mathematically moulded object.' Knies, *op.cit.,* p. 503—'The science of economics is, therefore, mathematics applied to the concept of human action and to its subspecies.' Croce: *Filosifia della practica,* p. 261 (1906). (My translations).
18. Cf. Hans Albert: 'Modellplatonismus', in Narrenberg, Friedrich & Albert (eds.): *Sozialwissenschaft und Gesellschaftsgestaltung* (1963).
19. A strictly parallel error is that of constructing a continuum of prediction acts, as Herbert A. Simon does in a well-known article 'Bandwagon and Underdog Effects and the Possibility of Election Predictions', 1954, reprinted in his *Models of Man* (1967). Cf. an article by Audun Øfsti and myself: 'Self-defeating predictions and the fixed-point theorem', *Inquiry* No. 3, 1982, and Simon's reply in the same issue.

a way of participating in socio-culturally determined contexts of meaning *(Sinnzusammenhänge)*, in cultural forms, where preference acts are infrequent, unless the word preference is inflated so as to become devoid of meaning. To be sure, this objection has already been met, since the mathematical doctrine of mathematics is expressedly presented as a 'model' of what consumer behaviour would be like *if* consumers acted according to the assumptions. On the other hand, the application of these models in and on everyday life has not been undertaken, and this calls forth the urge to treat consumption as a topic of sociology and social research.[20]

The mathematical approach to economics often blurs the distinction between money prices and sums and that which the sums and prices refer to, the goods, services and means of production, all the kinds of *matériel* and materials.

On the most advanced level this basic ambiguity was the topic of the so-called 'Cambridge' or 'Capital controversy' a few decades ago, between neo-classical and 'neo-Ricardian' economists.

Neo-classical economists conceive of 'capital' as an entity which enters into a production function together with (wage) labour. The price of capital is likewise thought of as determined by *its* marginal productivity. If so, the term 'capital' must denote some determinate *matériel*—a machine, or some other equipment, raw material, etc. As such, each piece of capital- as *matériel*—may be of its own kind. Yet the different kinds of capital are dealt with as homogeneous, in so far as they have their market price measured in money. Then capital turns into a homogeneous stuff.

Further, neo-classical doctrines assume that under perfect competition the purely technical combination of 'men and machines' that yields the highest or best output in terms of products will also be the one that fixes the prices of the production level for the market as a whole, thus avoiding waste. (This assumption may be altered through the disturbing impact of trade unions, monopolies etc.)

This means that there is no harm in the *double-entrendre* of

---

20. Cf. Veblen's *Theory of the Leisure Class* (1899), or the recent work of Bourdieu: *La distinction, critique social du jugement* (1979).

the term 'capital', denoting now some *matériel*, and now a money magnitude, since there is a correspondence between productivity and profitability.

The neo-Ricardians proved that this is not necessarily so. They constructed cases where the technical composition of labour power and *matériel* had no necessary connection to price and profit. This leads to a paradox in relation to neo-classical doctrines: a production technique may be replaced by another requiring more intensive use of capital at a given wage level (in consonance with neo-classical common sense), but there may perfectly well occur a switching back to this technique at a higher wage level (impossible according to neo-classical teachings). This is meant to show that one should not conflate the economic 'concept of capital with the stock of physical means of production',[21] and that neo-classical Liberal economics works with an untenable concept of what capital is.

One important corollary is that the price of capital cannot be determined independently of the class conflict between wage labourers and capital owners. To measure capital in terms of its market price is circular reasoning, since prices are determined by the distribution ratio between wage labour and capital.

This entails that one cannot always refuse to raise wages by giving the reason that this will make production unprofitable, since that may, or may not, be the case.[22]

According to Joan Robinson, who initiated this discussion, the unfortunate habit of thinking of capital as a homogeneous stuff is contracted and reinforced through extensive use of mathematical language in economics.

5. Ad marginal utility

An array of objections to reasonings about marginal utility and utility in general were posed by widely different thinkers in the aftermath of the so-called Marginalist Revolution.

Veblen attacked what he discerned as the underlying presupposition, that economic activity is driven solely by pursuit of pleasure (hedonism). Instead, in a way reminiscent of the young

---

21. Cf. Johan Robinson: Contributions to Modern Economics, p. 122 (1978).
22. Cf. M. Dobb: *Theories of Value and Distribution since Adam Smith* (1973), pp. 262–3.

Marx, he emphasizes the human being's urge to objectify and express himself through activity.[23]

More specifically, he attacked J. B. Clark's marginalist account of the determination of wages, on the ground that the painstaking work of the wage labourer and the consumer's pleasure in consuming the goods produced are not commeasurable.

Croce affirmed that Gossen's law of decreasing pleasure did not pertain to what goes on in life, since strictly speaking all acts are unique and diverse and hence not quantifiable. Just as Bergson had shown that instead of saying, for instance, that one fruit tastes sweeter than another, we should say that its sweetness is (qualitatively) a *different* one, Croce points out that the second or last mouthful does not procure a lesser enjoyment, but a (qualitatively) *different* one, and that the last was in its way just as necessary as the first one.[24]

Also, in his exchange with Pareto, he objects to the notion of a scale of economic values, in the sense that we visualize ourselves in different (economic) situations, and make a choice according to our scale of values. This, Croce maintains, is strictly speaking impossible. Values are constituted through our choice, which does not imply a (quantitative) comparison, but our will.[25]

A third point of disagreement concerns Pareto's notion that the relation of utility (or 'ophelimity') is simply a relation of pleasure, not entailing any judgment of economic approval. Against this, Croce asserts that there is such a thing as *economic remorse*, which means that I act in a self-contradictory way, yielding to a temptation, which afterwards leads to an economic disapproval of my choice.

Schumpeter, by his emphasis upon the creativity of at least *some* human actions, implied a break with the reasonings of

23. 'Man is not merely a bundle of desires that are to be saturated ... but rather a coherent structure of propensities and habits which seek realization and expression in an unfolding activity.' *The Place of Science* (1919), p. 74.

24. '... otherwise, he would remain unsatiated as to his normal needs, his habit, his whim'. *Filosofia della pratica* (1908), p. 259. (My translation).

25. 'a is worth b, the value of a is b does not signify (the economist's of the new school are well aware of it) a = b; but nor does it mean, as they say, that a > b; but that a has *value* for us, and b *not at all*.' (My translation).

marginal utility, as noted by Andre Piettré.[26] The entrepreneur is described as one who has an urge to create, to bring forth something new, without paying heed to the validity of marginal costs. Marginal reasonings seem to be confined in their validity to the actions of repetitious economic life.

Sombart also refers to cases where the conception of marginal utility does not apply, such as the passionate collector of stamps, coins or vases. Each new piece gives greater pleasure than the foregoing, and there will be no saturation or oversaturation. The same goes for avarice and covetousness.

Comparisons of utilities can only be undertaken through the medium of money, Sombart affirms. But money prices do not correspond directly to or reflect mental states of feeling. Therefore, he states that 'in economic reality the economic behaviour of men is not determined by the doctrine of marginal utility'. The doctrine may at best serve as a Weberian 'ideal type', as a conceptual tool through which we obtain a provisional order out of the unsurveyable weave of economic connections.[27] Hilferding and Bukharin, among the adherents of Marx, considered the main weakness of marginal reasoning to be its turning away from the realm of production and the objective, and towards consumption and the subjective (tastes).[28]

6. *Ad the rewards of the factors of production*

As mentioned earlier, classical Liberal economics conceived of rent, interest and profit as a deduction from the economic value created by labour. Neo-classical economists instead treat land and capital on a par with wage labour as factors of production, each of them being 'rewarded' according to their productivity or cost. Thus, there is a marginal productivity of both land and capital and money as well as wage labour.[29] This presupposes the property structure of land owners, capital owners, and property-less wage-labourers and a corresponding differential

---

26. A. Piettré: *Histoire des doctrines économiques* (1959).
27. Sombart: *Allgemeine Nationalökonomie* (1960), pp. 72–74.
28. The various objections to the concept of marginal utility set forth within the Marxian tradition is resumed in A. Mátyás: *History of Modern Non-Marxian Economics* (1980). For my part, I have discussed the concept in 'Two notes on consumption', in Otnes (ed.): *The Sociology of Consumption* (1988).
29. The sometimes mentioned marginal productivity of a manager is a *non sequitur*.

structure of wealth. Given this structure, it may be demonstrated that each factor of production in a competitive market gets what is its due.[30] But this begs the question in so far as it does not explain why this property structure should be accepted. To be reckoned with as one unit of additional manpower and as a factor in a production function shows that wage labour is alienating. As to exploitation, this seems to have been reinterpreted as the only reasonable payment of this production factor. But this may lead one to question the justice of this property structure, why there are owners and non-owners and, even if this be admitted, why the proportion of owners and non-owners should be that which happens to exist, and why the consumption of the owners exceeds that of the wage labourers.

And this easily leads one to pose the more general question whether this property structure depends for its persistence on an armed custodial force (the 'police') or 'ideological apparatus', in other words, whether the relationship between owners of land and capital and wage labourers is not that of common 'interest', but that of 'class conflict'—which may bring one to Marxian conceptions or other forms of 'institutional' economics.

Apart from this objection one may point out that this market determination does not suffice to account for income distribution in society as a whole. Besides and complementary to the market economics there is the public sector, where a considerable part of the citizens are employed. This sector consists to a large extent of non-profit organizations, that is, their products and services have no market price. The payment of civil servants and other employees is fixed according to the characteristics of 'bureaucracy' (in the Weberian sense), according to rank, prestige, seniority, etc. The differential remuneration within the public sector should therefore be understood as an integral part of a system of *social stratification*, that is, it belongs to sociology. Moreover, the market's dependence upon the public sector is itself a topic for sociology.

---

30. 'The salary of a professor of economics measures his contribution to society and the wage of a garbage collector measures his. Of course this is very comforting doctrine for professors of economics but I fear that once more the argument is circular. There is not any measure of marginal products except the wages themselves.' Joan Robinson: *Op.cit.* p. 12.

7. Flaws in the doctrine of equilibrium

a) *Limited validity*—The long period of extended, involuntary unemployment nourished doubts among many neo-classical economists as to the functioning of a Liberal economy when left to itself (though the majority perhaps maintained their conviction.) The most prominent spokesman was Keynes, who endeavoured to show that neo-classical economics is valid only for a special case of Liberal economy, and therefore should be supplemented by a 'general theory', covering the cases where enduring (not transitory) under-employment and over-production occur, unless the government intervenes in various ways (public investments, deficit budgeting, deliberate, if modest, inflation etc.) According to Keynes, a Liberal economy may be in stable equilibrium at a level below full employment for reasons unknown to neo-classical economics. He further submitted that such a state of under-employment would not remedy itself, and that therefore the market was not generally self-regulating. Through the 'multiplier effect' (a device originally invented by Kahn) it was shown how effective demand could be stimulated so as to secure full employment.

b) *Statics vs. dynamics*—Long before this most influential Keynesian revolt or reform, Schumpeter had expounded a doctrine of economic development which implied a break with the equilibrium doctrine.[31]

Economic development, he tried to show, came about not so much through steady augmentation and accumulation, but through ruptures, discontinuous inventions of 'new combinations' that get the economy out of its equilibrium. It is *entrepeneurial* activity that creates something new, breaking routines and habits of acts and thoughts, supported by a certain kind of credit that creates purchasing power *ex nihilo*.[32] Thus, before he worked out his *élite* doctrine of politics, Schumpeter had already presented an *élite* conception of economic evolution.

31. Though Keynes himself remained committed to Liberal politics and economy, thinking of the above-mentioned kind could with good reason be taken as an indirect confirmation of important tenets of Marxian economics, as shown by one of his pupils. Joan Robinson: *An Essay on Marxian Economics* (1942).

32. Schumpeter: *Theorie der wirtschaftlichen Entwicklung* (revised ed. 1926), p. 109. The similarity between Bergson's and Schumpeter's thought is obvious,

c) Sociological assumptions—In order to explain the apparent failure of a Liberal economy, Keynes introduced some new assumptions about the market participants, such as their 'liquidity preference' of their 'marginal propensity to consume'. These were psycho-sociological assumptions, which made Liberal economics more dependent upon other branches of knowledge than it had been before. Thus, the Keynesian investigations indicated that economic sociology may greatly enhance the understanding of a Liberal economy.

Shortly after Keynes' *General Theory* had appeared, Parsons published his *Structure of Social Action*, showing how two leading neo-classical economists, Marshall and Pareto, had adopted concepts transcending the original Liberal frame. Thus, Parsons pointed out how Marshall skipped the presuppositions that each participant's ends (wants, tastes) were independent of other participants—an insight which may be stated in terms of social norms. Two decades later Parsons went further in the same direction, discussing Keynesian economics in sociological terms. For instance, he (and his co-author Neil Smelser) made an effort to improve upon Keynes' doctrine of 'the propensity to consume', by sketching a consumption function derived partly from sociological considerations.[33]

8. Conclusion

Liberal economics—classical and neo-classical alike—investigates and defends the free use of individual property, a freedom protected by the Liberal State. The individual's political freedom and his economic freedom (in the sense of participation in an essentially free market) are intertwined.

Among the manifold objections which have been levelled against Liberal economic thought, three fairly distinct kinds have been presented:

and their *chef d'oeuvres* were published nearly simultaneously, in 1907 and 1911, respectively. Both concentrate their attention on the qualitatively new, the spontaneous; both affirm that evolution is a creative process, led by unique, outstanding human beings, who differ essentially from the mass of men and women.

33. Thus, they refer to 'class and prestige symbolization (...) a major area of role involvment for the consumption unit. In so far as the specific items in a family standard of living are culturally defined as symbols of class prestige, differential spending on class symbols obtains from class to class.' (*Economy and Society,* p. 223).

The first kind challenges the narrow conception of economic activity as a relation of utility in the sense of employing tools and other material means (even human labour power) so as to obtain a maximum of effect. Against this is affirmed that the 'wealth of nations' comes about through processes that are cultural and moral. This points towards a broadened conception of economics as a cultural science, or to its necessary supplementation by socio-cultural conceptions. To affirm the importance of culture means to lessen the importance of strict (intellectual) computation and utilitarian activity. This corresponds to the opposition presented in chapter 2, between the primacy of tradition and the primacy of decision.

The emphasis on historicity is closely connected to these considerations. Partly as a national defence, partly as a rejection of Liberal economics as the final, true economic order, it underlines the changing cultural settings of economic activity through the centuries.

The second kind corresponds roughly to the second chapter's opposition between community and individual. To the extent that production and consumption cannot be taken as strictly individual activities, but as collective—(for instance, to the extent that tastes and preferences are not strictly individual, but expressive of socio-cultural norms), this points once more to a socio-cultural science as a substitute for, or supplement to, Liberal economics.

The third kind concerns the conflicts inherent in any economy constituted by the relationship between the propertied and the propertyless. Against the assurances that a Liberal economy benefits all and everybody it is asserted that it conceals oppression and conflict. Superficial, formal equality and liberty cover basic, real or material inequality and lack of freedom for those who perform wage labour. The highly abstract, mathematical design of recent Liberal economics sometimes contributes to blurring these conflicts (as shown in the case of the 'Capital Controversy'). This shortcoming makes apparent the need for an economics of oppression and struggles, as a substitute or complement.

When these kinds of objections are combined, several possibilities of economic thought that are different from Liberal economics arise. In accordance with the Introduction, two of them are singled out for lengthy exposition, that is, Sociology as the Science of Social Integration (chapter 4), and Historical Dialectial Conceptions (chapter 5).

*

Social Statistics and Sociography on the one hand, and Liberal politics and economics, on the other, together make a *bloc*, since their oppositions are founded upon a unity—the triad of the State, the Market and the Individual. The following chapters try to expound topics which, as it were, lie beyond this *bloc*.

4

Sociology as the Science of Social Integration

1. The fundamental concept of sociability
a) An initial exposition: Comte
Auguste Comte continued the endeavours of Bonald and de Maistre, both of whom he profoundly admired. His aim was to make their insights the foundation of a new science of the social, *la sociologie*, while leaving out what to him appeared as obsolete Christian faith. This new science should confute once and for all Liberal politics and economics,[1] and give precepts for the establishing of a new order of human relations. 'L'Ordre pour base, le Progrés pour but, vivre pour Autrui'.

His main objections to political economy have already been mentioned: the market is unable to create order. Likewise, he never gets tired of attacking Liberal political writers such as Voltaire and Rousseau and their likes. Their talk of 'rights' he deemed 'metaphysical' in a derogatory sense, as intellectual constructions abstracted from the 'positively' given situation, and from knowledge of the 'positively' given human constitution. Political constitutions, enacted in General Assemblies, Parliaments and similar political *fora*, cannot create order either. What is needed, is a *social* order, based on a specific human *sociability*.[2] Neither the political state, nor the economic market, but society is the fundamental domain.

1. Comte was also opposed to the probability calculus, which founds (inductive) social statistics. In the *Cours de philosophie positive,* he rejects reasonings about the probable as 'purement chimérique'. This may be seen as a contingent feature of Comte's doctrine, in the sense that he might just as well have been favourable towards this new branch of mathematics (in which he himself was generally an expert). But his disapproval can also be interpreted as expressive of his predilection towards the understanding of wholes or totalities (the *polis*, the organism, the church).

According to Comte, the human being is both selfish and sociable, both affective and intellectual. But selfishness and affectivity are initially preponderant, though only a dominant sociability, led by the intellect, can provide for a good and happy life. This circumscribes the most general task of sociology: to show how the affections and the intellect, the selfish and the sociable, can be brought into an equilibrium so as to make a social order.

This is obtained firstly through family life, 'the eternal school of social life', which mediates between the individual and society at large. The married couple makes a basic social unit of complementarity. If women are the feeble sex with respect to intellectual strength, they are endowed with a superior capacity of sympathy and sociability. From these alleged truths Comte infers that the man shall have dominance, while the woman, though being the subordinate and obediant, shall be the moral centre of the family. The two sexes need each other; husband and wife form a union in the strong sense of the word. The child's relation to its parents implies a 'gradual education of the social sentiment' The child comes to love and venerate the parents as its superiors, while fatherly love is the purest expression of what it is to love our inferiors. Both relations teach us sociability through time, the one 'to respect our predecessors, the other to cherish our successors'.[3] Relations to brothers and sisters also develop in us our inborn propensity for being attached to others, devoid of protection and competition; they are most susceptible of being extended to universal love.

Domestic relations, Comte says, are first and foremost moral, not intellectual, and differ essentially from the social bond proper, which is the sentiment of co-operation, co-ordinating the relations of families to each other. Concerted efforts in order to achieve a common end, specialization of occupations and work tasks—this constitutes above all *social solidarity*, making every family feel both its importance to and dependence on all the others. However, the very specialization which makes possible the development of a general society, threatens its unity.

2. '... la sociabilité fondamentale de l'homme', 'la sociabilité essentiellement spontanée de l'espèce humaine ...', 'penchant instinctif à la vie commune ...' *Cours de philosophie positive,* 50th lecture (1842).
3. *Système de politique positive,* II (1854), pp. 184–90.

Diversity may turn into dispersion and disintegration. To counteract this tendency is the purpose of government in society. Upon government falls the social task of thinking and acting along general lines, 'to recall unceasingly the thought of the whole and the feeling of common solidarity'. To accomplish this is urgent not only in economic life, but all through social life, hence government must be both temporal and spiritual.

In the domain of co-operation and government the intellect is preponderant; it stretches, as it were, sociability so as to cover the entire social domain.[4] While still an affective attachment, the social bond is marked by understanding (of the social).

Although the bulk of Comte's assertions must be discarded in the light of our present knowledge, the general features of his sociology cannot be as readily brushed away, since they are also discernible in more recent expositions of what social integration essentially is.

b) The social self
Opposing the pedagogy of the eighteenth century and the concern with the development of the individual's personality, Durkheim affirmed that all education involves a *socialization* of individuals. The aim of pedagogy must differ in different societies, since they have different conceptions of what is important and valuable in life. The child's development is not solely biological and psychological, but social. The self is social, egotism and altruism being 'two concurrent and intimately intertwining aspects of all conscious life'.[5]

Relations to others are therefore constitutive of the human being, and therefore beyond or beneath considerations of utility. What is given as *datum* in our experience is not the abstracted individual, the single human being, but some kind of social whole, whose ways of integrating and disintegrating are the topic of sociology.

The contributions of G. H. Mead fit neatly into this doctrine

---

4. 'C'est donc exclusivement dans la vie domestique que l'homme doit chercher habituellement le plein et libre essor de ses affections sociales, et c'est peut-être à ce titre spécial qu'elle constitue le mieux une indispensable préparation à la vie sociale proprement dite: car la concentration est aussi nécessaire aux sentiments que la généralisation aux pensées'. *Cours,* 50th lecture.
5. Durkheim: *Moral Education* (posth. ed. 1925, English ed. 1930).

of the social: the self evolves through 'taking the role of the other', through the exchange of gestures, words and facial expressions arises a mutual understanding which is primordial. 'We must be others in order to be ourselves.' Social interaction integrates its participants into a whole, out of which develops the consciousness of being a distinct self, relatively separate from the original social matrix.

c) Anomie

This conception is also underpinned by way of contrast, by showing how social disintegration is harmful to the individual, as in the case of *anomie*.

Anomie, as introduced by Durkheim in his study of *Suicide*, is a trait of the social environment, and hence, it might be thought, something *external* to the participants of society. But this inference is wrong. In an anomic situation social pressure — *la contrainte sociale*—diminishes to vanishing point. Precisely because of this, the individuals will experience acutely their *internal* relation to society. They themselves become anomic. The structure of their need-dispositions, to employ a more recent term, undergoes a change towards dissolution. The reason is that there is no auto-regulation of human needs and desires. Unfettered by the social order, left to itself, 'our sensibility is a bottomless abyss' and becomes defective as to inner structure.[6] The individual is part of a whole in a way analogous to the *Gestalt*-psychologists' unity of figure and background. The original, irreducible unity is the individual on the background of society in general.

d) Social need as facticity

Utter, protracted loneliness can have mortal effects upon the human being, but even less extreme isolation is harmful when

6. This conception was presumably taken over from Rousseau, to whose work Durkheim had devoted part of his doctoral dissertation. Cf. the following passage: 'L'Etre suprême a voulu faire en tout honneur à l'espèce humaine: en donnant à l'homme des penchants sans mésure, il lui donne en même temps la loi qui les règle, afin qu'il soit libre et se commande à lui-même ...' (*Contrat social* (1762), book 5, the opening). Further evidence of this influence is adduced by Phillipe Besnard, who has written the hitherto most thorough and extensive book on the anomie concept, *L'Anomie, ses usages et ses fonctions dans la discipline sociologique depuis Durkheim* (1987).

it lasts long. These well-known truths are usually referred to or presupposed when one speaks about human beings' social need, that is, a need for some kind of contact with other human beings. This need is essentially diffuse; it is part of our facticity, and only felt as need in situations tending towards the inhuman. For this reason, appeal to our inborn need for social relationships will have a very limited impact upon our choice regarding what kind of social relationships we prefer or want to establish. Even the war of all against all suffices to transcend our social facticity so that we do not experience our need for the social as such. On the other hand, this facticity shows that when carried to the extreme, the cult of the self-sufficient individual human being becomes self-destructive or dishonest (as when one enjoys telling someone how delightful solitude is).

2. Primordial and derived social integration

While the science of Mechanics set its mark upon Western thought in the eighteenth century, the science of Biology had a similar impact upon the nineteenth century. The distinction between the lifeless and life, the mechanical and the organic appears in all realms of discourse.

a) Gemeinschaft and Gesellschaft

In the domain of the social, Ferdinand Tönnies constructed a typology based on the distinction between an organic society and a mechanical and artificial one, *Gemeinschaft* and *Gesellschaft*.

Gemeinschaft denotes the primordial internal relation between human beings. Its first and simplest forms are family relationships (relations between mother and child, between siblings and spouses). Neighbourhood, based upon habit, comes next, and as the third, specifically human, form, friendship, affinity of minds. The house is the simplest *Gemeinschaft* unit, from which develops (analogous to, but not identical with, organic growth), the village, the (small) town, the corporation and the religious community. The most general and complex *Gemeinschaft* concept is that of the people: those who belong to the same people are united through internal bonds, by language, customs and beliefs—*consensus*.[7]

To this form of sociality corresponds a form of will (or activity) which is termed *essential will*. This concept is best understood within the Romantic tradition's concern with expressive totalities: The essence of, say, a woman expresses itself through her bearing, her acts, which in turn are understood as expressive of her essence (or 'character'). The expression is internally related to what is expressed, as is the phenomenon to the essence.

Essential will is closely connected to organic life, as the 'psychological equivalent to the human body'. Corresponding to the three levels of sociality mentioned there are three levels of essential will—pleasure, habit and memory.

The inborn pleasure (Gefallen) at certain objects and activities Tönnies considers to be the animal form of human essential will: breathing, eating, drinking, biological reproduction and so on. They are close to instinct, since they are intentional or teleological, albeit not deliberate nor even conscious.

Habits are a more developed form of essential will, though still on the level of animality. They consist in pleasure at certain objects or activities acquired through experience and practice.

Memory is the third level of essential will. If habits are second nature, Tönnies says, memory is third nature, and corresponds to the spiritual forms of *Gemeinschaft*.

Gesellschaft is the general name for various social relationships that presuppose and stem from the *Gemeinschaft* forms. *Gesellschaft* relations are external relations between human beings, whose mutual attitude is that of fundamental indifference.[8] Everybody treats others merely as means to his or her own ends, and hence that kind of exchange from which both sides

7. 'Reciprocal, binding sentiment as a peculiar will of a Gemeinschaft we shall call understanding *(consensus)*. It represents the special social force and sympathy which keeps human beings together as members of a totality.' Tönnies: *Gemeinschaft und Gesellschaft,* Book I, §9 (1887).

8. 'The theory of the Gesellschaft deals with the artificial construction of an aggregate of human beings which superficially resembles the Gemeinschaft in so far as the individuals peacefully live and dwell together. However, in the Gemeinschaft they remain essentially united in spite of all separating factors, whereas in the Gesellschaft they are essentially separated in spite of all uniting factors.' Book 1, §19.

expect to gain, permeates the realm of *Gesellschaft*. Thus, all market relations as conceived by Liberal economics belong to this kind, and so does urbanity as the relationships between people in great towns.

The mode of will corresponding to this mode of sociality is termed 'arbitrary will' (Kürwille) and should be connotative not of *arbitrarius* (the contingent, uncertain) but of *arbitratus*, to the acting at one's discretion, at pleasure. While acts that spring from one's essence flow unreflectively ('naturally' as it is often said), arbitrary will involves the deliberate position of a purpose, a goal to reach, in relation to which external means are sought. Parallel to the forms of essential will, Tönnies delimits three forms of arbitrary will.

Its simplest form is deliberation (Bedenken), as when we represent to ourselves the pains and obstacles connected to some desired state of affairs, and hesitate. A more developed form is termed intention (Bestrebung), where planning and calculation constitute a 'system of thought', an 'apparatus in one's head', by means of which one pursues one's aims. The figure called the climber clearly exemplifies this form of will. The third form is termed *consciousness* (Bewusstsein), comprising all the assumptions and bits of knowledge one possesses to help one master the environment, 'theory and method for dominating nature and human beings'. The general aim of arbitrary will is *happiness*, which is chased or pursued or run after. Happiness is thus represented as an external object or state to be possessed through the use of intellect or even cunning.

The distinction between essential and arbitrary will should be understood within general Romantic thought, for which the relation between the naive and the experienced, the immediate and the reflective is so important.[9] *Gemeinschaft* denotes the young and fresh social life, which inevitably changes into a mature, reflective and tired mode of social life, *Gesellschaft*, where 'cool self-love' (in Bishop Butler's phrase) and second thoughts and afterthoughts have crept in. Thus, in History, youthful Greece is followed by the world-weary Alexandrian

---

9. Cf. the famous story contained in Kleist's text 'Über das Marionettentheater': A young man is praised for his graceful bearing, becomes aware of it, and for this reason loses it and never regains it. His efforts only make him less graceful; he has been spoilt by his reflection.

and Roman sociality, or Germano-Christian feudal society by the more cynical Enlightenment and its capitalist mode of production. For the same reason, women generally express essential will, while men's will is essentially of the arbitrary kind.

One of the most important specifications of the *Gemeinschaft–Gesellschaft* distinction is the interpretation of the natural law doctrine. The validity of the Liberals' natural right pertains to the domain of Gesellschaft; however, there is also another sense of natural law, the law written in men's hearts, and as such it expresses *Gemeinschaft*.

Going one step further than Tönnies, we may venture the assertion that *Gemeinschaft* refers to primordial sociality or the spontaneous sociability of which Comte spoke. It must always permeate social life to a certain (not exactly assignable) degree. If, on the contrary, social life consisted in mere *Gesellschaft* relations, it would break down, disintegrate. Essential will and its corresponding activities therefore bring forth the original and basic social integration, while the unity and totality of arbitrary wills presuppose and exploit this primordial sociality, and should perhaps be termed a (Liberal) political and economic integration. Intellect is nourished by feeling; deliberate constructions presuppose customs; explicit agreement presupposes tacit consensus. To grasp (or fail to grasp) that a pure *Gesellschaft* is impossible, is the *shibboleth* test of sociology.

b) Primary groups and their derivations

A similar doctrine was presented by Charles Horton Cooley a little later. The general background for Cooley's sociology was a certain way of conceiving wholes which he liked to call 'organic'. Organic wholes are such that their parts are interdependent, and each part expresses the whole in its singular way, as the whole expresses its parts. The organic whole is an expressive totality, and the need of expression is fundamental to life. This outlook Cooley had taken over from poets such as Thoreau and Goethe ('in endowment, almost the ideal sociologist'). In this sense, Cooley continues the Romanticist movement.

Society, according to Cooley, is a kind of organic whole. The relation between the individual human being and society is one of mutual dependence and expression. The individual and the social are as it were two sides of the same thing or entity. From one point of view society appears as composed of individuals, from another it appears as a whole. For instance, a school class can be experienced both as a whole and as a set of separate pupils, but these two experiences are interdependent. The individual human being is strictly inconceivable abstracted from others, and on the other hand a society cannot be thought of as something distinct from its composite members.[10]

Cooley thus repudiates Liberal conceptions of the individual: between the individual and the social there is no priority, logically or evolutionarily. There is no individual becoming a social being, nor a social whole developing into individuals. If we go back to the time when our ancestors were such that we would not call them social, it must be equally wrong to call them individuals or persons, Cooley wrote. A deficient or inferior individuality is correlative to a deficient or inferior sociality.

That is, an individual is a human being connected to a collectivity by an internal relation. If there has been a pre-collective era, which is dubious, that era was also a pre-individual one.

Cooley applies the often used analogy of orchestral music,[11] and expressly rejects a *utilitarian* conception of society: 'It should not be conceived as the product merely of definite and utilitarian purpose, but as the total expression of conscious and subconscious tendency, the slow crystallization in many forms and colours of the life of the human spirit.'

10. This reasoning stems from the Aristotelic-Thomistic logic with its so-called 'moderate conceptual realism'. The general concept—*in casu* society—is said to be neither a name *(nomen)* for a number of individuals (thus escaping conceptual nominalism), nor an entity other than the individuals and endowed with an independent being (thus escaping conceptual realism). The middle position is to affirm *universalia in rebus*, which means that society exists 'in' and through its individuals. Moderate realism lost its grip on Western thought when mathematical physics won through in the seventeenth century. Nominalism and more Platonic conceptions became dominant. But moderate conceptual realism was an important trait of the Romanticist movement and its attempts at a revival of medieval culture.

11. 'No one would think it necessary or reasonable to divide the music into two kinds, that made by the whole and that of a particular instrument, and no more are there two kinds of mind, the social mind and the individual mind.' And further: 'The unity of the social mind consists not in agreement but in organization ... whether, like the orchestra, it gives forth harmony may be a matter of dispute, but that it sounds, pleasing or otherwise, is the expression of a vital cooperation, cannot well be denied.' *Social Organization,* pp. 3–4 (1906).

This relationship between the individual and the social is manifested in the clearest possible way in the kind of contexts which Cooley terms *primary groups* and which he describes as intimate fact-to-face association and cooperation. The outcome is, he says, 'a certain fusion of individualities in a common whole' which he calls the experience of belonging to or being a 'We', of mutual identification with others.

Such groups come into being in a more or less spontaneous way. They are not established like contracts (according to Natural Right doctrine). Neither are they instrumental in their orientation, but first and foremost they are ends in themselves, not something else. Furthermore, Cooley claims that primary groups are nearly universal in the history of mankind, to be found at all times and places. They express Comte's fundamental sociability.

The family, the neighbourhood, the community, the peer group of adolescents and the play-group of children—these may be particularly clear instances of primary groups when they are not marred by selfishness and struggle for domination. These expressive totalities exemplify the limiting concept of complete social integration, as distinct from, for instance, the economic integration which (according to neo-classical doctrine) is obtained through markets of perfect competition. Life in primary groups does not exclude conflict and self-assertion. 'It would be a poor conception of the whole which left out the opposition, or even one dissential individual.' But discordance will in the end be transcended by unity. In the primary group each member expresses the group in its own, singular way. Self-expression is at the same time group-expression. The 'I' expresses the 'We'. And therefore Cooley is able to state that to sacrifice one's self might at the same time be self-assertion, in so far as it is assertion of the group.

Convinced that primary group life is the good life, not only for himself, but for all other men, too, Cooley is led to ask how the essential traits of the primary group could be preserved in larger social settings. Being thoroughly acquainted with Evolutionist thought, Cooley believed that the primary groups were a primitive stage in society's evolution toward an all-encompassing organization of all human beings. We have and can have face-to-face relationships with only a dwindling part of humanity, but for many reasons we are ever more aware that we do have an impact on others geographically distant, and conversely. The question then arises how the social world could develop into an expressive totality, uniting all larger and smaller groups through a common commitment to what Cooley terms the 'primary ideals'—the primary group itself, and, derived therefrom, other universal virtues such as 'loyalty, lawfulness, freedom', truthfulness and kindness. Cooley's general answer is: through the new means of *communication*.

As in the section on Tönnies, one may take one step further and state, *mutatis mutandis*, that, like 'essential will', the attitudes of primary relations constitute the basic social integration. Whereas—on the other hand—the derived, secondary relations between people who are distant from each other and strangers, cannot by themselves make a social whole. The aloofness, coolness, utility-oriented ('impersonal', 'formal') attitudes of secondary relations may be tolerable, even pleasant in some contexts and to a certain degree (as when we are on holiday abroad). But if we imagine that nearly all our relations to others were of this kind, so that we never felt any internal relation to others, but constantly found ourselves external to any group whatsoever, the situation will appear as socially impossible, as disintegrating.[12]

This chain of thought purports to show that the Liberal conceptions of the individual and utility are untenable or at least secondary, and presuppose a social integration.

3. Integration and disintegration of differentiated societies

The doctrine of biological evolution included the concepts of integration and differentiation. The process of evolution entailed the emergence and survival of ever more differentiated integrated entities, 'organisms'. Spencer applied this thought not only to the realm of the organic, but also to what he termed the 'super-organic', the subject matter of 'sociology'.

Durkheim took over from Spencer the notion of social evol-

---

12. Nils Christie, the Norwegian criminologist, speaks of primary and secondary social control. The police exert secondary control, but if undue recourse to the police takes place, the primary control breaks down and calls for more secondary control, leading to a socially disintegrating, vicious circle. Cf. for instance, his *Limits to Pain* (1982).

ution as a process of differentiation, but diverged markedly as to the specificity of social integration as distinct from biological.[13] According to Spencer, the evolution had been from ceremonious and military societies to utilitarian and industrial ones, integrated through contracts between independent individuals. Durkheim agreed on the prevalent religious and ritual character of archaic societies, but forcefully objected that the social bond uniting human beings in differentiated societies like his own was not mutual advantage and selfishness, but an 'organic solidarity' transcending or founding relationships of mere utility. On this subject, he rather lent upon Comte's writings on primordial, spontaneous solidarity, which he elaborated. The general proposition is that while undifferentiated societies are integrated through rituals, differentiated societies are integrated through morality and law.

a) The social integration of occupational life
The division of labour in society is a specification of the general notion of differentiated wholes. Everybody who accomplishes a special task thereby contributes to the general goals of society as a whole; the relation between the specialists is one of *solidarity*. Durkheim tried to show peremptorily that this solidarity could not be reduced to mutual advantage of the individual participants, as Spencer had maintained. According to Spencer, solidarity in industrial society arises spontaneously from the free actions of exchange between the members of society. Now, exchange usually takes the form of contracts, and therefore, Spencer conceives of solidarity in industrial society as contractual solidarity. In this case, Durkheim resumes, 'social solidarity would then be nothing else than the spontaneous accord of individual interests, an accord of which contracts are natural

13. Durkheim (and also Cooley) claims that society originally consists of an undifferentiated social mass, an anonymous social existence, in which human beings take part, without any idea of being, each of them, a 'self'. When a differentiation takes place, Durkheim further claims, the first individual human beings, that is, the first with a feeling of 'I', will be the leaders of the society. These leaders, often described by Liberals as despots, are not really despotic. True, they dominate, but they do not suppress the others' individuality and freedom, since they have not yet acquired individuality and freedom. This reasoning purports to show the genealogical priority of the collective over the individual; it is an *anti-robinsonnade*, and, probably, more true to history.

expressions'.[14] Thereupon, Durkheim attempts to show that this is impossible.

As a preliminary, Durkheim objects that the legal obligations imposed on the members of society, and the legal apparatus as such, should have diminished if Spencer's view was correct. But, he contends, the opposite is the case: 'It is very evident that, far from diminishing, it [the legal apparatus] grows greater and greater and becomes more and more complex'. Therefore, he maintains, Spencer is wrong in taking the contract relationship as the more and more prevalent kind of social bond. True, the number of contract relations augments, 'But what Spencer seems to have failed to see is that noncontractual relations are developing at the same time'.

This reference to what is given does not suffice for Durkheim. He hastens to add that contracts themselves are not free exchanges. That is, even if contracts were the ever-spreading type of social relationship, Spencer would be wrong. Durkheim affirms that contracts are *legal* relationships, and therefore regulated by society and not by individuals. This implies that a contract binds the partners in unpredictable ways, depending on the course of events. There are also *customary* elements in law, rules of what is equitable, which are tacitly assumed by the contracting partners. Durkheim goes on to add further support for his assertions stating that legal regulation of contracts is no substitute for exchanges proper, except in a purely theoretical sense. For if we were to regulate all our interactions by way of explicit contracts, social life would be practically impossible.[15] Contractual law furnishes sufficient permanence and previsibility to social interaction, by establishing norms, based on experience.

In other words, to engage in a contract transcends to a large extent *individual* intentions. Any act of contracting refers to *common* attitudes, conception and customs which, as it were, absorb a great part of the contract, which resembles the famous

14. *Division of Labour in Society,* p. 203 (1893).
15. 'If, then, it were necessary each time to begin the struggles anew, to again go through the conferences necessary to establish firmly all the conditions of agreement for the present and in the future, we would be put to rout ... if we were linked only by the terms of our contracts, as they are agreed upon, only a precarious solidarity would result.' *Ibid,* p. 214.

iceberg—the individual part of the contract is the visible part. Social norms or folkways are constitutive of a contract, and—*mutatis mutandis*—of exchange as such. Purely individual engagements must be *ponctuel*, instantaneous, almost devoid of meaning. For our acts are partly defined by their possible fulfilment in the future, and this fulfilment will be determined to a great extent by social norms. To make exchanges or act at all outside the legal sphere would be like acting in a no man's land with no cues in the action field. To put it another way, the legal rules form part of tradition, and to act without a base of tradition is not possible. And, finally, in addition to the legal rules, the *mores* exert a certain pressure on us, at the same time as they provide a setting, conferring meaning on our activity.

In this way Durkheim wants to show that the picture of a society of individuals engaging in exchange activities is superficial and fallacious. These exchange acts are part of, and ox pressive of social solidarity, of a social, normative life, a moral life transcending the individual as such.

But does not this reasoning itself lead to a utilitarian interpretation of institutions? Does it not seem that the legal system is useful for social interaction? No, the legal system is rather a *condition of possibility*, a transcendental condition (in the Kantian sense) for contracts and agreements. This is a more reasonable interpretation of Durkheim's argument, among other things because he contends that contractual law 'is no longer simply a useful complement of individual conventions; it is their fundamental norm'. Thus utility is contrasted to norms.

The integration of occupational life through market exchange is therefore merely apparent. The integration is specifically *social*, expressive of a specific solidarity which is non-utilitarian and non-individual. This is why Durkheim pleads in favour of a revival of the occupational guilds or corporations. They will be adequate to express and articulate the concerns and conflicts of a differentiated economy.

b) The social integration of political life
Durkheim also challenges the Liberal political order of his time—representative democracy based on elections where each voter casts his or her vote in secret. This political institution

produces disorder, just as the market within the economy. Liberal politics is detrimental to the making of social solidarity, since it rather stimulates selfishness and narrow-mindedness. The electorate becomes or may end as a mass of separate, selfish or self-oriented individuals, constantly tempting and tempted by politicians who make promises that cannot be kept. To amend this deplorable, disintegrated situation, Durkheim recommends founding government and politics on the corporations, that is, founding the political on the social. If mass elections were replaced by representatives chosen and delegated by the corporations, the sense of the social whole would be preserved.

The government and its administration—which together constitute what is called the State—should not be conceived as something external to the citizens, but as the self-reflection of society.

Starting from the concept pair of society and individual, Durkheim later on thinks in terms of the triad of society, State and individual. The state protects the individual from a possible tyranny of the smaller social group, but this social group constitutes the individual through its adherence to its collectivity, the organic solidarity. Social relationships in the strict sense remain fundamental in relation to political relationships.

4. Social integration of undifferentiated societies: rituals

The specific way through which social wholes with little or no differentiation are integrated—such is Durkheim's proposition —may be termed *ritual*. Ritual calls forth and expresses a certain social experience to which Durkheim gave the much decried name 'collective consciousness', but which, as will be shown, might also be interpreted in a way less outrageous to (Liberal) common sense.

One may distinguish between negative and positive rituals.

a) Punishment as negative ritual

Durkheim gave the following interpretation:

What we call punishment is an outburst of rage. He who is punished, the offender, has done something that elicits rage. Those who punish are usually specific organs, or authorities. They do not, however, punish on their own behalf, but on behalf of the entire society, the collective. Punishment is thus a collective undertaking.

Further, this collective undertaking has an intention or a purpose, like every other action, but this intention usually appears in a disguised or encumbered form. It usually looks as if its purpose is to deter the offender, or members of society in general; punishment readily seems to be a preventive measure, a deterrent and warning. Yet punishment does not work preventively in this way, and in this respect punishment fails to achieve its effect. It is not senseless, however, because it has another sense. It reinforces those who inflict the punishment in their own obedience to the law. By giving expression to anger and abhorrence at some misdeed, others are strengthened in their resolve not to do likewise. This effect is further reinforced by the fact that punishment is undertaken in community; the outburst of indignation of one is reinforced by that of the others, creating a collective rage, an experience *sui generis* incomparably more powerful than the indignation of the individual alone.[16] Punishment thus forges solid bonds between those who punish; they aver their community and solidarity with one another. Punishment's 'true function is to maintain social cohesion intact, while maintaining all its vitality in the common conscience ... We can thus say without paradox that punishment is above all designed to act upon upright people...'

But this takes place in such a way that it appears as if it were society itself, that unique entity, that was demanding revenge and atonement. Punishment thus appears in an illusory form, but, says Durkheim, it is a necessary illusion. What this implies, it would seem, is that the *esprit de corps*, the great 'we,' the collective, can only exist and exercise its peculiar kind of power by virtue of a kind of self-deception on the part of each individual participant which does not appear to derive from an exertion of willpower. The feeling that the collective constitutes something different from ourselves, something exalted and of an

16. 'If anyone expresses before we do an idea which we have already thought of, the representation that we gain from it contributes to our own idea, superimposes itself, confounds itself with it, communicates to it whatever vitality it has. From this fusion grows a new idea which absorbs its predecessors and which, accordingly, is more vivid than each of those taken separately.' *Ibid.,* p. 113. G. H. Mead gave a similar interpretation.

essentially different nature, is quite simply overwhelming. These collective feelings, says Durkheim, 'appear to us as an echo in us of a force which is foreign to us, and which is superior to that which we are. We are thus forced to project them outside ourselves, to attribute what concerns them to some exterior object'.

b) Religious practice as positive ritual
Again, one may consider the most general or simple case, where the religious customs and beliefs are shared by all members of the social whole in question, and hence do not call forth or aggravate internal conflicts. Here, the participation in cult activities has a specific fortifying and unifying effect on the group as a whole. Disregarding the great varieties of such activities, they all have in common to express one's commitment to or even adoration of one's group. The overt object of the cult may be a goddess, an animal, an artefact, a stone and so on, but this object is a symbol of the group itself. Therefore, the religious cult is the group's self-adoration as a group. 'Society is the soul of religion.' If the religious rituals and beliefs appear strange to the outsider or the non-believer, this is because the language of religion is the language of the collectivity *sui generis*, and therefore unintelligible to the individual who does not participate in the group.

The structure of ritual is the same as in the foregoing case: There is an overt, expressed intention or purpose, and an implicit, tacit, subconscious or unrecognized purpose, that is, to strengthen the group's integration. The chants, the dances, the prayers, the mortifications and afflictions all have this significance, which may be understood by the participants, but most often will pass unnoticed.

5. Latent social function and amphibious interaction
These and similar accounts of social integration are often connected to the thought that customs such as rituals have or perform an integrating function for the social whole in question in a way that at least resembles organismic functions. That is, rituals go on as if the social whole as such acts with the aim of re-establishing or reinforcing its unity. The notion of function, or more precisely *latent* function, expresses not that the single

members of the group (the 'individuals') act, but that their acts must be understood as expressing a non-individual or super-individual intention, that of the group mind, the collective consciousness or the like. The social totality seems to act as if it pursues its own self-preservation or good. Thus, to say that the function of punishment rituals is to reinforce social integration means that such rituals are the means by which the group in question reinforces itself.

Simmel and Weber were both among the first to repudiate this reasoning. Weber wrote that the 'functional' consideration of the 'part's' relation to 'the whole' could at most serve as a preliminary, on the condition that one avoided 'the false conceptual realism'. In other words, he maintains that a given social whole, a 'State' or a limited company is just a name *(nomen)* for certain individual human beings and their actions. To this conceptual nominalism corresponds an ontological individualism, the conception that solely individual human beings exist, not totalities of human beings.[17] Ever since, the struggle over the functional approach or 'functionalism' has been endemic. On the one side, those who contend that all actions can be ultimately traced back to individual agents, on the other side, the proponents of a collectivity *sui generis*, acting as such. The one side claims that descriptions of social functions are just descriptions of consequences of actions, and, in particular, that latent social functions refer to what Merton termed 'the unintended consequences of social action'.[18] The other side retorts that strictly individual actions do not and cannot take place, since they are always mediated by collective structures, such as language and cultural symbols. A possible way of surpassing this opposition is to consider the significance of *amphibious* action and interaction in social life:

17. Weber: *Economy and Society,* pp. 14f.
18. Popper, a declared Liberal thinker, also claimed that the proper topic of social science should be the unintended consequences of action, as a means to resist thinking that deplorable social conditions are always produced by people who have 'a vested interest in hell' *(The Open Society and its Enemies, vol. II* 1941). Recently he has been followed by Raymond Boudon, who rejects expressions such as 'Capital requires labour power with certain qualifications', 'the dominating classes mystify the exploited classes', and wants to substitute references to such collective or non-individual agents by interpretations of individual agents and unintended consequences of actions. Cf. for instance Boudon: *Les effets pervers* (1981).

All of us, presumably, have had the experience that our actions may fail because we try too hard, are too intent on success, and that in such cases it is advisable to have an oblique intention, to act as if we did not act, carelessly or the like.

Especially within artistic performance this topic is much discussed, since in the domain of art (at least *les beaux arts*) action should not dwell on toil, eagerness to succeed, apprehension of failing, but flow gracefully, elegantly or 'spontaneously'; but the intention to be 'spontaneous' spoils spontaneity, it seems, and the unlucky artist is caught in a vicious circle of over-achieving. Nevertheless, a kind of 'reflective spontaneity' does exist. It is a great concern of the wisdom of the East—as in the Tao teaching of action as non-action—and is also described from time to time in the West.[19] One can succeed in doing one thing provided one seemingly tries to do another thing, or perhaps better: by shifting, amphibiously, from the one to the other. Action should not be intended by intellect, nor driven by will, but nevertheless, or precisely for that reason, express an intention.

Ritual settings are such as to suggest social interaction where all participants act toward each other in an amphibious way, that is, not deliberately, but nevertheless intentionally (kneeling, singing, dancing, etc. together). The often rigid prescriptions of conduct that are applied, make it especially easy to switch back and forth from the true topic and the faked topic, and to forget to be preoccupied with one's own achievement. The ritual process passes as if not every member of the group acted for himself or herself, but as if the group itself acted. This happens when the expert dancing couple performs at its best, or the group of musicians, or the football team. This is what the expression *esprit de corps* refers to, everybody acts as if they were members of the same body *(corpus)*.

This makes it intelligible why Reformed Christians have a more reluctant attitude towards rituals than Catholics do. This reluctance is an aspect of their general emphasis upon intellect, will and self-control of the individual. To participate in rituals may be experienced as losing oneself in a way that afterwards

19. For instance *The Art of Seeing* by Aldous Huxley; *Zen in Archery* by Herrighel, and the books of F. A. Alexander.

brings remorse and shame. And the same goes for the place of rituals in a socio-cultural world dominated by instrumental action orientations: They tend to be regarded with suspicion, as intellectual dishonesty or bad faith, self-delusion; and, perhaps, tend to be badly performed in a way that makes them stiff or clumsy, that is, a caricature of themselves.

6. Social integration by opposition and from the outside

The integration of a social whole can be reinforced through a relation of opposition to another social whole in the environment. The adversary or hostile group makes the members of the other group aware of what they have in common, and especially when they perceive a threat, appeal is prone to be made to basic commitments (cultural values, way of life etc.). The awareness of being a 'We' or an 'Us' in relation to a 'They' may arise (although there is also the possibility that the group will disintegrate when exposed to an external threat).

Now, the experience of reinforced integration can be exploited in the following way. In a situation where a social group tends to dissolve or is involved in grave internal conflicts, integration may be restored by the attention being directed at an external enemy, real or feigned or imaginary. Then the previous internal tensions and disagreements may be felt as less important in face of a common threat. In this case, too, the integrating activity is amphibious, achieving one aim while overtly doing another thing. But if the intention to restore inner unity is too overt,[20] to point at an external threat or enemy will be perceived as a subterfuge, as a deliberate attempt to divert attention from important inner struggles.

As to internal group conflicts, they too, may have integrating consequences; as such, they lead to a crisis: The aggravation of the discord may reveal that disagreement was at bottom more important than agreement, and the group falls asunder; or going through a conflict may show that what united the members was, after all, of greater moment than what split them, and hence the group may be better integrated after the crisis is overcome. Again, this insight may be present during a conflict,

---

20. This is one of the meanings of Faust's famous: 'Man merkt die Absicht und wird verstimmt': Some intentions, if they are to succeed, must not be deliberate and reflective.

and make the process more complex and the outcome more ambiguous, since some or all of the participants may surmise that the conflict was—deliberately or amphibiously—somehow induced to bring the group to the point of crisis.

Finally, unity of a social whole may be preserved by the group's concern with conflict issues of little significance, while it would probably disintegrate if more fundamental conflictual topics came to the fore. Thus, the group continues to exist by a precarious unity that cannot bear scrutiny and attention. Once more, the avoidance of the endangering topics may stem from both a deliberate and an amphibious intention.

7. Social integration of thought, perception and memory

The exposition so far has revolved around the conception that human beings are somehow united or fused together through conduct that does not spring from the intellect and the will (without for that reason being 'irrational'). This section deals with how the intellect itself is conditioned by sociality, and integrated socially into a whole.

a) Perception

To perceive the world is not detached from what we are doing in the world. We perceive, not a flickering of externally related impressions, but a situation, that is, a structured whole, a *Gestalt*, of meanings, signs, exigencies or suggestions, that address our capacity to act in the world. We perceive the world differently in so far as we have different projects or protensions. Further, I do not experience my perceptions as mine in the strict sense that nobody else could perceive the same. On the contrary, the world's structured landscape of signs, tools, *matériel* is given as perceivable and already perceived and partly produced by others. The perception of Others is partly constitutive of my own perception; I perceive a shared world, and to this extent, perception is basically social. This does not preclude perceptual differences. Humanity as the totality of human beings, past, present and future, is given as a diversity of more or less loosely integrated groups, nations, cultures, among which I myself belong to some. The recognition of this diversity reinforces the experience of being integrated into a social whole; since it reminds me of the fact that to perceive the world differently would involve shifting my social adherences through getting integrated into a new reference group or culture.[21]

Perceiving in the broad sense also includes sensations, to hear, to smell and taste and so on, and these experiences, too, are partly constituted by our sociality. Sounds are heard as order or noise according to the language we know and the musical scales and rules we are aquainted with. Tastes and smells are saturated with socially determined meanings, as shown by the great variety of what is considered edible throughout the world.

b) Thought

Thinking is internally connected to speaking, and to speak is a social relationship; it is speaking to and with others, by dint of a commonly understood language. The unity of our thought is for this reason shaped by sociality. Moreover, our criteria for what shall count as a valid statement are partly determined by our reference group (in Merton's sense). This will usually pass unnoticed, but in cases of profound disagreement we will be reminded that the truth of our thoughts is partly constituted by a *consensus* among those considered competent. One will then be aware that one's conceptions have risen within a specific context (a 'school', a 'tradition'), since they lose their obviousness when confronting strangers. To be sure, one may be stubborn and still regard one's own conceptions as true, and wish or claim that those who disagree should undergo a re-education. But one may also have second thoughts, and consider the difficulties connected with such a re-education (translations, interpretations, connotations, sub-textuality etc.), and arrive at the, perhaps uneasy, conviction that knowledge can never be completely dissociated from its social conditions. One may also proceed to take one further step and state that the notion of universal truth is internally related to the notion of a united humanity, and that no proposition can be fully true as long as there exist repressions and oppressions among human beings (and between human beings and other living beings.)

21. Within French culture, Bourdieu has recently shown how class oppositions express themselves in the realm of taste, which is structured as a field of oppositions, both in the sense of conflict and domination, and in the sense of linguistics. (Cf. Bourdieu: *Op.cit.*)

c) Memory

To remember something may at first glance appear as a psychic act or event that as such does not refer to any social relation. But Halbwachs undertook a painstaking work to show the opposite. When we remember something, we explicitly or tacitly refer to collective experiences, and especially to language.[22] But also the memory of music can not be a strictly individual feat, as Halbwachs tried to show; it is connected to the existence of collective schemes, such as the written score.[23] Generally, he states that 'a person remembers only situating himself within the viewpoint of one or several groups and one or several currents of collective thought'.[24]

8. The syntheses of Sorokin and Parsons

Two attempts to weave together these affined strands of thought were undertaken around the middle of our century, first by Pitrim A. Sorokin and then by Talcott Parsons.

a) The general sociology of Sorokin

(i) The point of departure is what he terms 'the general social phenomenon', which is said to be *meaningful interaction* of human beings. By interaction he means 'any event by which one partly tangibly influences the overt actions or the state of mind of the other'. In order to be social or socio-cultural, interaction must also have meaning or value 'superimposed upon the purely physical and biological properties of the respective actions'.[25] Next, meaningful interaction is dissolved into three parts; those who do the interaction (its 'subjects'); the meanings, values and norms for the sake of which the interaction takes place; and 'the overt actions and material vehicles

---

22. 'Nous parlons nos souvenirs avant de les évoquer; c'est le langage, et c'est tout le systeme des conventions sociales qui en sont solidaires, qui nous permet à chaque instant de reconstruire notre passé' *(Les cadres sociaux de la memoire)*. These reasonings have an affinity to those undertaken by Wittgenstein in his lectures at Oxford, published posthumously in *Philosophical Investigations* (1953).
23. 'La mémoire chez les musiciens', in *Revue philosophique,* 1939.
24. Maurice Halbwachs: *La memoire collective* (posth.), p. 33. (My translation).
25. 'Stripped of their meaningful aspects, all the phenomena of human interaction become merely biophysical phenomena and, as such, properly form the subject matter of the biophysical sciences.' *Society, Culture and Personality* (1947), p. 47.

through which the meanings, values and norms are objectified and socialized'.

(ii) A slightly different way to describe this is to affirm the unity of the *cultural* system, the *social* system, and the *personality* system. The cultural system is a totality of meanings and values, which together make a consistent whole. However, this integration is never complete; there are always contradictions and inconsistencies within culture. These make for the dynamics, the change of culture. Further, the cultural is objectified in social and personal systems. The social system is a relatively integrated whole of human beings, which, in turn, mirror the social system to which they belong. The social system consists of interactions between human beings, according to various forms of social norms, expressing cultural meanings and values. It also consists of vehicles and artefacts embodying cultural values. The interdependence between the spiritual and social and material aspects of the socio-cultural world is fundamental. (This fuses together propositions to be found in the works of Durkheim, Cooley and many others).

(iii) Distinguishing between organized, unorganized, and disorganized groups and social systems, Sorokin states that the organized groups are integrated through law-norms, that is norms that prescribe what are the group members' rights and duties, what is obligatory, and what is prohibited. These norms are not necessarily legal (formal); they may just as well, and even more often, be part of the (informal) customs and mores recognized in the group. To these norms correspond on the part of the personality system a *normative motivation,* different from motives of purpose and utility-orientation.[26] Thus, when they are ongrafted, one does not comply with law-norms for fear of punishment, but from conviction.

(iv) These law-norms, through determining every member's rights, duties and tasks, *differentiate* and *stratify* the group. Social stratification is claimed to be an inherent trait of all such groups, in the sense of a rank order that involves various other forms of inequality. Stratification is interpreted as being *functional* for the group, in the sense that it preserves and reinforces the group's integration.[27]

26. *Ibid,* p. 76.
27. *Ibid,* pp. 377–78.

(v) There are at work specific 'mechanisms' through which groups maintain themselves, and which are similar to the self-regulations of organisms. Such 'mechanisms' are functional or perform an integrative function.

(vi) Cultic acts, rites, reinforce group integration through the members' affirmation of ultimate values and meanings, that is, their ultimate solidarity with each other.

(vii) Solidary groups (as distinguished from antagonistic ones) are divided into *familistic* and *mixed* or *contractual*. These concepts are meant to supersede those of *Gemeinschaft* and *Gesellschaft* and Cooley's concept of primary groups and other social relationships. The familistic group is a 'we', and their mutual concern extends to most of the members' life; while the opposite holds for the contractual group, where mutual concern is limited, and everybody acts in a selfish way.

(viii) This broad distinction between solidary groups specifies one still more general, the fundamental distinction between *ideational* and *sensate* cultural systems.[28]

Sorokin devoted a voluminous work (*Social and Cultural Dynamics*) to the task of showing that Western history moves in a cyclical way, passing from the ideational, *via* the idealistic to the sensate form of culture, and then repeats the movement. He asserted that we are approaching the end and break-down of a sensate era, and forecast the adventure of a new ideational one.

b) The general sociology of Parsons
(i) The point of departure is the concept of action and the conclusions drawn from a discussion of what he termed the 'utilitarian dilemma'.[29] In order to be action, and not behaviour (an organism's reaction to environmental stimuli) there must exist a normative orientation on the side of the human agent, that is, a choice between different kinds of action norms. This is a *conditio sine qua non* if there is to be an actor in a situation (as different from an organism in an environment). (Like Soro-

28. This distinction presumably stems from Sorokin's Orthodox Christian upbringing and faith. Orthodox Christian Churches emphasize the Spirit (pneuma), while the Roman Church emphasizes God, and the Protestant churches the Christ and the Cross (cf. G. B. Shaw's 'Crosstianity').
29. 'The utilitarian dilemma' is expounded in chap. 6.

kin, Parsons is zealous to make clear his disagreement with behaviourist tenets.)[30]

(ii) The interaction between two human agents or 'actors'—Ego and Alter—is described as a relationship of mutual orientations and expectations.[31] This complementarity presupposes communication through a common system, which makes for stability and enables actions and gestures to have approximately the same meaning to both actors. For these reasons, an existing symbol system tends to acquire a normative significance for the actors; they will tend to act so as to preserve it for the purpose of communication. A shared system of symbols is therefore constitutive of a social interaction situation.

Thus, the human being as a psychological system, a 'personality', is internally related to the cultural system. The cultural system is a whole, a relatively consistent order of values—cognitive, moral and cathetic—to which action is oriented. The social system is a relatively coherent order of social roles, which express and objectify the cultural values. The role-expectations are internalized by the personality system, especially through child socialization but also later in life. Personality is a system of need-dispositions which correspond to the social and cultural systems. These three systems or orders together make a totality, and can be described separately only through an act of abstraction.

(iii) As already shown, the human being has a choice of several action orientations. Tönnies' *Gemeinschaft-Gesellschaft* and Weber's four action types were attempts to conceptualize these orientations; Parsons endeavours at the same time to give a more general and specific exposition. Any action and situation is dissolved into a number of choices between alternative features (variables), which can be combined into different structures and 'patterns'. The ensuing set of possible combinations,

30. Sartre and Merleau-Ponty faced the same task as Parsons, to develop an anthropology beyond both Idealism and Positivism. Following Kierkegaard and Heidegger, they described the human being as neither pure nature nor pure spirit, but as 'existence'. But they concur with Parsons in their notion of the *situated* action.

31. '... since the outcome of ego's action is contingent on alter's reaction to what ego does, ego becomes oriented not only to alter's probable *overt* behaviour but also to what ego interprets to be alter's expectations relative to ego's behaviour, since ego expects that alter's expectations will influence alter's behaviour.' 'Values, motives and systems of action,' in *Toward a General Theory of Action* (1951), p. 105.

claiming to be exhaustive, was called the 'pattern variables'. Every actor, it is said, is faced with five choices or even dilemmas. He or she must decide whether to act in a way that is (1) universalistic or particularistic, (2) specific or diffuse, (3) affective or affective neural, (4) achievement-oriented or ascription-oriented, (5) self-oriented or collectivity-oriented.

Through choosing from between these alternatives, different actions, roles, and cultural patterns emerge. The total number of combinations is 36, though there is a tendency for some of the variables to cluster in actual social life. The pattern variables confer greater generality on sociology, compared to the efforts of Weber, Durkheim, Cooley and others.

(iv) This doctrine of social action is connected to a 'structural-functional' approach to the topic of social integration. Partly influenced by systemic thinking within biology, Parsons ventures on some assumptions concerning a social system's inherent tendency to maintain itself. He also poses a sociological equivalent to physics' 'law of inertia'.[32] From this he derives the further assumption that social systems display several integrative devices or 'mechanisms' to preserve their equilibrium. Especially, internal differentiation is a process by which a social system copes with internal conflicts and tensions, and external changes and challenges: New specific roles develop, new specific institutional contexts, new specifications of the value pattern, which at the same time achieves greater generality. Thus, the ultimate values that found the unity of actors belonging to the same society, their consensus, tend to transcend more narrow boundaries of kinship groups, ethnic groups, estates, classes, nations, and, as in the case of the USA, to approach a 'supra-national consensus'.

Further, any social system is seen as differentiated into four sub-systems, each of which performs a specific function for the system as a whole. The first function is adaptational to the system's internal and external conditions. On the level of society this function is performed by the economy. The second function is goal attainment; on the societal level, this corresponds to activities within the political system. The third function is the integration of the social system as such. Religion and, more generally, cultural activities perform this on the societal level.

32. *The Social System* (1951), p. 251.

The fourth function is the latent maintenance of the socio-cultural patterns, where family life and socialization processes achieve this within a society.

On the basis of various kinds of experiences and experiments the general proposition is set forth, that any system passes through phases where one of the four functions is emphasized, and that this movement has a definite order, A-G-I-L. (This doctrine of differentiation, developed in terms of the pattern variables, brings to a provisional close the various efforts made in this direction.)

(v) *Social stratification* is interpreted as a specification of the general concept of a social system as a normative order.

Stratification is ultimately a rank order, where the members of the social system in question are ranked according to the esteem or prestige they receive, with respect to the dominant value orientations. The unit of the stratification order is assumed to be the kinship unit (in the Western case, the family). The value orientations may vary according to the 'pattern variables' in Western society; the universalism-achievement orientation is paramount. Wealth and power are not in themselves constitutive of social stratification; they serve as status symbols and indicators of high rank, even if in actual social life they tend to have an independent impact. Hence the integration of the stratification order will be rather loose in a society of a Western kind.

(vi) The presentation above outlines how a social system functions as a self-maintaining, self-reproducing whole, an integration of differentiated parts. As a rule, it is submitted, the members of a social system act in conformity with the expectations attached to their social roles, and thus respond approvingly towards each other. But there is, of course, also a lot of non-conformity, of deviance from the norms of the social system, the interpretation of which devolves upon sociology.

Basically, deviance is conceived as the consequence of *ambivalence* in the face of thwarted expectations; there is resentment, but still emotional attachment to the one who did not fulfil the expectations. Such an ambivalent attitude may develop in mainly two directions; either as a repression of the (positive) attachment towards the Other, or as repression of the resentment or the experienced offence. When these repressions are generalized, they become general dispositions towards others. Either one tends to reject every social norm, expressing thus an alienative attitude, or one tends to approve of everything that is normatively expected, thus expressing an attitude of compulsory conformity. These dispositions may turn into vicious circles and issue in deviant behaviour patterns such as neuroses, psycho-somatic illness, criminality, etc.[33]

In accord with the general conception it is assumed that any social system tends to respond towards deviance in a way that is conducive to its continued existence. This response is termed *social control*, processes that counteract deviant tendencies. Some kinds of social control are devised to prevent certain acts through coercive measures, deterrence and the like, but though conspicuous, they are not the most important. Instead, psycho-therapy is described as the 'proto-type' of social control in recent Western society life. But in order to understand the functioning of day-to-day social life, one must take into account the control aspect of teasing, jokes, more or less tactful rebukes and so on, whereby minor deviances are noticed and met with sanctions. Only when these 'control mechanisms' break down, do the more specific kinds of controls begin to function.

In addition to these forms of social control dealing with deviant behaviour to cope with the strains of social life, there also exist specific institutions to cope with situations of particu-lar strain. One of these is institutionalized reactions to illness and death, mourning rituals that channel emotions in a cultural-ly prescribed way. Another important device of integration is to isolate deviants and deviance patterns; through encapsulating deviance it becomes less of a threat to the social system as a whole.

(vii) This amounts to a coherent, elaborate doctrine of so-cial integration and disintegration. But the obvious repetitious

---

33. This may be compared to Hegel's 'dialectic': every conception turns out to entail contradictions, which lead to the opposite conception. Next, it turns out that the attacked conception and its opposite are basically one and the same, and this leads to transcendence of the negation and the positing of a fresh conception, which engenders its opposite and so on. Parsons' doctrine of conflicts does not lead to the social system's self-transcendence and change by itself. He affirms that every rebel represses his (her) solidarity with those he rebels against, because the rebel basically shares the same fundamental value orientations.

character of the social system thus described calls for some doctrine of social change. This is offered in several versions, such as the proposal to treat science as a form of activity that institutionalizes inventions and thereby changes the social system, which adapts to the environment through steady differentiation of its structure, and through increased complexity.

9. *Sociological works par excellence:* Le suicide *and* Street Corner Society

Durkheim's celebrated book from 1897 is usually understood as an inductive investigation, a statistical social research that establishes step by step general statements or law-like propositions, susceptible to corroboration or refutation by confronting them with reality or experience. However, it is at least equally adequate to read the book as an explication of some fundamental social experiences, an explication the significance of which is elucidated through official statistics: Durkheim as a young man underwent the shocking experience of a crumbling nation, of failing solidarity within a whole society. Social disintegration and integration became the main topic throughout his work. His first contribution dealt with the forms of social integration; his next, the book *Le suicide*, with the forms of social disintegration. In a differentiated society such as ours the individual members are much more respected than in a less differentiated one. A well-integrated society cannot, therefore, consist of mostly mentally ill or otherwise disintegrated individuals. For this reason Durkheim takes the propensity to commit suicide as an expression of social disintegration. Suicide can have at least two, opposite, meanings: the suicidal agent's attachment to society was too weak, he (she) was too lonely and self-centred, and surrendered for this reason; or the suicidal agent was too strongly attached to other people, and succumbs to society's superior force. A third meaning of suicide, which is also considered important, is to be a response to a anomic social situation, that is a situation where there are no or ever-changing limits to aspirations and expectations, producing an ever-changing field of action where everything seems possible. Such social *anomie* leads to mental or psychic *anomie*, which shows itself as sudden temper and lack of balance. Beside himself (herself) because of bad luck or even good luck, the anomic agent may put an end to his (her) life. Such is Durkheim's general doctrine of suicide as a response to and expression of various forms of societal disintegration. It is intelligible, it is not water-proof or tautological, it shows us a way to interpret our lives. But it is not based upon the adduced statistical data, which serve merely as illustrations; it is based upon or makes explicit Durkheim's own, deep experiences. He conceptualizes his own experiences and thereby a conceptual whole (a 'theory'), a doctrine of social integration by which he interprets the social institutions of family, economy, religion and politics. This is not sheer arbitrariness, since Durkheim's experiences are common experiences. His propositions are so fundamental that we all understand them, and at the same time we do not see how they could be falsified or disconfirmed through reference to experience. It is generally acknowledged that the singular human being is internally related to others and cannot live without them; it is also one of mankind's general experience that one may wish to die from a sense of shame. Statements about such experiences may be termed *categorical;* they (partly) constitute the domain of the social, in the same way that the law of inertia and other of Newton's laws constitute our experience of lifeless matter ('nature'). Now it is asserted by experts that Newton's conceptions have been superseded through a scientific revolution; as a parallel, it is conceivable, as an undetermined possibility, that Durkheim's would be superseded, too. But no such sociological revolution goes on at present, the concepts of loneliness and shame are still accepted as both evident and basic. Hence, the conception of egocentric and altruistic suicide are understood, and consequently the concepts of too weak and too strong social integration. What Durkheim did in *Le Suicide*, was to deepen and develop some of our essential experiences with social life and give them the form of concepts.

Street Corner Society by W. F. Whyte, a case study of a slum district in Boston around 1940, vindicates a sociological interpretation as compared to both a Liberal and an administrative conception of human relationships.

The district is essentially a community, a *Gemeinschaft*, integrated through ethnicity (Italian background), language, kinship and family relations and rituals, religious belief customs, and feasts. Since the Anglo-Saxon culture is dominant, this subculture's integration is also strengthened from outside; the Italians' mutual solidarity is reinforced by their Otherness.

The value-orientations of achievement and universalism ('equality of opportunity') do not suit the condition of the district well, since its inhabitants are obviously handicapped in such Liberal competitions. Hence they do not seek upward social mobility through the activities recommended and endorsed by the Anglo-Saxon dominating strata, but address other kinds of people, semi-criminal politicians ('racketeers') and other influential figures within more or less legal business.

The consequences for the district of some of the New Deal reforms illuminates the difference between social integration and integration through the State. A settlement house is created with officially employed social workers whose job it is to give help and get people out of a mess. However, their services disturb and compete with the already existing patterns of solidary activities; the secondary relations interfere with the primary relations of the community. (The social workers' alienated position is accentuated by their lack of knowledge of Italian; they speak only English.)

The district is severely stricken by unemployment, which threatens especially the male population's sense of identity. The existence of street corner gangs of unemployed young men both expresses this fact, and countervails it. The gangs are primary groups in Cooley's sense, or perhaps even, or also, groups in the Durkheimian sense.[34] Thus, the rank in the group is strongly influenced by each gang member's achievement in the bowling competitions, while these achievements in turn are influenced by the rank, as brought out most vividly in Whyte's account of how his friendship with the gang's leader literally helped him perform well in bowling.[35] *Street Corner Society* contains all the topics of sociology as the science of social integration.

34. Note incidentally that the gang's leader disapproves of decisions through voting (this Liberal institution): 'It is better not to have a constitution and vote on all things. As soon as you begin deciding questions by taking a vote, you'll see that some fellows are for you and some are against you, and in that way factions develop. It's best to get everybody to agree first, and then you don't have to vote' (*ibid.*, p. 96).

10. The fascination of caricature: Brave New World *and* Ape & Essence

Aldous Huxley's two novels, *Brave New World* and *Ape & Essence,* both revolve around the conception of social integration carried to its extreme; the first novel depicts a happy social life where a fundamental *consensus* has been arrived at, the ultimate values cherished being 'community, identity, stability'; the second (in the guise of a screenplay) shows a society wholly integrated through misery and hate.[36]

In *Brave New World,*[37] the happy society has managed to reconcile completely the individuals with their society. The solution to the task was, firstly, devices such as (Pavlow'ian) conditioning and subconscious teaching ('hypnopaedia'), through which everybody comes to enjoy the position assigned to him or her beforehand by Society (i.e. its leaders of social control). 'The greatest moralizing and socializing force of all time'. This is a prerequisite of a class society in which each social class has its own, specific, and happy consciousness. Nobody wants to belong to a superior, nor to an inferior social stratum. The differentiation of working tasks and other functions goes on without conflicts worth mentioning. The tension between ascription and achievement is done away with through the abolition of family and kinship bonds. Second, sexuality has been detached from procreation (the words 'father' and 'mother' have become obscene)[38] and established as a purely social enjoyment (everybody belongs to everybody, promiscuity being obligatory). There are no sexual inhibitions which can make for resentment and hostility towards the social order. (This alludes

35. 'I felt my friends were for me, had confidence in me, wanted me to bowl well. As my turn came and I stepped up to bowl, I felt supremely confident that I was going to hit the pins that I was aiming at. I have never felt quite that way before—or since. Here at the bowling alley I was experiencing subjectively the impact of the group structure upon the individual. It was a strange feeling, as if something larger than myself was controlling the ball as I went through my swing and released it toward the pins.' *Ibid.,* App. A.

36. He also wrote a third novel about a possible, future good society, *Island*, published in 1963.

37. 'Miranda: O, wonder! How many goodly creatures are there here! How beauteous mankind is! O brave new world, that hath such people in't!' Shakespeare, *The Tempest*, Act V, scene 1.

38. There is extra-uterine conception and production of human beings. I leave out of account most of Huxley's amazing anticipations on recent trends in biology (gene technology etc.).

to Freud and Malinowski's work, which caused such a furore in the 1930s.) Deviance is dealt with through mild narcotics and psychotherapy. Third, there are regular gatherings, 'solidary services,'[39] where The Greater Being (Comte's Grand-Etre) is worshipped through psalms, narcotics and copulations. Fourth, knowledge is subordinated social integration, and scientific research is only allowed in so far as its findings do not endanger social stability. (This is the sociologism towards which Durkheim's thinking sometimes leads.) Fifth, knowledge of the past is transmitted to a very small degree, preventing any far-reaching comparison between the prevailing social order and preceding ones. This 'oversocialised conception of man' has erected a kind of sociocraty, led by experts in social integration.

Ape & Essence[40] renders another, but this time, horrible and ugly version of Durkheim's statement: 'Society is the soul of religion'. Huxley visualizes how the inhabitants of North America, more than a century after an atomic World War, are still plagued by its devastating effects, above all, by radiation's impact on the genes, causing the birth of babies with all kinds of deformities. Living under the yoke of utter misery, the inhabitants are integrated by bodily and verbal violence into a social totality where all individuals are subordinate to this whole. Every individual's wish must be subservient to the collectivity's most pressing goal, to purge the race biologically. This endeavour takes the form of severe repression of sexuality save a couple of weeks annually (to control the number of conceptions) and through ritual slaughter of the newborn that do not fulfil the criteria of normalcy (too many toes, nipples, etc.) These rites are led by a priesthood (of castrated men) who have constructed an inversion of Christian theology, based upon the conviction that the Devil, or Belial, finally became victorious in the great struggle between Good and Evil. From this belief it follows that one has to adore Belial, and inflict upon oneself Belial's punishments. This worship with all its cruelties is inter-

---

39. Huxley alludes to the emergent corporate economics, to what Gramsci called 'Fordism' through a pun with the expressions Our Lord/Our Ford.
40. This title, too, alludes to Shakespeare: 'But, man, proud man, drest in a little brief authority—most ignorant of what he's most assured, his glassy essence—like an angry ape plays such phantastic tricks before high heaven, as make the angels weep'. *Measure for Measure*, Act 2, scene 2.

nalized by the inhabitants, and permeates all living together. Moreover, social integration is reinforced by the hatred of deviants, in accordance with a well-known proposition of sociology (cf. Durkheim's interpretation of the integrating power of punishing on those who participate in the punishment).[41] To this spiritual authority is joined that of the polity (in the double sense of police and politics), posing as the will of the Proletariat.[42]

In both stories, the dangers and limits of the science of social integration are forcefully brought out, turning into nightmares the dreams of Auguste Comte.

11. The fascination of hope: Non-violence (ahimsa) as a sociological topic

As sketched above, social integration is often induced or reinforced by the real or supposed existence of an enemy external to the group in question. And actual warfare is often accompanied by an immensely heightened sense of comradeship, community, solidarity among those belonging to the same party of the struggle. One forgets to worry about one's petty ambitions, pleasures and annoyances, when participating in those kinds of vast, organized violence called (national or civil) war. This is one of the reasons why the prospect of war exerts an unmistakable attraction on many minds: it promises increased social integration and its concomitant experience of belongingness. But this sense of belongingness can be exploited for the very opposite purpose, of creating peace and abolishing violence altogether among groups. This was one of the prospects of the Pacifist movement which arose after World War I. One might re-educate oneself into a non-violent being through group training. Being in a group, it becomes easier to cast off fear of the enemy,[43] and fear is one of the principal sentiments which leads

41. 'If you want social solidarity, you've got to have either an external enemy or an oppressed minority. We have no external enemies, so we have to make the most of our Hots ... If anything goes wrong, it's always the fault of the Hots. I don't know what we'd do without them.'
42. 'A Democracy ... in which every proletarian enjoys perfect freedom.' 'True freedom'. 'Freely doing the will of the Proletariat.' 'And *vox proletarius, vox Diabolis.'* 'While, of course, *vox Diaboli, vox Eccleasiae'* (p. 168, first edition).
43. Cf. Gene Sharp: *The Politics of Non-violence* (1973), chap. 9, section on 'Casting off fear'. As is well known, Gandhi considered cowardice even worse than violent action.

to aggression and violence. By feeling oneself in unity with one's group, it becomes easier to feel in unity with the adversary group, transcending the relationship of hostility towards one of fundamental unity.[44] Through the refusal to hate one can un-learn the ingrained aggressive responses to frustrations, and come to think and feel about humanity in an affirmative way.

In short, sociology may help finding that 'moral equivalent to war' of which William James wrote, developing the tech-niques of peace and peaceful conflict-solving which would final-ly render warfare obsolete.

12. Final remarks

Sociology as the doctrine of social integration emerged when the notion of Society as distinct from the State became important. Instead of the dyad State-Individual, some thinkers would set the triad State-Society-Individual. Or one could say that Soci-ology arose when there occurred in fact a change in human relationships and the human condition in the West so that one could with good reason speak of Society and of the State as two different areas, the reciprocal relation between which becomes important to understand.

To emphasize the social level of being was part of the Con-servative riposte to Liberal thought. The attraction of Sociology as the science of social integration is, therefore, the attraction of Conservative political thought, stripped of its religious garb.[45]

The process during the last century has been such that the distinction between State and Society as separate domains has become ever more difficult to uphold. Rather, the two have permeated each other. The consequence of this is that Sociology can no longer be the science of Society, but of the social as such, as abstracted from a larger whole of human existence.

44. ' "Unity", he said in an articulate whisper.—He was committed to them, as a hand is committed to the arm. Committed to his friends, committed even to those who had declared themselves his enemies. There was nothing he could do but would affect them all, enemies and friends alike—for good, if what he did were good, for evil if it were wrong. "Unity", he repeated. "Unity.—Unity of mankind, unity of all life, all being, even." ' Aldous Huxley: *Eyeless in Gaza*. p. 612 (1936).
45. 'Social Liberalism' is a compromise, its best spokesman was John Stuart Mill (together with his wife), who, as mentioned in chap. 1, advocated his own kind of sociology, very different from the latter's anti-Liberal doctrine, and became a forerunner of our century's 'Social research'.

The basic conceptions of Sociology having now been set forth, their relation to Social statistics and to Liberal thought has, it is hoped, become apparent.

Sociology interprets those projects and forms which Social statistics both saps and takes for granted, since sociological thought is essentially concerned with wholes and internal relations.

With regard to Sociology's relation to Liberal thought, these essential features may be recalled: The distinction between primordial and derived sociality encompasses those between Society and the State, the social and the political level, economic calculation and pre-economic activity.

The concept of social integration of an economically differentiated whole was expressly worked out to refute the Liberal contract doctrines of politics and economics. Likewise, the interpretation of rituals bears on topics beyond the Liberal frame of mind: the fusion of individuals into something approaching a collectivity *sui generis*, the ceding of intellect and will to feeling and unreflective conduct, foreign to the self-controlled Liberal individual, and tacitly conducive to social integration.

The syntheses of Sorokin and Parsons both describe a socio-cultural whole where the conceptions of Liberal politics and economics are reinterpreted as valid for specific social contexts, dependent on more fundamental integrating social structures.

5

Historico-Dialectical Thought

A. The Contributions of Marx and Engels

The attack on Liberal politics and economic thought is persistent throughout the work of Marx and Engels, even if their bellicose writings also aim at other enemies. The following exposition will briefly restate Marx's and Engels' objections to the basic Liberal doctrines presented in chapters 2 and 3.

1. The historicity of human rights
The Liberal doctrine underpinned its claims for freedom by referring to the human being's natural, that is, inborn rights, rights which had always been there, even if not recognized at all times and places.

To this, Marx and Engels object—as did many other thinkers—that there are no timeless (eternal) human rights, but that each time in history has its own conception of what is right and wrong. The human being and species are essentially historical and changing.

The specific form of this objection in Marx and Engels is the charge that this historicity is connected to change in the human beings' productive relation to their material environment[1] (and not, as in Hegel's *Phenomenology of Spirit*, an unfolding of truth through the Spirit's struggles with itself.)

Thus, the abolition of slavery should not be seen as a consequence of having arrived at the insight that it is wrong to treat a human being as an *instrumentum vocale*. Instead, slavery came into existence at a certain level of development of the productive forces, and came to an end at another level.[2]

Likewise, the declarations of universal human rights in the

1. Marx and Engels: *German Ideology* (1845).
2. Engels: *Anti-Dühring,* chapter on the role of force in history (1877).

eighteenth century presupposed the universalistic features of the mode of production of the West at that time. To treat the citizens legally on a more equal footing becomes both a necessity and a possibility as wage labour becomes ever more prevalent in economic life. Thus the *Code Napoléon* was more appropriate to the rising commodity economy.[3]

2. The Liberal State as the State of the bourgeois class

While Liberals reconstructed the State as the outcome of an original contract between (naturally) free human beings, Marx and Engels assert that any State is the instrument of the proper-tied dominant class, and, in particular, that the Liberal State is the State of the burghers, a class of merchants and tradesmen that had arisen in the thirteenth and fourteenth centuries, and become the dominant class in Western society through the centuries. No pact is at the origin of this State, but fierce class struggles, whereby the class of the nobility and landlords lost their dominating position. Nor do the laws of this new Liberal State protect all citizens equally well. Private property is the condition for enjoying to the full extent the rights of the Liberal state.[4]

Human history is engendered not solely through the develop-ment of new means of production, but also by the inherent conflict between immediate, alienated producers and the owners of the means of production. The conception of this inherent opposition is the counterpart to Liberal economics' conception of a basic unity and consensus between the market participants. By designating these relations of production 'class' relations, it is held that 'class struggle is the motor of History'.

Productive forces (tools, implementations, machines) and the relations between immediate producers, i.e., the relations of production, are internally related. Change and development of productive forces call forth a change of relations of production, as the producers adapt to the change.

Above, as it were, this basic structure there is a structure of property rights, incorporated or embodied in legal codes (writ-

3. 'The idea of equality, ... is therefore itself a historical product ...' *Ibid.*
4. 'The State has become a separate entity; but it is nothing more than the form of organization which the bourgeoisie necessarily adopts both for internal and external purposes') *German Ideology* (Feuerbach).

ten or oral). These rights most often reflect and mirror the immediate relations of production, as their justification and legitimation. But they may also differ, deviate from or contradict the relations of production, in the sense that those who legally own and command or appropriate the means of production may in fact be without any immediate control. This distinction between *de facto* and *de jure* expresses that the mode of (immediate) production may stand in various relations to the structure of legal property. Generally, legal property relations adapt to actual relations of production.

The State—considered as a set of governmental and custodial apparatus—is also conceived as a structure that mainly adapts to the changes in the mode of production. Even if or when it appears and pretends to be in possession of power to decide about everything, including the material production, it generally is dependent upon, reflects and justifies the relations of production, appropriation and property.[5] Hence political struggles, conflicts—in which the combatants aim at control over the State apparatus—are never fundamental.

Political power in turn is—in the last instance—dependent upon domination within the mode of production, bearing on its development and change. The (political) State poses as a power that acts on behalf of or to the benefit of all its subjects or citizens, but in fact sides with the class that dominates within the domain of production.[6] Its pretended universality is false and partial. 'The State is an instrument of the ruling class.'

The bourgeois class spreads the erroneous notion that everybody has equal opportunities to lead a happy and rich life by virtue of the fact that estate privileges are more or less abolished, thus overlooking or concealing that class adherence maintains the old inequalities. Finally, the political institution of a secret ballot at parliamentary elections is deceptive, even when the right to vote is extended so as to become nearly universal. This form of democracy can never amount to more than a choice of rulers, not a rule by the people itself. The bourgeoisie will never

5. 'Only the political superstition imagines in our time that bourgeois life is sustained by the State, while on the contrary the State is sustained by bourgeois life.' Marx and Engels: *The Holy Family* (1845).
6. Cf. the objection concerning the superficiality of Liberal politics, chap. 2 *supra*.

be overthrown through parliamentary politics, only through political revolution.

3. The family as a bourgeois class institution

The 'subjection of women' is apprehended also by Liberals as one of the weak spots in a State professing to be liberal, that is, granting freedom to everybody. The Feminist movement began within the bourgeois class itself, demanding the same legal rights and the same opportunities for women as for men. This, of course, implied demanding the same rights for women as for men to participate in class oppression. Marx and Engels' interpretation of the relation between the sexes differed from the Liberals' by placing the question within a more general frame.

According to this interpretation, the bourgeois family emerged concomitantly with the rise of the burgher class and its mode of property relations and commodity economy.[7]

Within this family pattern the relations between capital owner and wage labour are repeated. Just as the propertyless consent freely to enter into a wage-labour contract, women consent freely to enter into the marriage contract; in both cases free consent is superficial and masks the coercion of prevailing conditions. The wife is the *prolétaire* of the family, the husband the capitalist. The condition of womens' liberation is the abolition of private property of the means of production, and the participation of all adults in society's necessary tasks, executed through public, collectively owned institutions. (This implied that society should collectively take charge of the upbringing of children.) Since women and men belonging to the wage labour class were on a more equal footing than women and men of the bourgeoisie, Engels, while refusing to forecast what the relationship between free woman and men might be in the future, ventured to affirm that the wage labourers anticipated to some degree the liberated love relationship between the sexes.[8]

7. 'Historically, the bourgeois gives the family the character of the bourgeois family, in which boredom and money are the binding link.' *German Ideology* (Saint Max).
8. Engels: *The Origin of the Family, Private Property and the State* (1881).

4. Bourgeois domination in Liberal public life

The Liberal State conceives of its citizens as an aggregate of independent units, *individuals*. Thus, in the legal code, only actions committed by or imputable to individuals can be punished. This legal individualism is apt to propagate the illusion or erroneous conception that a society consists of individuals, not of classes, constituted in terms of their relation to the various forms of capital. Hence, individualist morality dominates within bourgeois culture. Moreover, in its initial period, the Liberal State forbids coalitions between individuals, as a kind of *divide et impera*, thus trying to maintain each citizen in a state of impotency in the face of the State and the market. Now, the unpropertied have a greater need to unite than the propertied, therefore this prohibition indirectly supports the class domination of the bourgeoisie. Further, the Liberal rights and democratic practices are dismissed as mystifying or delusive. Freedom of speech and thought may be granted to one and all, but only a minority can make use of these rights, those who dispose of sufficient property or wealth to be relatively independent, and therefore can afford to speak their mind. (Kant was therefore consistent when he made property a condition for admission to the university.) The Liberal public sphere, with its opinions and discussions, its celebrated writers, painters and other artists, its politicians, is in fact open only to the bourgeois class, the nobility (the former ruling class), and a few aspiring propertyless individuals, zealous to be accepted by and adopted by the *bourgeoisie*.

5. The market as capitalist domination

The economic order brought about through the market institution and praised by the Liberals for its unconstrained working (its 'spontaneity') is in fact sustained by the armed forces of the Liberal State, especially its police and prisons. It is not true that all citizens accept the market as the best mediator between individuals in questions concerning the production and distribution of material necessities. The unpropertied masses, the poor, the wage labourers would not freely respect the private property of the rich and those who legally own the means of production. The market order is not established and upheld by an 'invisible hand' or 'the cunning of Reason', but by the State as the instrument of the ruling, propertied class.

Second, the order established by market prices according to the 'law of supply and demand' does not signify universal satisfaction, but oppression. The 'effective' demand is a very distorted expression of the wants, deprivations, sufferings of those who have but feeble purchasing power.[9]

Historically, the wage labourer is a new figure or 'character mask', since wage labour presupposes human beings that are legally ('formally') free citizens, with the right to enter into contract relationships such as the 'labour contract'. Thus labour is closely connected to the Liberal State and its legal structure. The labour contract engages two mutually independent partners: the capital owner, who has no authority over the propertyless, nor any responsibility (of charity etc.) and the legally free, who disposes only of his or her own working capacity, and who is supposed to weigh advantages and disadvantages before the contract is agreed upon. Important as this legal liberty is in human history, it should not divert attention from the fact that the freedom of the propertyless is limited. They may choose between labour contracts, but are forced by bodily needs to do some kind of wage labour, unless they choose to steal, to beg for alms or starve. This has nothing to do with freedom in the sense of objectivating one's intentions or wishes, or the expression of one's character, or the acting according to moral obligation. The legal freedom of wage-labourers cannot compensate for the constraints of their living conditions, therefore a Liberal economy gives liberty only to the propertied classes, while it means lack of liberty to the majority, the wage labour class.[10]

9. 'It should here be noted in passing that the "social demand", i.e., the factor which regulates the principle of demand, is essentially subject to the mutual relationship of the different classes and their respective economic position. ... It would seem, then, that there is on the side of demand a certain magnitude of definite social wants which require for their satisfaction a definite quantity of a commodity on the market. But quantitatively, the definite social wants are very elastic and changing. Their fixedness is only apparent. If the means of subsistence were cheaper, or money-wages higher, the labourers would buy more of them, and a greater "social need" would arise for them, leaving aside the paupers, etc., whose "demand" is even below the narrowest limits of their physical wants.' Marx: *Capital*, III, chap. 10 (1894).
10. 'We saw also that capital—and the capitalist is merely capital personified and functions in the process of production solely as the agent of capital—in

Even if it may be a good thing that goods produced are getting sold on the market rather than decaying, becoming rusty, getting obsolete, and so on, market clearance and equilibrium does not mean that any optimum is arrived at. Beneath the allegedly free, but in fact forced, competition between buyers and sellers in the market is discernible the conflict between social classes.

Social classes essentially are historical entities, liable to historiography, not (merely) sociography. They are constituted by their past actions and struggles, objectivated in the shape of associations, buildings, books, newspapers, monuments etc., and by their attitude towards this past.

6. The value doctrine of labour and the surplus product

Marx and Engels developed the great Liberal economists' labour doctrine of value showing how the contract relation between capital and wage labour inevitably leads to the capital owners' exploitation of the wage labourers.

The wage-labour contract is ambivalent: On the surface, it is a legally just contract between two free citizens whereby the one buys the right to dispose of the other's labour power for a stipulated number of hours; moreover, the wage will tend to cover the expenses of the reproduction of this labour power, and the deal should therefore be fair.

But since the wage labourer creates more than is needed to restore his (her) expense of labour power,[11] a surplus is created that must accrue to the capital owner, and hence the wage-labour contract will imply an exploitation (except in those rare cases where the wage labourers enforce a wage equal to, or higher, than the value of their labour product).

The wage–labour–capital–economic order is therefore inher-

its corresponding social process of production, pumps a definite quantity of surplus-labour out of the direct producers, or labourers; capital obtains this surplus-labour without an equivalent, and in essence it always remains forced labour—no matter how much it may seem to result from free contractual agreement.' *Capital*, III, chap. 48.

11. Cf. Comte's enunciation of these two 'economic laws', that 'chaque homme peut produire au delà de ce qu'il consomme; et ensuite, les matériaux obtenus peuvent se conserver au delà du temps qu'exige leur réproduction.' *Système de politique positive*, II.

ently oppressive. It must lead to increasing (relative) misery[12] and poverty on the part of the wage-labour class. The equality between the propertyless and the propertied is therefore mere appearance; delusively, the wage-labour market hides or masks class oppression.

7. The utility doctrine in politics and economics and the conception of alienated practice

Liberal economics considers the wage labourers as beings that have to be fed, clad and sheltered in order to be useful in the production process. Even if a few thinkers worry over the harmful effects of an extreme division of labour, too long working hours, etc. they fail to conceive of wage labour as such as a distorted mode of human productive praxis. They overlook the fact that labour power is the *facticity* of human activity. Through a Liberal economy the wage labourer is not only deprived of the surplus product (in the form of surplus value), but suffers a double alienation: being supervised and bossed about during the production process, and being without any influence upon the investment decisions as to what to produce and how to produce it. The notion of the disutility of labour is valid in so far as it expresses that wage labour may be so alienative as to be experienced as an evil, but it is delusive in so far as it suggests that productive activity as such is unpleasant. On the contrary, production is one way, if not necessarily the major way, for the human being to objectivate, express and develop himself and discover the environment, in short, a major way of cognition. The under-consumption of the wage-labour class and its concomitant sufferings must be emphasized, but poverty and misery should not make one ignore the significance of being barred from participating in the productive consumption of society (planning, projecting, producing) as one who has a share in the decisions. Moreover, the utilitarian conception of consumption neglects its cognitive significance

12. Cf. Marx on relative misery: 'If the working class has remained "poor", only "less poor" in proportion as it produces for the wealthy class "an intoxicating augmentation of wealth and power", then it has remained relatively just as poor as before. If the extremes of poverty have not lessened, they have increased, because the extremes of wealth have.' *Capital*, I, chap. 22 (1867).

as a way of knowing the world through sensuous experience. Consumption in the form of sheer restitution of bodily energy or as mere pleasure and fun, are distorted forms of what it can be. The very institution of wage labour is oppressive and implies a negative relation between capital owners and wage labourers, a class conflict.

8. The Liberal doctrine of (linear) progress and (dialectical) class struggle

The Liberals claim that, provided the market is allowed to operate unconstrained, protected by the State's armed forces, the wealth of nations will increase continually. There will be a steady accumulation of capital, a rise in productivity and total product. The market brings about an oscillation between ever new levels of equilibrium, and if there are disturbances of this progress, they are due to interference with the market's self-regulation (its 'mechanism').

Against this it is asserted that a mode of production based upon the opposition capital–wage labour is characterized by disorder, ups and downs, crises, over-production, underconsumption and chronic unemployment ('reserve army' of workers). A Liberal economy cannot last forever; it is no eternal order, but transitory, historic. It displays a number of historic tendencies which manifest themselves through class struggle and contradictions. Capital accumulation is a dialectical process in the Hegelian sense: Contradictions inherent in this mode of production engender changes of productive forces and relations of production which will lead to an essentially new mode of production. In the first place, the opposition between capital owners and wage labourers in the production realm (the 'industry') spurs the former to apply and urge the invention of new, work-saving means of production, in order to keep down the running costs of wages. The competition between capital owners also acts as an incentive towards development of forces of production. But contrary to the Liberal interpretation, these developments do not go on smoothly; they are violent, sudden, causing unemployment and bankruptcy and other damage.

In the second place, there is the tendency towards increasing centralization and concentration of capital. Not only do individuals own ever larger amounts of capital as a consequence of the drive towards large scale industrial production, but market competition tends to reduce the number of productive capital units. 'Every eapitalist is responsible for the death of many others'. The market thus tends to abolish itself through its internal conflicts and change into 'monopoly' (or rather oligopoly) capital. This also implies a concentration of the at first more dispersed wage labourers and more collective forms of work, prefiguring in a way the collectivity of the future mode of production (where the immediate producers associate).[13]

In the third place, there is the tendency towards relative impoverishment and proletarization. The above-mentioned centralization implies that the number of wage labourers augments; the former peasant, tenant, artisan or capital owner is turned into a wage labourer. This heightens the tension within the Liberal economy between the capital owners' class and the wage-labour class, a tension which becomes ever more outspoken as the wages tend to fall to the level of mere subsistence or to rise, but not to keep up with the momentous increase of material wealth in society as a whole. The capital owners take possession of a relatively greater share of the production surplus, partly for their own luxurious consumption, partly for the purpose of productive consumption (investments etc.). Thus, for internal reasons a Liberal economy engenders ever more glaring and hostile relations between the two basic social classes. In the fourth place, the organic composition of capital tends to rise, with the consequence that the rate of profit tends to fall, which threatens the Liberal economy with stagnation. This makes the image of the Liberal market economy as analogous to some self-regulating physical mechanism, determined by economic laws analogous to those of mathematical physics, utterly false. The Liberal economy, emerging through cruel struggles with the former econ-

13. 'The isolated workers are united together in large factories to particular jobs that mesh with one another. The tool becomes the machine. This mode of production permits no longer the splitting up of the instruments of production that is characteristic of small property, just as little as it allows isolation of the workers themselves.' *Capital,* vol. III, chap. 36.

omic order, is ridden by all sorts of contradictions and tensions, and will have to succumb in due time to a new mode of production, more in accord with Reason, and to participate in this revolution, is to 'make history'.[14]

9. Illusory ('ideal') freedom and basic ('material') necessity

Liberals tend, as noted in chapter two, to emphasize how intellect and will can and ought to be strengthened, in order to obtain a mental or spiritual freedom in addition to the liberties acquired through political and economic measures. Marx and Engels are eager to object that to those who are oppressed by the Liberal order (because of insufficient wealth), it is highly misleading to try to concentrate on their mental, spiritual freedom, since that freedom will be merely an inner one, not a complement to, but a poor substitute for, economico-political freedom. This will amount to a withdrawal into an imaginary world of 'representations' and 'ideas', shut off from the world of real, material existence. This split of the unity between the human being and its environment is one side of human alienation, destroying the essential, internal bond between thought, feeling and action. Such a cleavage gets its epistemological expression in the distinction and hiatus between 'subject' and 'object', or 'the ideal' and 'the real' or 'material'. Hence 'idealist' thinking should be combated.

Especially those who are oppressed should instead think of human liberation as something dependent upon material (economic) conditions, and strenuously oppose the suggestion that they have themselves to blame for their misery, caused by low morals and weakness of will. For to pull oneself together by an effort of will can have no lasting effect. We are not free to think and feel regardless of the mode of production and the relations of production within which we live. Human beings are not free

14. Marx claimed to have superseded the opposition between a-historical Liberal economics and Historical economics. With the first he shares the pursuit of law-like relationships between economic events and entities, repudiating the latter's compilation of historical facts without moulding them conceptually. But he shares the Historical school's conviction that every historical time has its specific economic mode, repudiating the ahistoric cast of mind of Liberal economists. Marx purported to have uncovered the law or conceptually intelligible direction of the mode of production as an historical process.

when they live under the yoke of material necessity, or when the product of their work turns into an 'alien, hostile force'.[15]

Therefore, Marx and Engels side with the French 'materialists' of the eighteenth century, who advocated the improvement of humanity through the changing of its external, material conditions, and were convinced that the human species is not essentially immutable, but perfectible.[16]

The 'materialist conception of history' also emphasizes the distinction between living under the impact from unnoticed material conditions, and becoming aware of this impact.

A 'materialist' interpretation of one's situation means to be attentive to one's place within the structures of production, that is, within the class structure. Those who disregard the class structure may experience a superficial, accidental freedom,[17] which any moment may be overthrown by events called forth by structural changes of the mode of material production.

10. Conclusion

The basic concepts—or 'categories'—of the Liberal doctrine are free citizens who have erected or constructed a State to protect themselves and, especially, to safeguard their economic transactions through the Market. The Market, in turn, is said to be the medium through which economic transactions obtain a form that accords with human reason, conducive to universal wealth and well-being for all.

Marx and Engels substitute for these basic concepts another triad—*mode of production, class struggle,* and *history* (historicity).

To Liberal politics as a framework for the living together of human beings, they object that this framework is not favourable

15. Marx: *Grundrisse* (written 1857–8); cf. the *Phenomenology of Spirit:* '... not as a superior power which is only alien to it, but one which is hostile.' (Section on the Heart's law and the madness of vanity').
16. '*Ideas* can never lead beyond an old world order. Ideas *cannot carry out anything* at all. In order to carry out ideas men are needed who can exert practical force.' And: 'There is no need for any great penetration to see from the teaching of materialism on the original goodness of and equal intellectual endowment of men, the omnipotence of experience, the great significance of industry, the justification of enjoyment, etc. how necessarily materialism is connected with communism and socialism.' *The Holy Family.*
17. 'Thus, in imagination, individuals seem freer under the dominance of the bourgeoisie than before...' *German Ideology.*

to all citizens, but mainly to that minority who own the means of production and affined kinds of property, that is, the bourgeois class. Therefore, the State is a bourgeois State, an instrument of domination and oppression in the hands of the bourgeoisie. Liberal democracy is sham democracy, it pretends to be the rule 'of the people, by the people, for the people', but is the rule of a numerically small part of the entire population. For this reason the relationship 'individual citizens—Liberal state' is superficial and unimportant compared to the relationship 'class struggle—Bourgeois State'.

To Liberal economics as an interpretation of what goes on in the domain of production and consumption of means of subsistence and other utilities, Marx and Engels object that this interpretation is both superficial and distorting. In the first place, the market is secondary in relation to the mode of production, its productive forces and relations of production. In the second place, the individual contract is secondary in relation to the fundamental class opposition which is inherent in the mode of production constituted by capital and wage labour. The essential feature of this class opposition is the wage-labour class's alienation from the production process and its product, in particular the exploitation on the part of the capitalist class of the surplus product in the form of surplus value.

In the third place, the economic order is not able to go on indefinitely; on the contrary, it is a historically specific mode of production, and has in it a number of contradictions which will lead to its collapse and subsequent transition to a historically new mode of production, the socialist or communist. How this transition will take place will heavily depend on how the class conflicts will be fought. A sharpened class consciousness on the part of the wage labourers will help to make the transition quicker and less painful.

Thus, Liberal doctrines are the dominant misinterpretation ('ideology') of the capitalist mode of production.

B. Some Later Contributions

1. Introductory remarks
Up to the outbreak of World War I, the historico-dialectical thought of Marx and Engels was fairly well confirmed and

verified by the historical process, as the self-interpretation of the wage-labour class. Since then, what has happened in the world generally and in the countries with a capitalist mode of production especially, has made these conceptions much more ambiguous as to their truth and validity. If they were not to be rejected outright as an obsolete guide for historical action, many later followers of Marx and Engels have deemed it necessary to restate, amplify, and bring up to date the 'materialist conception of history'. This part of the chapter presents some of these endeavours.

2. State and Monopoly Capital

Marx's and Engels' interpretation of the Liberal State was often dismissed as out-dated, on the ground that this State had undergone important changes towards the Social Liberal State and the Welfare State, and even towards a Socialist State which is rather the State of the wage-labour class.

Against this charge, the vindication of Marx's and Engels' conceptions has been that the State has adjusted itself to the monopoly stage of a capitalist mode of production, and has taken upon itself the task of protecting and furthering this new class of capital owners, so different in many respects from the preceding.

a) The State undertakes to facilitate the activities of the large capital owners by a series of measures: devaluation and revaluation of the currency; regulations of the money flow within the country; loans and transfers to firms temporarily in difficulties, subsidies to whole branches such as agriculture or export trades; intervention in class conflicts over wages; implementation of tax systems which ensure that the wage labourers pay while the capital owners get away with it; financing of education and research that are instrumental to capital accumulation and recruitment to the wage-labour army; maintenance of a military apparatus directed primarily against anti-capitalist foreign states ('cold war' between the Free World and the Communist World), involving very profitable contracts with the military industrial capitalists; financial aid to economically under-developed countries which endeavours to forestall political revolution and a subsequent socialist mode of production, an aid which also (and sometimes only or above all) assists the development of the dom-

estic economy; warfare or compliance with warfare against pop-
ulations trying to free themselves from the overexploitation of
multi-national concerns ('neo-imperialism').

b) The State poses as above or impartial in relation to class
conflicts; in many questions it even appears to be on the side
of the propertyless. Thus, most Western states are publicly
committed to assuring approximately full employment of the
labour force supply through public investment and the like.[18]
However, there is always much concealed unemployment.

The disablement benefit scheme has been a major device to
conceal unemployment, transforming a part of the propertyless
into a powerless stratum: Living 'on the dole' is a serious
threat to one's social identity,[19] and makes it difficult to become
accepted by the wage-labour class.

Further, free or very cheap, public health and medical services
apparently are advantageous to the wage-labour class; but in
the first place, they are already paid for through the tax bill,
and in the second place, these institutions cannot by far satisfy
the demand for medical care. The poverty of public hospitals
and medical aid is notorious, and so is the poverty of the public
schools on all levels, including the university.

c) The apparently benevolent welfare state often changes into
a stern corporate state imposing decisions which are disadvan-
tageous to the wage-labour class, such as declarations of a wage
freeze or settling of wage negotiations through enforced wages
arbitration.

d) Under the monopoly capitalist mode of production the
State may own a considerable bulk of the means of production,
transport and distribution.[20] Many of them are run on a non-
profit or deficit basis. Nevertheless, their general outlook and
orientation do not differ from that of a capitalist mode of
production; the authority structure of state-owned firms and
organizations and the income differentiation is quite similar.
Hence, the State acts as a capital owner and does not anticipate
a socialist mode of production.

18. During the last decade several Western countries seem to have renounced
this commitment, having high, constant rates of unemployment.
19. Cf. Cato Wadel's study of living 'on the dole': *Now, whose fault is that?*
(1971).
20. In Norway, the State owns half of the total shares.

This does not imply that the State apparatus of the monopoly capitalist mode of production is univocally an instrument for the capital owner class. On the contrary, it is ridden by all kinds of tensions and conflicts, and tends towards a 'segmentation' which threatens its unity. But on the whole, this State is neither the State of the propertyless nor the State of the whole population regardless of class adherence, but the State of monopoly capital.

The parliamentary system had had its influence weakened. 'Votes count, but resources decide' (Rokkan).[21] In general, the political participation of the population as a whole is markedly below what should be expected in an alleged liberal democracy.[22]

Political power has been shifted from parliament to the State administration, and the people who hold the leading positions in the state administration have their origin in the capital owner class and affined classes to an extent that make these classes grossly over-represented. This background will to a varying degree have an impact upon their decisions, making them—deliberately or subconsciously—act in favour of these classes.[23]

3. Socialization and the reproduction of class structure

Liberal doctrine claims that if there are great differences as to property and wealth in States with universal suffrage and a parliamentary system, this is because the majority think such inequalities are either just or preferable or both, and consider the liberty to improve economically to be a paramount value. The equal opportunity of (upwards) social mobility is one of the basic traits of a Liberal democracy. If it is a fact that there is a high degree of self-recruitment within the different socioeconomic strata, this cannot be taken as a proof that this equal opportunity is a fake, since the self-recruitment may be the (just) outcome of competition between individuals with unequal biological heritance.

Over the years a considerable body of research has been carried out which invalidates this Liberal tenet, even if much

21. Cf. Rokkan: 'Norway: Numerical Democracy and Corporate Pluralism', in *Citizens, Elections, Parties* (1970).
22. Cf. W. Martinussen: *Distant Democracy* (1975) for the case of Norway.
23. Cf. Milliband: *The State in Capitalist Society (1966)*, and *Capitalist Democracy* (1984).

of it has been undertaken in order to strengthen a Liberal economico-political order, and not to adduce evidence in favour of the dialectic-historical conceptions of Marx and Engels.[24]

The research in question relates to what is termed *socialization*, that is, the way children are raised and educated, and the hypothesis put to the test and corroborated is that socialization is class-specific in such a way that there is a considerable self-recruitment of the social classes, which contradicts the widespread belief in ('ideology' of) equality of opportunity.

The class specificity of socialization is described in different ways. One is to emphasize how the achievement orientation is fostered in children growing up in 'middle class' families, to a much larger extent than in 'working class' children. 'Middle class' children are encouraged to be independent, competitive and planning—these are personality traits conducive to success in an economy based on a capitalist mode of production.

Another way is to concentrate on the distinction between an independent bent of mind and a tendency towards conformity. The middle classes tend to transmit to their children the very personality required and reinforced in middle-class professional life: self-respect, trust in one's own capacities, and discernment.

The working class, by contrast, do subordinate jobs, and acquire the habit of obeying orders without having to understand the reasons for the orders. This conformity orientation—a specification of alienation—tends to be inculcated in working-class children through an education that stresses obedience. These different patterns of socialization tend to the self-recruitment of social classes.

A third way is the attempt to demonstrate how there are class-specific differences in speech, which tend to favour middle-class children in the schools. They are brought up in a social environment where it is more usual to give reasons for one's decisions and behaviour (regardless of whether they are valid or mere subterfuge), while the working class tend to appeal more directly to authority or solidarity. The relation of speech to action being different in the two classes, the school's demands are more easily fulfilled by middle-class children by virtue of

24. An apt summary is given by Kurt Huch in his book *Einübung der Klassengesellschaft* (1972). Major works in the field include Jencks: *Inequality* (1973) and Bourdieu & Passeron: *La reproduction* (1971).

their more 'elaborated code'. (Conversely, it is shown that the school's structure of values and norms are Liberal, putting the accent on individual achievement and competition, self-control and intellect.)

A fourth way is to develop the notion of a 'hidden curriculum' in schools, consisting of Liberal, middle-class virtues and values. It is shown how school teachers, themselves often coming from the middle-class, unwittingly favour middle-class pupils because of their speech habits and general bearing.

These approaches have in common the intention to show how (primary and secondary) socialization acts like a mediator between the class opposition in the mode of production, and the mental and bodily traits of individuals belonging to opposite classes.

4. Sexual repression and class oppression

Another mediation of class oppression which has been investigated, is the repression of carnal desire and lust through the inculcation of austere moral codes, such as the bourgeois-Christian morality, which prescribes pre-marital abstinence and monogamy, proscribes contraceptive devices and abhors homosexuality, seeking to limit sexual activity to its progenitive function.

This repression can be traced in at least two important directions: In the first place, the human body loses its overall sensuous-erotic quality (which we enjoy as children, in a way), and becomes more like a tool, an instrument fit for (wage) labour, with special 'erogenous zones' (Freud) to be activated in the proper contexts, and not permitted to disturb working hours. By internalizing this repression the human being exerts self-constraint and fosters a sufficient motivation for work.

In the second place, sexual repression is internalized in the form of the acceptance of forbidding authorities. One learns to be ashamed of one's desires, and to be proud of resisting them. One comes to admire authority and obedience as such, and the rigidity of these attitudes. The acquisition of an 'authoritarian personality' makes part of the wage-labour classes reluctant to join Socialist and Communist movements, and they may even, in times of crisis, adhere to Fascist movements, which offer opportunities for the release of suppressed hatred of oneself and others.

During the last decades this strict sexual morality, which had come to be attributed to the bourgeois way of life in general, has lost much of its unquestioned authority. This might be interpreted as greater sexual freedom, but also, as Marcuse did, as a new form of repression—*repressive desublimation*.[25] Through permitting or even encouraging sexual behaviour which has severed its bond to the Erotic, the transcending feature of longing, its pointing beyond what is given towards what might be, becomes extinguished. The sexual loses its force as a possible negation of the world as it is, since any sexual craving may immediately be satisfied. This is not to say that unimpeded sexual activity brings joy and pleasure. The release it gives may very well involve that aggression is dammed up, since pseudo-liberation of the sexual amounts to its domestication.[26]

5. *The doctrine of reification*
Simmel described at considerable length in his *Philosophy of Money* how calculation tends to enter into ever more of human relationships in a mode of production that is what Marx termed 'capitalistic'. Lukacs developed this insight further, connecting it to Marx's comments in *Capital* on commodity fetishism, whereby relationships between human beings appear as relations between things, that is, dividable, measurable, calculable and predictable. Things—exemplified by the kind of objects dealt with by classical mechanics—are given as unchanging, inert, identical over time or changing according to a calculable rule or 'law'. Relations between things are external; they constitute no totality of internal relations.

25. Kolakowski writes: 'Thus, when Jerry Rubin, the American hippie ideologist, says in his book that machines will henceforth do all the work and leave people free to copulate whenever and wherever they like, he is expressing, albeit in a primitive and juvenile way, the true essence of Marcuse's Utopia.' (*Main Currents of Marxism*, vol. III, p. 406). This passage imputes to Marcuse precisely that 'desublimation' which Marcuse combats.
26. This immediately makes intelligible the to many minds astonishing wave of all sorts of pornography which has accompanied the new sexual morality. If sexual desublimation were truly liberating, a decreased consumption of pornography should be expected, as a no longer necessary substitute.

Reification means that human beings act, think and feel as if they were like the things of mechanics. The so-called Taylor system within industrial organization (by now obsolete and replaced by other forms) carried reification of wage labour to its extreme. The 'laws' of demand and supply, the 'market mechanism' also reify human relationships. The fluctuations appear as movements going on independently of human volition, and to which one has to adapt, even if one knows that market processes are ultimately to be traced back to human action. Calculation and prevision of given, fixed, magnitudes are analogous to a stiffened gaze at the world, instead of a flexible look. This gaze Lukacs terms contemplation: the human being stands as a subject before an apparently alien object—the processes and products and exchange media of a capitalist mode of production—in a way resembling those who look at the stars. But this subject-object relationship is delusive and forced upon those who live in a society with a capitalist mode of production; since the apparent objects are not given, but produced, they are the subjects' objectivations. But because of the fundamental constitutive relation between capital and wage labour, these objectivations impose themselves upon the members of society as independent forces. Human creativity is suppressed and distorted. In the flux of activity, the objectivation process, there is no object confronting the subject as external, independent reality. Instead, the human being expresses himself through his praxis, changing himself through changing the world in an unceasing movement.[27] This objectivation is not calculable, since calculation presupposes fixed, given magnitudes. Human activity that is not alienated and reified is unpredictable, since it brings about something new. But in a society with a capitalist mode of production, there is little creativity. Thus, contrary to Schumpeter's contention, the entrepreneur is not really creative, but contemplative, since his (her) activity consists in manipulating given magnitudes. Reification embraces all the realms of social life. The legal structure shows the same reified traits; it is like a mechanism which produces predictable decisions about right and wrong. (Here Lukacs draws on Max Weber's sociology of law.)

27. The reasoning about adaptation versus action was given its final clarification by Parsons, in his treatment of the utilitarian dilemma, cf. chap. 7.

Philosophy from Descartes onwards also testifies to the reification of thought. To understand the relation between subject and object becomes the main and insoluble task. In Kant's critical idealism the failure is acknowledged through the exposition of the antimonies of reason and the notion of the 'thing-in-itself'. According to Lukacs, bourgeois thought reveals itself through its most outstanding proponents as mere or empty form, unable to grasp reality. The *Ding an sich* is the unattainable matter, and it troubles reified, formalist thinking in the same way as grim economic realities trouble reified Liberal economics, as in the case of crises, where the formalism of Liberal economics suddenly becomes apparent.

Only action—collective, class action—can overcome reification and the reified subject-object relationships, Lukacs asserted. Collective action is dialectic and historic, and liberates one from the yoke of reified existence.

This doctrine—even if disavowed by Lukacs himself in later years—was the point of departure of an array of historico-dialectical contributions in our century. It is a vast synthesis of Marxian conceptions and the capitalism studies of the original German sociologists (Tönnies, Simmel, Max and Alfred Weber, Sombart etc.) and Bergsonian conceptions of time and freedom.[28] The Critical Theory or Frankfurter School evidently owes much to Lukacs. Thus, Horkheimer's critique of instrumental reason attacks its reified character. The notion of *'quasi-Natur'* is also a specification of reification: When human relationships appear to be liable to treatment by social statistics, showing uniformities that resemble the uniformities of non-human nature, this is no proof that the sciences of humanity do not differ from the sciences of nature. For the uniformities of human behaviour are not at bottom natural, but the result and sign of oppression and constraint, taking the form of reified

---

28. Just as Simmel was deeply impressed by Bergson ('He knows more than I') Lukacs probably learnt much from the French thinker's interpretation of human freedom as the creation of unpredictable novelty and rupture with everyday routine, and with its fixed, spatialized relations and entities. Bergson opposes the vital and the mechanical, the 'spontaneous' and the 'ready-made', fluent duration and clock-time measurable in a way that anticipates Lukacs' doctrine on many points. But since Bergson is entirely foreign to any workers' movement, militant or not, and never spends a word on Marx, their divergence becomes very great.

existence. Reification makes human existence appear as quasi-nature. Lukacs' doctrine has also been developed further by Marcuse's investigations into the 'ideology of advanced industrial societies', to be considered in the following.

6. The doctrine of one-dimensional man

Marcuse's doctrine of one-dimensionality presents a condensed expression of the various attempts to explain how a society with a basic class opposition can nevertheless be without overt political conflicts.

One-dimensionality signifies the suppression of dialectics in a double sense: In the first place, negative thinking (negations, questionings, doubts, phantasies of the seemingly impossible, 'Utopian') is sought to be replaced by positive, affirmative thinking. (This is the 'positive philosophy' of Comte, expressly developed to refute the 'critical' thinking of the Revolutionaries.)[29]

This precludes conflicts becoming manifest and a topic for reflection and discussion. The consensual appearance of social, political and cultural life is confirmed.[30]

In the second place, the transcendence of the given and existing is counteracted by modes of behaving and thinking that neglect the changeable character of all *data*. The training in 'operational' thinking is a case in point: It defines and determines concepts in terms of determined sets of operations, in order to avoid any reference to universals. But universals are the trancendence of the particular *datum*. Operational thinking narrows the outlook and fixes the attention on what is.

One-dimensionality as a feature of 'the ideology of advanced industrial society' makes one forget or overlook or deny the split or cleavage of Being, makes one accept one's situation and suffering as unavoidable, makes liberation impossible.

Oppression in advanced industrial society takes the form of administration (Weberian bureaucracy)[31] and technology, in a

29. Cf. the excellent exposition in *Reason and Revolution*, 1941.
30. As Raymond Aron once remarked, Marcuse and thinkers like him worry over an excess of social integration in Western industrial countries, while Parsons worries over a *lack* of it.
31. Cf. Marcuse's contribution in Stammer (ed.): *Max Weber und die Soziologie heute* (1965).

way that minimizes conflicts over ends and means. The instrumental interpretation of knowledge ('science') leads to a deerotization of life and to a corresponding emphasis upon and exploitation of human sexuality (in a restricted, genital and aggressive sense). The 'pacification of existence' and its concomitant erotic existence will never be reached by progressive affluence of the kind offered by advanced industrial society.

The conception that domination over nature can no longer be separated from domination over man by man, leads one to question the technological apparatus as such. Instead of positing that a machine in itself is neither good nor bad, since it all depends upon the uses to which it is put, Marcuse affirms that technology in our society is in itself a mode of domination and social control.[32] Technology springs from a historic project or logic of domination, and as such constitutes our fundamental relations both to other human beings and our environment.

To be sure, Marcuse sides with Marx against Fourier and makes it clear that he does not envisage the possibility of 'the abolition of labour' and its transformation into play. On the other hand, he states that our technology does not serve to reduce human toil, but rather hinders our enjoyment and development of our needs and capacities.

7. The doctrine of the practico-inert field

Marx showed how the outcome of human productive activity under a capitalist mode of production stands before the immediate producers as 'a hostile, alien force' and outside the control even of the capital owners. Sartre generalized this insight through his descriptions of what he termed the *practico-inert field* and the *worked matter*. The concept of worked matter.

32. 'In the face of the totalitarian features of this society, the traditional notion of the 'neutrality' of technology can no longer be maintained. Technology as such cannot be isolated from the use to which it is put; the technological society is a system of domination which operates already in the concept and construction of techniques.' *Introduction*, Or: 'Today, domination perpetuates and extends itself not only through technology but *as* technology, and the latter provides the great legitimation of the expanding political power, which absorbs all spheres of culture,' chap. 6. And: 'In other words, technology has become the great vehicle of *reification*—reification in its most mature and effective form.' chap. 7. Marcuse: *One Dimensional Man* (1964).

denotes all kinds of matter that has been shaped or altered by human activity and intention, and not only products that appear in the form of capital in the usual, restricted sense. This extension involves that the fundamental distinction between use value and exchange value and its corollary, that between the material and the value dimension of capital, is put in parentheses.

Given the capital—wage-labour opposition and the condition of material scarcity, one may consider the *exigences* of artifacts such as a machine in the factory. It demands to be operated in a certain way, and addresses the worker as anybody, as an Other than himself. It is not the machine as a purely physical structure that is exigent; the machine transforms and embodies the expectations of the owner of the machine, making them inert and alienating. Likewise, a dwelling is the owner's interest[33] (in a specific sense) as a specification of an exigence: it makes demands on the specific owner who has his (her) being outside himself in this thing. One is owned by one's house. The social classes are constituted fundamentally by such alienating materiality; we are born into a social class with its specific kinds of artifacts, environment, general place in the production process, as a synthesis of exigences (or interests and destinies). In this practico-inert field one also experiences *counter-finality*, that is, how the products of one's activity turn against oneself (as the deforestation of China by the peasants brought about the recurrent inundations, or the import of precious metals from America to Spain produced a disastrous monetary inflation). Sartre further introduces the concept of the *collectives* and their corresponding mode of sociality, *seriality*, to solve the task he set himself of providing mediations between the contradictions of the mode of production and the happenings of the individuals' everyday life: The tramway, the broadcasting system, and other objects of collective consumption condition mutually alienative relationships between human beings, through making them a *series* of people where everybody is the same as

---

33. 'Interest is being-wholly-outside-oneself-in-a-thing in so far as it conditions *praxis* as a categorical imperative'. *Critique of Dialectical Reason*, p. 197 (Sheridan-Smith's translation). The factory is the interest of the industrial capitalist, but the *destiny* of the worker (whose interest is not to work in the factory).

(identical with) all the others (in the pertinent respect) without for that reason constituting a community.

Seriality is a specification of alienation and Otherness (Anderssein) which makes a large part of the practico-inert field.[34]

8. A general interpretation of socio-matter and domination

The doctrine of the practical-inert field makes intelligible the position of the State in the following way: the State is not legitimate, but nor is it rejected as illegitimate. There is an acceptance of the impossibility of rejecting the State, in other words the powerlessness of the serialized citizens, conditioned by the practical-inert field is the basis of the State's pseudo- (or quasi-) legitimity.[35]

I have ventured to elaborate this reasoning à propos Dahrendorf's well-known attempt to refute Marx's doctrine of classes.[36]

As noted earlier, Marx asserted that when the State poses as the ruling and dominating force in society, this is mere appearance, since, in reality, the State is produced by, founded on and serving the class that owns the means of production, the ruling class. Dahrendorf pays Marx back in his own coin, affirming that this presentation of the relationship between the State's power and property relations is itself mere appearance brought about through a 'trick of definition', a conceptual fallacy.

To show this, Dahrendorf begins by stating that to own something is a *right* over one or more objects and therefore a kind of rightful domination or authority. But if so, it becomes a mistake to designate the dominating class as the class that owns the means of production, since property is only one of many forms of authority. The ruling class is composed of all those who rule, regardless of what form this rule or authority takes. He thus maintains that it is possible to refute Marx's theory 'if we replace the possession, or non-possession, of effective private property by the exercise of, or exclusion from, authority as the criterion of class formation.' Further he says, that 'whoever tries, therefore, to define authority by property defines the general by the particular—an obvious logical fallacy.

34. This exposition continues in chap. 8.
35. Sartre, *ibid.*
36. Cf. my 'Notes on the concept of *matériel*', *International Journal of Sociology* vol. 9, no. 4.

Wherever there is property there is authority but not every form of authority implies property. Authority is the more general social relation.'[37] This fallacy may have been easy to fall into in Marx's time, when property was probably the primary means for the exercise of authority. But the evolution of society has since changed all this in two ways.

Moreover, Dahrendorf claims that while ownership of the means of production can evidently be abolished as a particular form of authority, it is not conceivable that authority in general—every form of authority—could be abolished. There will always, therefore, be social classes: those who rule and those who are ruled. The task of sociology is to describe which layers of society are constituted into classes at any particular time, and at any particular time what the relations between the classes are.[38]

We are thus confronted by two conceptions each of which claims to vanquish the other, and the discussion seems to have reached a deadlock, but for the concept of *matériel*, which indicates a way out of the impasse.

To own something does not necessarily mean simply to have a purely legal right, or to take some utility article or some other kind of *matériel* into possession. *Matériel* in itself may call forth a tacit property relationship, by suggesting, indicating, or appealing to certain ways of handling it, and thereby, contribute to the emergence of a right to disposition relative to it. The car as a transport vehicle may serve as an example: since it is dangerous for children, it tacitly excludes them as car owners. Generally, the structure, size, and design of *matériel* silently indicate directions of use and property forms. Marx's statement to the effect that owning the means of production is neither a legal relation nor something that comes about by direct or indirect use of force, can thus be interpreted as a statement that any piece of *matériel* indicates certain modes of use as particularly near at hand, which, in turn, indicates certain legal forms of property as especially near at hand or reasonable. Such

---

37. Dahrendorf: *Class and Class Conflict in Industrial Society* (1961) pp. 136–7.
38. His own proposal is this: The ruling class in today's industrial society 'consists of two constants, bureaucracy and government, and one variable, the veto group whose claims are, in particular situations, incorporated in government policy'. *Ibid.* p. 305.

an indication or suggestion never strictly determines modes of use and concomitant property forms. One can never clearly and unambiguously show how and to what extent a kind of *matériel* anticipates and determines legal property forms, even if we can see that such an influence exists.[39]

The same goes, *mutatis mutandis*, for the spatial distribution of the structures of *matériel* within a society, inducing those who do not have access to the most important kinds of *matériel* to accept others' access to it, from sheer powerlessness. Hence justice, legitimacy and consensus may rest on a tacit, amorphous powerlessness in the face of society's structures of *matériel*.

Prolonging this reasoning, the affirmation that the economy, or more precisely, the mode of production and its internal struggles determine other regions of human life can now be stated as two protensions:

The first is the 'barely expressible' thought that changes of matter and of *matériel* change our conditions of understanding. Understanding these changes calls for an 'informal' economics, a 'material' or 'socio-material' economics which tends towards formalization, without ever becoming entirely formalized and thus entirely accessible to 'formal thought'. It is what goes on beneath, as it were, the level of formal law and calculable economic magnitudes that ultimately concerns the facticity of human existence and history.

The second basic protension is that of conflicts as internal negations within a totality of human beings, such as pain, hatred, contempt or perverted solidarity and unity. Understanding these conflicts calls for a conflictual economics, which describes and furthers the essential conflicts within the mode of productions, which—*per definitionem*—are the class conflicts. While most economics doctrines speak of an affirmative totality, conflictual economics will speak of a negative totality, that is of an economy constituted by its conflicts.

Combining these two thoughts, the conception or protension

39. Investigations have shown that most citizens have a very poor understanding of legal texts such as the code of laws. Since it is often hard to disagree with a text one does not understand, one may choose to be silent, and this silence will count as acceptance. The legitimacy of the code of laws largely stems from its obscurity, which make legal books appear as huge masses of *matériel* inducing powerlessness.

of an informal and for that reason somewhat amorphous conflict between diffuse syntheses of human beings and their *matériel* and material environment, continually changing as the result
of human praxis, emerges as the topic of economics, or, rather,
of history. This level of conflictual materiality is the basis or
the background of all strictly economical reasoning, mathematical or not—and is what the distinctions between value of use
and values of exchange, and between productive and unproductive labour, point to. On this level, the protension of an existence
where all kinds of *matériel* and their handling are thoroughly
agreeable can emerge as a specification of the symbol of the
Resurrection of the Body.

9. New version of non-intellectual freedom (Sartre)

By developing the doctrine of the practical-inert field Sartre
also wanted to show how Marx' alleged 'materialism' is compatible with the assertion of the (unconditional, 'absolute') freedom
of human beings. To Sartre, human freedom shows itself above
all in the transcendence of everything that is given, including
the agent's own body. The human being is situated—at a
certain place, a certain time, with this particular past, language,
age etc., all of which are features of the facticity that is only
experienced through the human being's projects. Thus, a material hindrance does not in itself make me unfree; on the
contrary, acting in the world presupposes material hindrances
to be overcome.[40]

Therefore, matter as such does not determine my behaviour
in the sense of abolishing its freedom, making it predictable like
physical processes, and stripping it of its transcendence. On the
contrary, worked-up matter, matter stamped by human activity
may only limit my freedom, through mediating and transmitting
the intentions of *other human beings* with whom I am not in

---

40. This thought is rendered in altered shape by Giddens' conception of 'struc-
turation': Social structures are at the same time constraining and enabling:
They constrain me to use a certain language or code of behaviour if I am to
do something intelligible to myself and others; but they also make me able to
act at all in the social world, through constituting my activity as meaningful.
Even when I am 'left no choice' or have no 'real alternative' the structure does
not strictly determine my action, since my choice not to perish, but live on is
needed in order to constitute the act as an act. Giddens: *The Constitution of
Society* (1984), p. 177.

community. In a field of human conflict and dispersion, worked-on matter may distort and alienate the human being's freedom by way of mediation. Only a freedom can limit a freedom; the coercion that stems from the worked matter can be traced back to the actions and projects of human beings (living or dead), even if in actual, concrete life there is a circularity: Everybody may experience his (her) acts as forced by the 'circumstances', i.e. the practico-inert field.[41]

The 'idealism'—or rather 'intellectualism' and 'voluntarism'—of Liberal thought consists in its tendency to belittle the material necessity of human existence by insisting on the importance of a strong will, thought's independence of matter ('die Gedanken sind frei') and the like.

Instead, necessity in human existence is described by Sartre, not as incompatible with freedom (as in the old opposition between 'determinism' and 'freedom'), but as freedom violated and encroached upon, freedom experienced as alienated in the practico-inert field. The leap from the realm of necessity to the realm of liberty consists in the overcoming of this alienation.

Going perhaps further in this direction of thought than Sartre himself, one may note a sense in which the human being may experience lack of freedom, as in the case of fatigue. When the body is sick, exhausted, tortured or otherwise damaged, I may still retain the possibility of choosing how to respond to the damage, but only up to a point, beyond which my facticity overwhelms me (as when I faint from excessive pain).

10. Final remarks

These contributions in various ways enrich and bring up to date the original 'materialist conception of history'. Most important, of course, is the endeavour to show how industrial societies in the West can with good reason still be interpreted as based on a capitalist mode of production, that is, how the new relationship between State and Market, albeit involving a change, retains the State's feature of being favourable to the dominant class of capital owners.

The other developments of the original doctrine which have

41. 'The practico-inert field is the field of servitude, which means *not* ideal servitude, but real subservience to "natural" forces, to "mechanical" forces and to "anti-social" apparatuses ... 'Sartre, *op. cit.,* p. 331–2.

been set forth, mainly seek to make understandable why class exploitation and oppression is not experienced directly by wage labourers so as to provoke overt rejection and rebellion. The absence of an acute class struggle on the part of the wage-labour class is partly traced back to diverting mediations, such as the apparatus and discourses of sexuality and its morals, or the anti-dialectical logic taught within educational institutions on all levels. Partly, the said absence is interpreted by pointing to the impact of materiality in social life; through being social-ized and appearing as artefacts and signs of all kinds, matter *qua* socio-matter can make possible and strengthen a minority's exploitation and domination over the majority. The old 'mater-ialism's ambiguous and diffuse affirmation to the effect that matter determines human existence is here given a more limited and precise meaning: As *matériel*, matter may exert and mediate domination over human beings, thus leaving room for human freedom as veridical experience.

6

Attempts at Synthesis

Even if the conceptions to be presented in this chapter might perforce be inserted in the previous chapters, it is more exact to consider them as attempts to encompass all the preceding topics. Thus, the authors in question should not be called Marxists, Sociologists, or Sociographers, yet they apply notions from Sociology, the Materialist conception of history, and Social research, blending them in their own way.

A. The 'Critical Theory' of Horkheimer and Adorno

1. Introductory remarks

Basically, the Frankfurter School and its *Institut für Sozialforschung* endeavoured to reshape the historico-dialectical conceptions of Marx and Engels as a response to the weakening of the European labour movements and the corresponding rise of Fascism in the 1920s and 1930s.[1] This sinister chain of events indicated that these conceptions were insufficient both as an interpretation of recent History and as a guide to the making of History. It became urgent to understand what made people from all social classes susceptible to Fascism's inducements. The insertion of parts of Freudian psychology into Marx's and Engels' conceptual framework seemed promising (in the same way as Parsons' insertion of the same psychology into Sociology). Also, Hegelian notions of ossification of dialectical totalities were emphasized, to render intelligible the corporate structures of Late Capitalism.

During the ensuing world war, two of the leading figures, Adorno and Horkheimer, enlarged their critique (the word 'cri-

---

1. Cf. Martin Jay: *The Dialectical Imagination* (1973) for an ample account of the history of the Frankfurter School.

tique' having both a Kantian and a Marxian sense): The dialectic of Enlightenment had changed the instrumentally oriented sciences of nature from liberators of humanity to a means and medium of its coercion. Instrumental reason had turned into unreason.[2]

Now, it was of the utmost importance that this assertion should not be confounded with the usual critique of civilization and hatred of science that characterized part of the Romanticist movement. To forestall this misunderstanding, Horkheimer had already introduced the distinction between *traditional* and *critical* theory.

2. 'Traditional' and 'critical theory'

Traditional theory designates the search for general knowledge of regularities, functional relationships (of a statistic or deterministic kind) permitting predictions of future events and processes.[3] At the origin of this tradition Horkheimer places Descartes' *Discours de la méthode*. It presupposes that the topic of understanding is independent of those who attempt to understand, and that the topic contains a truth independent of human beings' actions and hopes.

Critical theory, by contrast, does not primarily aim at the discovery of uniformities, but at the change of the conditions of human existence through human action. This mode of thought—beginning, according to Horkheimer, with Marx's critique of political economy—rejects the notion that its subject-matter is given with merely an external relation to the praxis of human beings. Facts are not strictly speaking data; at least they are not given as data, since they ultimately refer to human activity, to *facere*. The data of the world can therefore be changed, and for this reason they are not univocal. They both refer to the past activity that made them, and point forward to possible action which may transform them. To be critical in this

2. Horkheimer and Adorno: *Dialektik der Auf Klärung* (1947).
3. 'One operates with conditional propositions, applied to a given situation. Supposing the circumstances a b c d, the event q must be expected, if d disappears, the event r, if g is joined, the event s, and so on. Such calculation belongs to the logical skeleton of history as well as to that of natural science. It is the mode of existence of theory in the traditionel sense.' Horkheimer: *Traditionelle und kritische Theorie* (1937) (my translation).

sense is to look for the condition of possibility of all that is given, and to discern the conditions of these conditions, i.e. their origin in human practice. To be critical also means to understand the actual facts in the light of the possible abolition of human distress and repression. Critical theory stands in an internal relation to liberation as intention and practice. The law-like necessity of social institutions and processes is the form of repression and alienation. The task of Critical Theory is to contribute to a world without such reified relations between human beings—a free world. Such contributions will not consist in 'social engineering', in the elaboration and application of insights that will serve as means of liberation as the end. Rather, they will consist in the elucidation of the actual forms of reification and powerlessness, and the awareness that to think always in terms of means and ends, the 'instrumental reason', it itself a form of repressed and unfree human existence.

Critical Theory repudiates both the Liberal notion of the individual and the Fascist notion of the totality. Critical theory maintains a third position, the 'ambivalent character of the societal whole', which it develops 'to conscious contradiction', the contradiction between the social world as created by human practice, and as comparable to processes of nature, mere mechanisms, owing to the lack of unitary, communal action. Critical Theory anticipates a society of free individuals living in community, reconciled with nature[4] and at the same time maintains the contradictions of the actual social world, above all, the class conflict determined by the opposition between wage labour and capital.

3. Relation to Sociology and Social research

One of Adorno's essays, written 20 years later, shares the same basic conception of Critical Theory, and furnishes precious amplifications.[5]

In this (and many other essays) he attacks the dominant forms of social research on account of their preoccupation with

---

4. Cf. the last words in Adorno's *Essay on Wagner* (1952), speaking of music's 'immemorial promise: Living without anguish *(Angst)*'.
5. 'Soziologie und empirische Forschung' (1957) reprinted in R. König (ed.): *Der Positivismusstreit in der deutschen Soziologie.*

the scattered facts and their refusal to think in terms of social wholes. He also objects to their superficial registering of attitudes, opinions and the like, and their neglect of objectivated and objective mind, such as economic institutions. He also points out the implicit compliance in the use of ready-made distinctions such as that between 'classical' and 'popular' music, without inquiring into the social conditions of such a distinction, and an interpretation of the music itself.

But he also attacks Sociology (in the sense defined above), a science concerned with the interpretation of meaningful social totalities. For these totalities only exist as repressive, dominating structures, reifying the great majority of human beings. To present social life as based upon an encompassing consensus is itself repressive, since what the members of society experience as coercion is interpreted as their mutual affirmation and unity. This is to conceal conflicts instead of clarifying them. In the same vein, he rejects sociology's protest against the allegedly dehumanizing ways of social research, on behalf of the spiritual being of humankind. For to speak of humanity as spiritual may also be repressive in a world where human beings are in fact debased and lead a life unworthy of themselves. The lofty, edifying considerations of sociology are hypocritical and (in the Marxian sense) mystifying and ideological, with the slightly menacing undertone inherent in all edification.[6]

Likewise, the paramount importance of exchange relations within a society with a capitalist mode of production makes the utilitarian, calculating orientation prevalent in social interaction, and therefore high-minded conceptions of a solidarity beyond any utility inevitably assume the character of exhortation on behalf of a false universality that does not exist except in the mode of hope and anticipation. All communities and organizations of human beings in our world are tinged by compulsion and coercion, regardless of the intimate affection of the unions. The complete integration of the singular human

6. 'The enraged, indignant protests and the subtler defensive gestures provoked by Kinsey's investigations are the most powerful argument for Kinsey. Wherever human beings are, in fact, reduced under the pressure of conditions to the "amphibious" mode of reaction, as they are in their capacity as compulsive consumers of the mass media and other regimented joys, opinion research, which infuriates lixiviated humanism, is better suited to them than, for instance, an "interpretative" sociology.' (*ibid.*, p. 74).

being into some social whole is therefore a threat.[7] Adorno insists on the ultimate, irreducible 'non-identity' of the singular human being's experience; in this respect, he takes over Kierkegaard's notions of 'existence' as that predicate of 'the singular' ('enkelte') which makes him or her elude integration into humanity as a universal, integrated whole. But again, he accuses Empiricistic social research of sharing Existential philosophy's conviction that everything depends upon the singular human being, who is burdened with a total responsibility for his or her existence. The measurements of attitudes and opinions suggest individual freedom, since they neglect the reification of freedom through capitalist production, markets and administrative apparatuses.

In a damaged world there are no beautiful expressive totalities, neither on the level of corporations and groups, nor on the level of individual human beings. Everywhere, there is ugliness and pain, distortions and perversions, bits of experiences and memories, habits and rituals that are torn out of their initial context; ambivalence permeates every human relationship and ridicules the hope of a life worthy of human beings. Under the prevailing conditions, all the procedures and findings of social research are highly important, provided they are understood in a critical way. The haphazard, the meaningless, the docile, the resigned—these features of the modern world are clearly brought out by Empiricist and Positivist social researchers. But in order to be true, and not only correct (as corresponding to the facts) these results must be interpreted by a transcending conception of human liberation.[8] This conception anticipates a world where instrumental action and reason are abolished, not only in relations between human beings, but also in humankind's relation to the non-human (physical) environment, that is, the reconciliation referred to earlier (ch. 4): The opposition between lust and toil, sexuality and instrumentality, gives way, in favour of a human existence that is erotic in the widest sense of the word.

Adorno defends the concept of totality against the objection that it simply means that everything is linked with everything

---

7. Cf. Adorno's introduction to the German edition of Durkheim's *Sociologie et philosophie*, where he attacks the French sociologist's authoritarian attitude.
8. Adorno: Introduction to *The Positivist Dispute in German Sociology*, p. 12.

else. On the contrary, it designates 'the sum of individuals' social relations which screen themselves off from individuals,'[9] and for this very reason acts as a force upon the individuals.

Totality is the reification of human relations, acting as a *contrainte sociale* in Durkheim's sense. Totality is the correlate of repression and lack of freedom. 'A liberated mankind would by no means be a totality'. Thus, capital, described by Marx as an 'anti-social force' is a totality concept, and so is commodity exchange, which mediates the domination of men over men. Totality preforms desires and thoughts of human beings, who thereby are profoundly alienated. The purpose of Critical Theory is to assist at the vanquishing of totality and the coming into existence of unalienated individuation.

4. An example: Adorno's interpretation of music

Arrogant and futile as these assertions may sound, their significance changes for the better when connected to Adorno's own work within sociology and social research, such as his investigations into music.

Being also a composer and a musicologist, Adorno's critical treatment of music best brings out his conception of a critical theory of history and society.

Adorno endorses the prevalent conception of the Vienna Classics (Haydn, Mozart, Beethoven) as composers who participated in the political, bourgeois movement of liberation. Especially Beethoven's music expresses at the same time individualism and universalism, the longing and urge for a new social synthesis and the conflicts between the subjugated individual and the established authority (in fact, the way we listen to Beethoven's music is imbued with images, slogans and aphorisms of Liberal politics). This music is not exclusively beautiful, but expresses turmoil, despair, restlessness, and precisely for this reason the music is true. Truth must express both harmony

9. Sartre's contention in *Question de méthode*, that Marxism must assimilate psychoanalysis and sociology if it is to avoid being reduced to its skeleton, brings him close to the position of the Frankfurter School. For by 'sociology' he does not envisage the contributions of Durkheim and his followers, but the 'social research' done in the USA. Its disconnected findings should enrich and confront the totalizing conceptions of historical materialism.

and dissonance, it must be both affirmative and negative, and indicate and express important conflicts and contradictions. True music must also be on a par with—apply and exploit—the possibilities of the musical means of production. As these develop, compositions cannot avoid becoming obsolete, as works once true, but being so no longer. The cultivation of music made before our own age therefore runs the risk of being a cult, an adulation and idolatry of 'flawless masterpieces' of 'eternal value'. This is an aspect of what Adorno terms fetishism in musical listening. From this chain of reasoning it follows that music after Beethoven tends towards untruth—as in the great example of Wagner. This he sees in connection with late capitalism and a bourgeoisie no longer a carrier of historical progress. Being himself a pupil of Arnold Schönberg and Alban Berg, Adorno conceives of so-called 'a-tonal' music as the true music of his own time. This is because the Second Vienna School (Schönberg, Berg, Webern) uncompromisingly skips every cliché, refuses every outworn musical formula[10]—thus avoiding fetishism and reification—and because it emphasizes conflict, pain, the unresolved contradiction.

The public's reception of this musical movement deeply impressed Adorno. Schönberg's music was scorned and scoffed at, as unspeakably ugly and meaningless. But this rejection was in bad faith, Adorno contends. This music was not refused because it was not understood, but, on the contrary, because it was understood only too well. In the same way as the Freudians pointed to deeply embarrassing facts, which for this reason were resisted and denied, the 'atonal music' expressed an anguish which musical public opinion refused to admit and recognize—and hence Adorno's abysmal bitterness. Through his music Schönberg (like the Bible's prophets) anticipated the coming horrors of Fascism, and for this reason met with resistance. Neo-classicism (Prokoviev, Hindemith, Castella, Poulenc

10. 'The diminished seventh is right and full of expression at the beginning of op. 111. It corresponds to Beethoven's whole technical niveau, doesn't it?—the tension between consonance and the harshest dissonance known to him. The principle of tonality and its dynamics lend to the chord its specific weight. It has lost it—by a historical process which nobody reverses.' *Dr. Faustus*, chap. 25. Adorno's contribution to the musical parts of this great novel is recorded by Thomas Mann himself in *Die Entstehung des Dr. Faustus. Roman eines Romans*.

and others) with its ironic play with old forms seemed to Adorno too easy a way out of the musical *impasse* facing composers.[11]

The music of Strawinsky was a more serious challenge.[12] Works such as *Le sacre du printemps* and *La symphonie des Psaumes* were archaic in a dubious and dangerous way, evoking primitive societies where rituals involving the sacrifice of human beings are practised, that is, the individual's total submission under the collectivity. This anticipates the doctrine of Fascism and National Socialism (Hitler: *'Du bist nichts, dein Volk ist alles'*), which to Adorno was a relapse into barbarism. The musical texture confirms this interpretation, as, for instance, the famous cluster chords of the *Rite of Spring:*

These terrifying rhythms and sounds strongly suggest the collective ritual's horrible acts, and Strawinsky's 'neo-barbarism' was hailed as a great achievement, after the uproar at the first performance was attributed to lack of understanding. But this neo-barbarism amounts to an affirmation of the undifferentiated social totality and its violent means of maintaining social integration.[13]

Thus, in the realm of music, the unresolved conflicts of economico-political life are mediated and reflected in a specific way, not only in the social relations between musicians, their audience, editors, the mass media and so on, but also in the musical scores themselves.

Adorno's typology of listeners conceptualizes other areas

---

11. '... I speak not of the folklorists and neo-classic stylists whose modernness consists in their forbidding themselves a musical outbreak and in wearing with more or less dignity the style-garment of a pre-individualist period. Persuade themselves and others that the tedious has become interesting because the interesting has begun to grow tedious.' *Dr. Faustus,* ch. 25.
12. Cf. Adorno: *Philosophie der neuen Musik* (1949).
13. This reasoning also casts doubt upon the truth of some of Bartok's music, such as his *Allegro barbaro.*

of his musical experiences, especially his participation in the Princeton Broadcasting Project. From this activity he learnt how little most people understand of the music they listen to, and why this is so. Modern consciousness does not have that synthetic unity presupposed by great music of the past, but is fragmented, divided, alienated. Accordingly, listeners are distinguished with respect to the adequacy of their perception of the musical object. The *expert* is defined by completely adequate listening, which, since it understands the structure of the musical flow, is also termed 'structural listening'. The *good listener* is likened to those who know their own language without knowing much about grammar and syntax. This type not only 'likes' music, but can properly be called 'musical'. The *consumer of culture (Bildung)* as a type is led either by a sense of cultural obligation or by some sort of snobbism. In both cases a relation to music as such is lacking, and this type has succumbed to fetishism, in the Marxian sense. The *emotional listener* as a type neither perceives the musical objects nor pretends to be a connoisseur. The relation to music essentially serves to release repressed or morally inhibited drive impulses, as a refugium where the human being is allowed to feel anything at all, which he or she is usually debarred from doing through the instrumentality of economic life. (Structural listening too, presupposes an effective cathexis, with the difference that what is cathected, is the musical object itself.) A reaction to this type is constituted by the listener of *resentment*, in Nietzsche's sense. Finally, there is the *entertainment* listener, who does not perceive music as relationships of meaning, but merely as stimuli to give comfort through diversion and deconcentration, interrupted by sudden moments of attention and recognition. This type of listening (compared to smoking by Adorno) is interpreted as one of several possible responses to the atomization of social life, and from a purely quantitative point of view presumed to be the only one relevant for a sociology of music.

This typology specifies alienated and non-alienated consciousness in the field of musical activity—modes of reification and repression and resistance—corresponding to the description and typology of the music itself (light music, opera, modern, jazz, etc.) and the various social institutions through which music is objectivated and mediated.

5. Final comment

Critical Theory remains committed to the fundamental conceptions of Marx (and, to a lesser degree, Engels) concerning
human self-expression and alienation, the fetishism of commodities, the class conflicts underlying free exchange on the
markets, the repressive feature of all appeals to solidarity beyond class cleavages. But the defeats of the movements guided
by historico-dialectic thinking have called forth a state of social
life where Social research is often more appropriate than the
interpretations of History as a totalizing process, and where the
concepts of Sociology must be considered relatively detached
from class conflicts. This attempt at synthesis does not endeavour to create a new whole where Marxian thought, Sociology,
and Social Research are the integrated parts; instead, it seeks
to take account of all three parts (and also a fourth, Freudian
'psychoanalysis') without pretending to fuse them into a smooth
unity.

B. Habermas's Theory of Communicative Action

1. Introduction

Habermas's concern with human communication is presumably
a response to his adolescent experience of Fascism and National
Socialism.[14] These movements scorned discussions in favour of
fisticuffs and other forms of bodily violence; they derided the
appeal to universal reason as bloodless intellectuality. Precisely
because of this, Habermas has throughout his career attempted
to vindicate reason in human affairs.

This is already clearly apparent in his first book, *Strukturwandel der Öffentlichkeit*. This work deals with the rise of the
bourgeois form of public life, its heyday and subsequent decay,
judged according to criteria of communication and truth. Feudal and absolutist princes led a public life that was representative in the sense that it consisted in a display of gestures and
rituals, in pomp and circumstances symbolic of political power.
They uttered their will, and dispensed their favour and dis-
favour; they commanded, scolded and pardoned, but did not

---

14. The end of the Hitler regime was a shock to him; he was at that time a
member of the *Hitlerjugend*.

reason with their subjects. With the development of the capital-ist mode of production and the concomitant political restructuring, a new kind of public life came into existence, marked above all by the formation of a public opinion. This public opinion was a mediator between, on the one side, the government (the king, the court, the ministers and their ambian-ce), and, on the other side, the class of industrials, merchants, lawyers, etc. The newspapers and the coffee-houses were the two important places where public opinion was made, and the form of its making was discussions. These are ways of convinc-ing other people through appeal to reasons that are valid for at least all who participate in the discussions and thus transcend particular 'self-interest'. Discussions aim at a *consensus* that unites and integrates the participants through the unconstrained use of their reason. This bourgeois public sphere and opinion presupposes a distinct private sphere, where individual opinions are fostered, the bourgeois home and family, and private prop-erty and enterprise.[15] This, of course, limits the validity of bour-geois public institutions. The later development of mass politics and mass media, of the interventionist State and the transform-ation of privacy into a sphere of intimacy, sapped the foun-dations of public opinion as the outcome of rational discussions. Any return to previous states of affairs is out of the question. The example of bourgeois public life serves Habermas as a point of departure, from which he can pose the more general question of the possibility and essence of communication be-tween human beings. Public discussions being a special case of reason in social intercourse, the task Habermas sets himself in his last works[16] has been to investigate the realm of such dis-course as a whole, to elaborate a general doctrine of communi-cative action.

2. Strategic and communicative action

The basic distinction in Habermas's doctrine of communication is between strategic and communicative action. Strategic action is a more generalized version of Weber's means-end action, and

15. As already noted, Kant considered, financial independence a prerequisite of academic study.
16. Above all, in *Theorie des kommunikativen Handelns* (1981), English trans-lation of the first part: *Theory of communicative action* (1984).

designates actions where the actor attempts to use Others as means to his (her) own ends, while taking into account that the Others seek to do the same. 'Strategic action' is also a generalization of Tönnies' *Kürwille* (arbitrary will). On the other hand, communicative action is action the intention of which is to agree with Others as to the truth and validity of a conception.[17]

This concept is intended to replace Weber's 'traditional', 'value rational' and 'affective' actions. The reason is that Habermas wants to show that communicative action is also a mode of *rational* action.

For it is not enough, he says, to share the same mood to be in a state of *agreement*. This requires the pronunciation of—or at least the possibility of—a proposition that makes explicit what there is unanimity about. Unanimity is mediated by language, which implies that those who agree do so by virtue of their reason. Unanimity can never be imposed, except on the basis of reasons.[18]

Thus, Habermas connects communication, speech and reason to each other by an internal, essential relation.

Habermas takes up Austin's doctrine of locutionary, illocutionary, and perlocutionary utterances, since it seems to him to show clearly that the co-ordinating aspect of communicative action is different from that of an instrumental co-ordination, and, consequently, that the 'orientation to reaching understanding' is the original mode of communication, upon which the strategic is parasitic. The perlocutionary act—'to bring about something *through* acting in saying something'—is a kind of strategic action, which presupposes and exploits the existence of locutions and illocutions.[19] Communicative action is interaction in which all participants 'pursue their illocutionary aims without reservation'. Interaction, where at least one of the

---

17. 'By contrast, I shall speak of *communicative* action whenever the actions of the agents involved are coordinated not through egocentric calculations of success, but through acts of reaching understanding'. *Op.cit.* pp. 286–7.
18. This reminds one of Russell's distinction long ago between persuading and convincing somebody.
19. *Ibid.*, I, pp. 288f. Strawson and Habermas may be right that as a basic mode perlocutionary actors must conceal their perlocutionary intentions in order to succeed. However, Hamsun showed in the novel *Mysterier* (Mysteries) in 1891 how a virtuoso of perlocution, Nagel, dazzles everybody through constantly declaring his perlocutions.

participants speaks in a perlocutionary way, Habermas terms lingually mediated strategic action.

The response to a communicative utterance (affirmative, declining etc.) has implications for one's further actions. Agreement refers to conventionally established obligations. Thus, what Habermas terms 'the pragmatic level' mediates between the semantic level of understanding of meaning, and the empirical level of action consequences of the unanimity. To elucidate how communication can be the basis of all human relationships is the task assigned to 'formal' or 'universal' 'pragmatics'.

To understand a speech act, Habermas states, is to know what makes it acceptable.[20] Some of these conditions of acceptability pertain to obligations which concern future action and interaction. However, more is needed in order to know when a request is acceptable. The hearer must also know 'why the speaker expects that he might impose his will upon him'. In addition to the conditions of fulfilment he must know the conditions of *sanctions*. The next step taken—which leads us into the domain of sociology proper—is to consider what it means to understand authorized commands or requests (such as a stewardess's order to stop smoking before landing). According to Habermas, the one who utters an authorized request guarantees that the claims to validity of the request will be given if needed. The hearer accepts on rational grounds if he expects convincing reasons for the uttered request. But the case of the imperative backed by sanctions makes it clear that one can perform illocutionary speech acts and nevertheless act in a strategic way. Therefore a more precise determination is given: 'Not all illocutionary acts are constitutive for communicative action, but only those with which speakers connect criticizable claims to validity.[21]

The claims to validity can be judged in three respects: as to correctness *(Richtigkeit)*, as to sincereness *(Wahrhaftigkeit)*, and as to truth (in the sense of correspondence with what is the case), in the sense of an 'existential proposition'. To these three corresponds the reference to what Habermas terms three worlds, the world of legitimate orders, the world of facts *(Sachverhalte)*, and the subjective world of experiences *(Erlebnisse)*.

20. *Ibid.* I, pp. 297f.
21. *Ibid.* I, pp. 297f.

3. Life world and systems

Through successive extensions one may attain the level of concrete social life, by taking into account not only explicit, but also implicit utterances, not only direct, but also indirect ones, not only isolated speech acts but also sequences, not only speech, but communicative *action*, and—finally—not only communicative action but also the resources of background knowledge, that is *life worlds*.[22]

In everyday life we make deap-seated and trivial background assumptions which, if altered, change the meaning of the conditions of validity of speech acts. We do not notice these assumptions, we make them pre-reflexively, and become aware of them through a kind of *problematization*, which may result from the shaking of our 'natural picture of the world'. A doctrine of communicative action must therefore be supplemented by a doctrine of the life world.

Habermas's conception of the life world is worked out through contrast with that of Alfred Schütz, who describes the life world's structures as it is given to (a phenomenologically trained) consciousness. Habermas presents a life-world concept based on language and culture as background knowledge, as *semi-transcendental* conditions. 'Language and culture are constitutive of the life world itself'.[23] While the lifeworld concept (and similar concepts, like Cassirer's 'natural world') was developed as a contrast to the world of (physical) science, Habermas's life world is expressly conceived as something which is not lived or experienced, but constitutes conditions of communicative action and interaction. These conditions are taken for granted, their validity goes without saying, but in rare moments they may 'explode'.

However, Habermas does not want to identify the life world with 'culturally inherited background knowledge'.[24] It consists also of traditions of solidary groups and of socialization processes. The life world is therefore conceived of as socio-cultural. The life world's structural components are culture, society and personality, corresponding to processes of cultural reproduction, social integration and socialization. This permits Ha-

22. *Ibid.*, II, pp. 441ff.
23. *Ibid.*, II, p. 190.
24. *Ibid.*, II, p. 204.

bermas to connect his doctrine of communication and life world to the basic topics of sociology, thereby giving them a new interpretation.

Taking over the notion of differentiation, Habermas considers the possibility of a rationalized life world as the outcome of an evolution.[25]

To those who belong to a socio-cultural life world, it may seem as if social life is integrated solely through action oriented towards unanimity, but it is also co-ordinated through functional connexions which are unintended. Such functional co-ordinations Habermas terms *systems;* in our society the *market* is the major example. In systems strategic action is adequate.

Society is conceived by Habermas as the unity of life world and system; a doctrine of society must therefore investigate the relationship between the two, that is, between communicative and strategic action. His general proposition is that systems have differentiated through historic evolution, thus relieving the life world of some integrative tasks, which have instead been undertaken by mediums such as money and power. However, developed on the basis of the life world, the systemic mode of integration may expand into the domain of the life world. This 'colonization' of the lifeworld is 'pathological', since it threatens the ultimate foundation of society.

Habermas restates a thought of Durkheim's, who distinguished between division of labour as part of the evolutionary process towards differentiation, and its pathological form,[26] and goes on to affirm that Marx overlooked the distinction between the differentiated 'systems' mediated through 'de-lingualized media', media like power and money as evolutionary outcomes, and their pathological forms, or rather, their pathological extensions (into the life world). Consequently, the major charge of alienation within the politico-economic sphere levelled against the strategic actions of a capitalistic mode of production should be withdrawn. Only when strategic action begins to permeate

---

25. 'The further the lifeworld's structural components and the processes contributing to its maintenance become differentiated, the more the interactional contexts depend on conditions of a rationally motivated understanding, that is, the establishing of a consensus which *in the last analysis* relies on the authority of the better argument.' *Ibid.,* II, p. 218. (My translation).
26. Cf. Durkheim: *De la division du travail social*, part III.

the life world, too, should it be condemned and opposed. The law of Value, moreover, is no longer valid,[27] he says, and therefore, the opposition between social classes (in the Marxian sense) is no longer fundamental to the understanding of society. Instead, pathological forms of consciousness and social interaction that are not class-specific crop up (such as 'fragmented' instead of 'false' consciousness).

The question of liberating the individual human being has become a question of communication.

4. Comment

While starting as a pupil of Horkheimer and Adorno and universally recognized as the most outstanding proponent of the Frankfurter School's second generation, Habermas has gradually changed the direction of his thought, making it more akin to Kant than to Hegel, and closer to Sociology than to Historico-dialectic thought.

His recent 'Theory of communicative action' is a great attempt to go beyond both the tradition from Comte *via* Durkheim and Mead to Parsons, and the tradition from Marx and Engels, *via* Weber and Lukacs up to the Frankfurter School. The basic, unifying and transcending conception proposed is that of Reason as linguistically mediated activity. When his outline of communicative action is compared to Parsons' and Shils' 'paradigm of social interaction' the essential difference is this, that to Habermas, values and norms are not just internalized, but must be 'in principle criticizable' according to universally valid claims. In other words, the intellect, reason and reasoning are reintroduced by Habermas as founding human intercourse. Acting with reference to Others, he states, presupposes an implicit recognition of them as rational and reasoning beings, since the use of language entails claims to reason. Kant's (and Fichte's) preoccupation with sincereness and lies recurs in Habermas's doctrine as concern with communicative and strategic action. Through the 'linguistic turn' Kant's teachings of practical reason are renewed by Habermas (and Apel). *Theory of Communicative Action* continues the thinking in *Metaphysics of Morals*. What is at stake in both works is the possi-

27. Cf. my remarks on this topic in chapter 7.

bility of Reason being constitutive of human relationships, the possibility of deriving from Reason the institutions of politics, economy, family and so on as they are given as experienced facts, and by the same token to judge these factual institutions as more or less deviant from or conformative to Reason.

C. Bourdieu's Doctrine of Habitus and the Socio-Cultural Fields

1. Introduction

The work of Pierre Bourdieu has progressed from special investigations towards more general questions regarding the human being's fundamental relationship towards matter and other human beings.

Class domination in the cultural field (in the large sense of that word) is one of his main topics, another being the internal relation between perception and cognition, on the one hand, and one's practice as activity in specific, material, socio-cultural contexts, on the other. In combination, they make him appear now as a follower of Marx and Weber, now as a follower of Durkheim and the sociology of knowledge. In addition, his books show him as an expert sociographer, applying all kinds of 'methods in social research' (surveys, questionnaires, factorial analysis, etc.)

2. Habitus and class structure

Bourdieu's main concern appears to be the persistence of marked class differences and oppositions, notwithstanding Liberal (or Social Liberal) political measures to alleviate and level class inequalities, above all through educational reforms aiming at increased social mobility rates. These attempts to make the old capitalist class society disappear have proved superficial to the point of hypocrisy; the reason why they failed Bourdieu traces back to a lack of understanding of how school curricula and culture generally have class affinity and favour pupils from the dominating classes. This thought he has developed into a general doctrine of differential class *habitus* and socio-cultural fields.

The basic conception, then, remains that of Marx and Engels: Liberal thought as a delusive ('ideological') mode of understanding which distorts and blurs the conditions and essence of class relations. In the same vein, Bourdieu also retains a 'materialist' conception of human practice, that is, he thinks of action as partly constituted by an understanding, a 'practical sense', which is not primarily intellectual.[28] This practical sense is class-specific, he contends, giving rise to class-specific modes of perceiving and acting in the socio-cultural field, each class having its specific *habitus*.

The socio-cultural field is therefore heterogeneous, consisting of differing and conflicting relations of property and kinship, and of the internalization of these relations in the form of specific habitus, and of these habitus's externalization into the social-cultural field, as cultural activities.

The habitus concept may seem to be derived from Merleau-Ponty's doctrine of the body (in *Phénoménologie de la perception*), placing the body in a social situation structured by class oppositions. Epistemologically, however, Bourdieu does not adhere to this special version of Husserlian phenomenology, but refers approvingly to Cassirer's doctrine of science. Following Kant, this German thinker tried to demonstrate how mathematics, physics and chemistry proceed, not by abstractions, but by *con*struction of concepts, evolving from 'substance' to 'function' concepts, defined in terms of relations.

Culture, in a broad as well as in a restricted sense, is perhaps given more importance in class struggle than is usually found in the writings and declarations of Marx and Engels. Bourdieu speaks of 'cultural capital', convertible into 'economic capital', and of cultural domination as one mode of the general class domination. However, the priority is clear, and is, once more, in accord with the materialist conception of history: Property of all kinds is the dominating form of capital, and cultural capital the dominated form; therefore the leaders of industry, commerce and finance are the dominating fraction of the dominating classes, while the artist, intellectuals, professors etc. belong to the dominated fraction.

---

28. 'Les conditionnements associés à une classe particulière de conditions d'existence produisent des habitus, systèmes de *dispositions* durables et transposables ... générateurs et organisateurs de pratiques et de représentations qui peuvent être objectivement adaptées à leur but sant supposer la visée consciente de fins' etc. *Le sens pratique*, p. 88 (1981).

Since culture is a field of class struggles and of symbolic violence, there are no class-neutral activities or products (cf. the next section).

Since class society, at least in France, tends to perpetuate itself, Bourdieu is led to pose the Parsonian question of how the social system maintains itself. Instead of pointing to internalized role expectations Bourdieu introduces the notion of 'orchestration of habitus': there takes place a subconscious or unconscious adaptation to and anticipation of the possibilities and exigencies of the socio-cultural field, a mutual 'tuning in' which make the structures of domination persist. On the level of daily practice, of one's habitus expressing itself in routine activity, class society reproduces itself.

This notion of orchestrated habitus has been the target of many attacks, accusing Bourdieu of a kind of 'sociologism' or 'functionalism' which deprives human beings of their capacity to act intentionally.[29]

But this charge seems groundless, or even far-fetched, since it is rather the opposite objection that comes to mind, that Bourdieu tends to present social life as a vast field of countless and endless strategic action on the part of individuals, similar to the *Gesellschaft* of Tönnies, the only difference being that the strategies are mostly carried out by virtue of *habitus*, and not deliberately. The endeavour to interpret economic practices as one kind besides other practices (cultural, ritual, symbolic etc.) which also have their essential 'economy' also suggests such a stance. However, this is exactly the choice or dilemma Bourdieu seeks to avoid, speaking of 'socialized individuals' with 'transindividual dispositions'.

The habitus concept intends to transcend the following oppo-

---

29. Cf. the following rejoinder: 'Ai-je besoin de dire que, ayant depuis longtemps dénoncé ce que j'appelle le *fonctionnalisme du pire* et fourni, avec la notion d'habitus, le moyen de rendre raison de l'apparance de téléologie objective que procurent certains collectifs, je ne me reconnais aucunement dans des étiquettes, comme celles de "sociologisme", de "réalisme totalitaire" ou d' "hyperfonctionalisme", qui me sont parfois appliquées.' And: 'Il faut échapper à la vision mécaniste qui réduirait les agents à de simples particules jetées dans les champs de forces en réintroduisant non des sujets rationnels travaillant à réaliser leurs préférences dans les limites des contraintes, mais des agents socialisées qui, quoique biologiquement individués, sont dotés de dispositions transindividuelles, donc portés à engendrer des pratiques objectivement orchestrées' etc. *Homo academicus,* pp. 194–6 (1984).

sition: On the one hand, social life is thought of as constituted by singular human beings pursuing their goals through deliberate activity (the utilitarian doctrine of Liberal economics): on the other hand, one interprets social life as constituted by collectivities having intentions of their own, essentially different from those of individuals (such as Durkheim's *conscience collective* or Parsons' 'social system'). Now, *habitus* is a disposition concept: habitus is acquired through the socialization process and hence springs from the social environment within which one is born and raised. For this reason, one's habitus is socially constituted and specifies how one's field of deliberate action is structured and perceived.

3. Two examples
a) Consumption pattern and class structure
In their work *La reproduction* and *Les heritiers* Bourdieu and Passeron showed how students issuing from the dominating classes were rewarded during their university studies on the grounds of a cultural heritage which strictly speaking should be irrelevant.[30]

The cultural differences acted as a reinforcer and reproducer of class differences. In the subsequent work, *La distinction*,[31] (which in may respects continues Veblen's *Theory of the Leisure Class*) this and other findings concerning culture and class were generalized.

Briefly, the outcome of this great and voluminous investigation into tastes and habits in France can be recapitulated in the following way: The dominant conception of good taste is the one already expounded by Kant in the *Critique of Judgement*, according to which the aesthetic experience—the experience of the beautiful and the sublime—implies a distance to the environment. Bourgeois taste is a taste of distance, it is distinguished and relational, it emphasizes the relation between things rather than the things themselves; it tends to give greater weight to form than function, and attaches importance to manners and the finer points. This good taste presupposes a material and economic ease that only the dominant social classes enjoy,

---

30. This has come to be designated as the effect of 'the hidden curriculum'.
31. English edition in 1984: *Distinction*.

while the popular classes are overwhelmed by material necessities and lack the required distance. These classes make a virtue of necessity and acquire a 'substantialist' taste. (liking to eat what they willy-nilly have to eat, etc.). The relational and substantialist orientations are internalized and incorporated as bodily schemes, to the effect that the great social classes are characterized by a specific *habitus*, the distinguished and the vulgar habitus of the dominating and the dominated, respectively. Distinction is a mode of class domination,[32] and for each member of the dominant classes a way of asserting oneself.

Between the dominant and the popular classes there is the old and new petty bourgeoisie, the *habitus* of which bears the marks of pretentiousness. Now, it is very unpleasant and embarrassing to acknowledge that one's taste is not simply one's taste, but either a virtue of necessity or self-assertion, social climbing, and a way to keep others down. Not only is good taste defined as the taste of the dominating class, but distinguished taste and class domination are internally related. No distinguished trait is neutral and beyond the opposition between the social classes. But to reject one's taste as to food, drink, clothings, music, furniture, etc., or better to recognize it as produced by and expressive of the class opposition of distinction and vulgarity is hard, also for the social scientist him (or her) self ('When dealing with such an object, scientific work on the object is inseparable from work on the working subject'.)

To achieve this, the language employed must at the same time mark a break with everyday experience and make 'those who don't or won't know this experience' *feel* it. The data of research must be reconstructed and reformulated in a language aiming at liberation. The subtitle of the work, 'a social *critique of the judgement of taste,*' refers to this intention to lay bare the social conditions of our judgments of taste, including those of Kant's critique.[33]

For this reason this investigation resembles a 'social psychoanalysis' or 'socio-analysis': It aims at *'forcing the return of the*

32. Sartre had already described distinction as a bourgeois mode of oppression in the nineteenth century. Cf. *Critique de la raison dialectique,* vol. I and *L'idiot de la famillie,* vol. III (1972).
33. Here, the resemblance to the 'strong programme' of some British sociologists of knowledge (Barnes, Bloor and others) is easily seen.

repressed' through *'denying denial in all its forms'*. These findings imply an attack on the assumption of Liberal economics that consumers constitute a homogenous mass, having the same habitus, perceiving the fields of possible purchases in the same way, differing only through the differential purchasing power. But consumption patterns cannot be explained solely in terms of prices and incomes; they must be set in relation to cultural differences internalized as habitus.[34]

b) University conflicts and class habitus
Describing the university as a socio-cultural field,[35] Bourdieu revives Kant's distinction between the temporally and the spiritually dominant faculties. The faculties of medicine and law are most affined to the dominant fractions of the ruling classes, since they are charged with discipline and order (not only legal obedience but also health and sanitary conditions being a governmental concern). Statistical analysis reveals that professors of law and medicine tend more towards right-wing political opinions; their class background is more often that of the dominant strata of the dominant classes; they are less often divorced, have relatively more children, and have more official commissions and decorations. They are, in short, more strongly integrated in the dominant social order than professors within the other faculties (where those working within the natural sciences are at the other extreme). This means that the impact of *habitus* is of greater avail within medicine and law than elsewhere in the university field.

Nevertheless the corps of professors taken as a whole also have their acquired habitus, having passed through the same established channel of recruitment, advancing from a diligent apprenticeship, by carefully and patiently preparing a doctoral dissertation, to full professorship at the protector's retirement.

---

34. For instance, statistics on consumption show that the wealthy fractions of the dominating classes spend relatively more on food than the less well-off fractions, such as academic people, contradicting Engel's law on consumption. This can be interpreted through habitus differences: Academic people have acquired a more ascetic habitus, and have learnt to distinguish themselves by leisure activities which are not expensive. This is confirmed, for instance, by their predilection for mountainneering, while the rich play polo, go on cruises etc. Cf. *Distinction*, p. 219.
35. *Homo academicus* (1984).

As a social system, the university was in a state of equilibrium between habitus and structure before 1960.

The demographical changes disturbed this equilibrium. The crowds of students inundating the universities in the 1960s led to a structural *déclassement*. University diplomas underwent rapid inflation, thus causing disappointment of the students' aspirations (fostered by their habitus, adapted to the former structure of the educational order). This dissatisfaction was one of the reasons for the students' rebellion. Their assault on the professorial reign in the spring of 1968 forced the professors to become aware of their habitus, instead of just living it out unreflectively, as routine and 'second nature'. This is testified by the professors' deliberate organization to defend their positions. This shift was trying, especially for those whose habitus were best adapted to the old social and academic order; (on the other hand, the faculties of medicine and law were those least affected by the inflatory habitus). The defence of the professorial rights and privileges was best undertaken by people who hitherto had been considered marginal, but whose deviating habitus responded better to the new situation.

Among the students, the inflationary wave threatened students from different social strata in different ways. Students with a habitus expressive of the dominant classes tended to find an expedient in choosing academic topics of such haziness that their habitus would be a dominant feature of their esteem and professional performance (for instance certain kinds of social science and psychology).

4. Comment

Bourdieu elaborates a non-intellectual doctrine of action, according to which deliberate and calculating behaviour is exceptional and casual. He may seem to treat the individual agent as one who pursues strategies isolated from the others (in accord with 'methodological individualism'). However, his notion of the 'orchestration of thousands of habitus' and of habitus being transindividual indicates a conception closer to Durkheim and Parsons. But, once more, it would be wrong to attribute to him an 'over-socialized conception of man', according to which members of society cannot but reproduce its main structure and order. For that would imply neglecting the reference to class struggles and oppositions, and the class aspects of all discourse and parlance, present everywhere in Bourdieu's writings. When Bourdieu shows how the propensity to answer (instead of abstaining from answering) questionnaires bearing on politics not only correlate with formal education, ('scholar capital') but also with the *habitus*-conditioned feeling of having the right to pronounce political judgments,[36] this reasoning involves more than simply pointing out an 'intervening' third variable. It warns against a certain tendency of accepting the data as data without inquiring into their conditions and foundations. This carries on the Frankfurter School's attacks on Positivist social research, and so do Bourdieu's sundry remarks on the use of everyday terms, *notions communes*, which are taken at face value, though they are the outcome of underlying social oppositions and conflicts.[37]

Since Bourdieu shows how the 'popular classes' have a 'substantialist' attitude, while the dominating classes are 'relationalist', the suggestion is near to hand that science is a feature of class domination. But this is by no means Bourdieu's conception. To him, class domination is his object of scientific investigation. He is convinced that science can approach indefinitely a truth of the social field beyond the participants' partial representations and distortions.[38]

36. 'Like every recording of "data" at face value, this endorsement of appearances would have the effect of preventing inquiry into the objective bases of these representations, and, more precisely, would prevent one from looking into the reality of the division of political labour for the truth contained in these representations of the division of labour.' *Distinction,* p. 409.
37. 'So reflective analysis of the tools of analysis is not an epistemological scruple, but an indispensable pre-condition of scientific knowledge of the object ... etc.' *Ibid.,* p. 94.
38. Cf. *Homo Academicus,* pp. 47–8.

7

Discussion and Evaluation

I have outlined five sciences or ways of thinking about human relationships. The first three deal with the State in three respects: as the governor and administrator of citizens; as a power apparatus the citizens seek to be protected by as well as protected against; as the sustainer of the market as a mediator of economic relationships.

The last two oppose and supplement in various ways the first three, by directing attention to Society and sociality.

Their interrelations and claims to validity will now be examined.

1. Social statistics and Sociography
The position and validity of the statistical treatment of human relationships and human behaviour seems easily determined. In the first place, statistical reasoning not only describes important features of the State's activity; it is also part of its administration. So long as there exist States with an administrative apparatus, statistical interpretations of human affairs will be a necessary part of the official's equipment. (Thus most States have their own Statistical Bureau.) As pointed out, statistics not only reckons with individuals, but also contributes to their construction and reinforces their existence as such. In the second place, statistics pertains more generally to fragmented human existence and human relationships, that is to the facticity of social life, as distinct from its culture, that is, from a meaningful whole of projects, values and symbols.

As such, social statistics is the epistemological mode appropriate to an ontological realm or level. But this is not how social statistics is usually understood. Rather, it is presented as a tool, a way of thinking which in itself does not make any judgment as to the constitution or essence of social relationships. It is said to be ontologically neutral.

This is one of the reasons why introductory books on social statistics—such as that of Blalock—often begin with remarks that seek to calm the readers by assuring them that a minimum of mathematics is applied throughout the exposition, thus taking for granted a widespread fear of mathematics. But if the readers are supposed to be really concerned with ('interested in') the social field, and if statistics (and or any other branch of mathematics) is supposed to render this field's relations more intelligible than prose writing, then there should be no reason why they should be afraid of the mathematics applied. On the contrary, learning to interpret social relations through mathematics should be a joyful experience, since it would clarify an otherwise dim understanding.

But, of course, the reassuring remarks alluded to are not groundless. They stem from experience with (academic and other) social science students, some of whom always show reluctance towards statistics. The reason for this reluctance is not, however, that they are 'too stupid to understand mathematics' (to use Russell's expression), but that they are concerned with those parts of the social realm which are not essentially statistical, as, for instance, organizations or class conflicts, and hence call for a different mode of understanding.

These differences are often expressed and even institutionalized as the distinction between 'method' and 'theory'. But this is misleading. Social statistics does not consist of mere means or ways ('methods') of knowing the social domain, while sociological theory is supposed to be the body of (hypothetically) known general propositions about this domain. Social statistics is a theory of the social in its own right, in competition with or complementary to what was originally called 'sociological theory'. Or conversely, sociological theory is itself a method, a way of understanding.[1] When all attempts to integrate or build a bridge between statistical 'method' and sociological 'theory' fail, the reason is that the task is not only impossible, but even unnecessary or meaningless.

1. This is one of the reasons why the term 'theory' was mainly avoided in this book.

2. Liberal politics

Liberal politics expresses highly important aspects of the self-understanding of citizens in most of the existing States, and to some degree also renders an account of what passes among the citizens. Above all, the notion of living in a 'free country' with legal protection, freedom of speech, the right to settle anywhere, take up any occupation one pleases and acquire property sheltered by law, participate in elections that designate political leadership—this notion is essential in the minds of a large part (perhaps even most) of the population. Moreover, it is part and parcel of the State's declaration of what it stands for: In official speeches and texts, in public and semi-public educational institutions, these liberties are praised and explained as to their content and origin. Finally, most of the books, newspapers and other printed matter overtly or tacitly convey Liberal conceptions. As to Liberal 'political science' (or *Staatswissenschaft*), it—like jurisprudence—is partly integrated into the State's activities, and partly acts more like a detached spectator of the political life that goes on, describing it in terms of struggle for power among diverse interest groups, according to the 'exasperated liberalism' alluded to above. Obviously, Liberal politics and political science is valid within limits.

As a mere reflection or mirroring of political life in parts of the Western world, the descriptions and discourses of Liberal political science are valid.[2] But the objections raised against Liberal political thought, in so far as it pretends to cover the whole ground of relationships between human beings, must be accepted.

3. Liberal economics

As in the case of Liberal politics, Liberal economics is obviously valid when understood as a mirroring of economic relationships, as they are experienced by a large part of citizens, and especially by those who dispose of any kind of capital assets. In order to understand the more or less grave struggles over economic matters which take place daily in the Western world, some acquaintance with Liberal economics is indispensable.

2. This is what Sorel termed *'la petite science' (L'illusion du progrès,* 1927).

But the claims of Liberal economics are much bigger. It does not content itself with mere descriptions and reflections of market relations as these are institutionalized through the State and interpreted by most, and especially the most powerful, participants in this market economy. It poses (in Samuelson's wording) as 'the Queen of the social sciences', as the most advanced of the social sciences, that is, the science that has most closely approached mathematical physics.[3]

All the cardinal and ordinal magnitudes of economic life may create a nearly irresistible impression that there are unknown regularities or 'laws' to be discovered about economic processes, similar to the regularities and 'laws' of physics. But these magnitudes refer to the *facticity* of economic life, which is transcended by human action.[4] The economic domain shows features of creativity, novelty and historical change, as do the other domains of human activity. Therefore, economics will never be like mathematical physics for the same general reasons that no social science will ever be.

Even such an acute observer of the weakness of her own science as Joan Robinson maintains in *Economic Philosophy* the pious hope that economics 'can make an advance towards science', taking the word in a Positivist (more specifically, Popperian) sense. Such pretensions are unfounded, and therefore, Liberal economics is rather more of a pseudo-science than the other social sciences, since its self-understanding is so bad. While the discussions revolving around the fundamental possibilities and limits of sociology (or psychology, or social anthropology etc.) have been very searching, corresponding dis-

3. Most text-books on economics make unjustified claims as regards the predictive power of its doctrines. One signal exception is Heilbroner and Thurow, who write in *Understanding Microeconomics* (1978): 'No other social science has this seemingly simple but enormously valuable predictive capacity. That is, no other social science can lean with confidence on functional relationships of the kind that underpin economics.—With just how much confidence can economics lean on those relationships? The answer is disconcerting. The actual predictive record of economics is spotty, even poor ... the predictive power of economics is a great deal more impressive in theory than in fact.' (pp. 70–71).
4. In this sense one may endorse the economist Schumacher's final judgement on the importance of economy in his last book, *A Guide to the Perplexed* (1977): 'There is no economic problem'. In the world to-day, economic 'problems' should be transcended as such and transformed into political, moral, esthetic etc.

cussions within Liberal economics have, since the *Methoden-streit,* been casual and superficial.

*

As two counter-sciences have been presented 'Sociology', as the science of social integration, and the historico-dialectical conceptions which originated with the writings of Marx and Engels ('historical materialism', the 'materialist conception of history').

4. Sociology as the science of social integration
The concepts of Sociology are superior to those of Liberal thought in the sense of giving a much better account of how human beings are united with each other so as to make wholes. The Liberal contracts and deliberated associations are deprived of their paramount position, becoming just a special case among many other cases of integration, and even presupposing them.

Also, Sociology is superior in its understanding of what makes totalities of human beings disintegrate, and what makes members of a whole withdraw, deviate, rebel or become ill. The Liberal conception of legal transgression, punishment and restitution (according to the slogan 'crime does not pay') becomes merely a not very prevalent special case of deviance from and sanctions of norms.

Through linking internally the human being's personality to the social and cultural system to which it belongs, a much more comprehensive and intelligible doctrine has been worked out, showing how sociality in its various modes is presupposed by Liberal thought.

Regarding Sociology's relation to Statistics and Social research, it was stated above that sociological propositions should not be understood as 'theory' to be confirmed or weakened by the 'methods' of social research, since these two activities are both 'theories' or both 'methods'. But if so, how should the validity of Sociology be understood?

As social beings we experience the social, and can think about it, reflectively. Sociology as the science of social integration claims to be a throughgoing reflection on social experience as an integral experience. Therefore, the propositions about social integration and disintegration expounded in chapter 4 express and conceptualize experience, and in this sense, they are empirical. (Thus, Parsons, for instance, speaks 'from experience' in his writings.) But these propositions are not empirical in the usual sense of referring to contingent states of the world. They do not *refer to* experience and its content; they *make explicit* experience.

Understanding social integration and disintegration cannot be kept entirely separate from one's practice and skill in social relations, in small groups or larger settings. The seemingly external relation between the knower (sociologist) and the known (social relations) reveals itself as an internal one. The concept of the subject-object relationship must cede to that of self-reflection as internal relation. In this sense, for all the strangeness of Vico's *Scienza nuova*, its basic protension is valid, not only for history, but for sociology too.

This does not mean that sociological propositions are true *a priori* and unassailable. On the contrary, not only are there other conceptions which challenge the social interpretation of experience, there are also (as will be shown in Part Two) attempts to supersede sociology on its own level, so to speak.

But it does imply that one should not think of, say, Parsons as a proponent of 'Grand Theory' (as Wright Mills said) with little or no contact with the world of experience. For Parsons' sociology does concern experience, but mainly the most general traits of the social realm. Moreover, his experience may be one-sided or miss certain highly important traits. Over against this conceptualized experience it is fully possible to assert another.

Those who consider this a mere pretext for nourishing all kinds of pet fancies about the social domain, and for sparing oneself the toil of 'empirical social research', mostly overlook that 'empirical research' nearly always presupposes general conceptions of the kind discussed in this part of the book, or other, equally encompassing convictions. To test these general propositions by singular instances is not feasible. It will lead to bottomless doubts and self-dissolving thinking. As said Cassirer, all true *skepsis* is relative. Sociography will never achieve a synthesis, a general doctrine of the social, arriving at an understanding of social totalities. It has to presuppose and lean on a doctrine of social wholes, on Sociology.

As stated several times, Sociology partly arose to compensate for the shortcomings and one-sidedness of Liberal thought, its individualism, intellectualism and utilitarianism. As a supplement it has sometimes been welcomed, but more often it has provoked a rejoinder: Liberal thought has rallied itself and launched a counter-attack, declaring that it can cope with all the topics pointed out by this new would-be science, and hence that there is no need for such a supplement.

Thus, in recent times, Liberal economics has tried to expand its domain, dealing with topics that have long been regarded as a concern of sociology. At least partly, this endeavour tried to meet the difficulties economics had run into and which had inflicted upon it a considerable loss of esteem. Instead of making more modest claims than before, granting sociology greater competence, some Liberal economists decided to take the opposite position and make bigger claims than before on behalf of their science. Instead of listening to the sociologists, one has tried to deprive them of their topics through making them part of economics.

This expansive attempt has mainly taken the form of transforming questions about economic, political and social relations into questions about strategic action, leaning heavily upon Morgenstern & Neumann's 'theory of games and economic behaviour', a work issuing from the Lausanne school (Walras, Pareto) of neo-classical Liberal economics.[5]

Clearly, this whole trend of thought begs the question and may be disposed of as merely a reiteration of assertions long since refuted. Durkheim's famous objection to Spencer's contract interpretation of industrial society—*tout n'est pas contractuel dans le contrat*—points to the insufficiency of Liberal

---

5. Two widely known contributions are Downs: *An Economic Theory of Democracy* (1957) and Becker: *The Economic Approach to Human Behavior* (1976). Another prominent spokesman for this attempt was Leif Johansen, the economist, who looked forward to the time when the 'theory of games' would be the general social science; yet another is Jon Elster, who considers the treatise of Morgenstern & Neumann as important for our time as Newton's *Philosophia naturalis* for his. (Elster: *Leibniz et la formation de l'esprit capitaliste* (1975), p. 121.) For my part, I have tried to show that not even the game of chess is played according to the 'game theory'. See my contribution 'Game theory and social interaction: The case of chess', in Bråten (ed.): *Methodology and Sociology* (1980).

thought, and so does Tönnies' distinction between *Gemeinschaft* and *Gesellschaft*. And those who still remain unconvinced can be referred, either to Schütz's account of how the social relation is constituted in the temporal flow, or to Parsons' treatment of the 'utilitarian dilemma':

a) Schütz developed within the social domain one of Bergson's and Husserl's basic propositions. They had shown how action evolves temporally as a vague intention or protension which becomes ever more determinate as it is carried out. When thinking on the acomplished act, we easily fall prey to the 'retroactive illusion' (as Bergson said) that the act was represented in the mind at the outset, and then reproduced in the external world. But careful or exacting afterthought will reveal the creativeness of our temporality. This experience is at odds with the (determinist) conception of human consciousness and activity as externally related states succeeding each other, and also with the utilitarian conception of action as application of means to obtain a preconceived, determined end.

Schütz's description of encounters between human beings emphasizes how the Other is bodily given to me as a field where all kinds of intentions express themselves through the temporal flow, as I am given to the Other. Such a presence constitutes the experience of 'growing older together', that is, being aware of one's own and the Other's stream of consciousness as a temporalizing, synthesizing activity. One's *durée* becomes intertwined with that of the Other's, there is a mutual perception of intentions, expressions and acts. To experience the Other involves perceiving his (her) perception of myself, my experience of this reciprocity and so on, all of which constitute the We-relationship.

During this We-relationship my previous knowledge of the Other is enriched at every moment through my experience. My scheme of interpretation changes as new features of the Other appear during our 'growing older together'. What is given to consciousness in a Here and Now is infinitely rich, and according to my attentiveness, I can always grasp new features of the situation.

Our relations to those who are absent, Schütz claims, are essentially different. We cannot but experience them as types or in a typical way, which entails that the creative temporal flow of novelty is replaced by fixed, determinate representations.[6] Part of these typical relationships may be liable to interpretation in terms of 'mathematical game theory' or the like, but the whole field of originary social intercourse (between human beings in each other's presence) will not lend itself to this treatment.

b) The general refutation of the utilitarian conception of society furnished by Parsons can be resumed in the following way:[7] The utilitarian doctrine of action conceives the means-end relationship as the general form of actions, so that all actions may be interpreted as utilitarian actions. But this is an untenable generalization, which overlooks the fact that a utilitarian action presupposes that there is at least one other kind of action. This becomes clear upon closer examination:

Let us take an acting person, an *actor*, with his *end*, his *means*, and his *conditions* for action. The actor here is an analogue to the natural scientist in his laboratory, or the technician who applies this knowledge in the course of his activity. But it can be shown that his scheme of action is inconsistent. For one thing, it presupposes that ends are random or incidental, that there are no reasons why they have been chosen, and that the relations between ends are random too. In other words, ends are given features—*data*—in the action situation.

But if the ends of action (or at least the final and ultimate ends) have no meaningful relation to one another, but are incidental, the notion of action breaks down, 'for there can be no such thing as choosing among random ends.'[8] On the other hand, if ends are not random, the actor's choice of an end for his action must be based on a scientific knowledge about some means-end or cause-and-effect relation, and then ends become part of the conditions of action, or the situation.[9]

For, if the ends of action are determined by applying knowledge about past and present states, ends will not be distinguish-

6. Alfred Schütz: *Der sinnhafte Aufbau der sozialen Welt* (1932).
7. This passage, slightly abridged and altered, is reproduced from my essay 'Sociological Theory and Utilitarianism', *International Journal of Sociology*. vol. IX, no. 4.
8. Parsons: *The Structure of Social Action*.
9. 'For the only possible basis of empirical knowledge of a future state of affairs is prediction on the basis of knowledge of past and present states. ... The active role of the actor is reduced to one of the understanding of his situation and forcasting of its future course of development.' (*Ibid.*).

able from the means and conditions of an action; yet they must be so distinguishable for the proposed concept of action to hold up. Consequently, concludes Parsons, the concept of action presupposes that ends are determined in another way than solely through reasoning in terms of ends and means. That is, the means-end relationships becomes a norm that guides action, and the scheme of action in question then presupposes that there are also other norms (or at least one other norm) of action. But then we have moved beyond the utilitarian doctrine of action.

This reasoning is transcendental: It purports to show why there must be more than one normative orientation for actions (the means-end norm) in order that human action may be possible at all. That this is so may be discovered upon reflection. But in everyday life, which is 'prereflective', this is not noticed before such reflection takes place.

As long as this refutation has not itself been refuted, Sociology's claim to supplement or supersede Liberal thought should, therefore, rest on safe ground. Nevertheless, the mentioned expansion of Liberal economic thought may well go on undisturbed, since Liberal economists pay little heed to contributions to their topic made by people outside their own circles, whether this stems from narrow-mindedness, arrogance or lack of competence (presumably Morgenstern and Neumann never heard of Parsons' refutation of utilitarianism.)[10]

However, another, and much stronger objection to Sociology has also been elaborated, based upon the experience that the social world does not consist of integrated wholes, but of damaged, fragmented ones. This, as already seen, is the basic assertion of 'Critical Theory', which will be considered again later in this chapter.

5. Historico-dialectical thought

As a 'critique of political economy' and of Liberal politics, the thought of Marx and Engels and their followers must be generally accepted.

10. Three great general works on games in general were undertaken in the 1930s and 1940s: Morgenstern & Neumann's *Theory of Games and Economic Behaviour;* Wittgenstein's *Philosophische Untersuchungen* (concerning 'language games') and Hesse's *Glasperlenspiel* (translated as *Magister Ludus*). Of these the first contributes less than the other two to the understanding of the human condition.

They have shown how Liberal politics interprets social life in a distorted way, overlooking the class feature of the existing liberties. They have shown, too, how Liberal economics interprets human life in a way that blurs the oppressive and coercive features of an economic order based upon wage labour for the bulk of the population, and a minority's legal possession of the means of production. This attack is founded on its specific labour doctrine of value, the validity of which has been often questioned, but which seems unrefuted still.

Among all the objections raised against it, two are considered especially decisive. The first states that it is impossible to calculate the value of some product, since it has been produced by tools, the value of which has to be calculated, and this value requires the calculation of the tools and labour power that produced these tools, and so on in a regress that is not infinite, but leads back to the dim origin of humankind. The second objection is that most (or all) products can be produced by more than one production process, that is, by the application of different amounts of labour power and tools and materials. In order to choose between different production processes (and the corresponding production functions) one has to estimate the value of the various technical coefficients, which leads to the same difficulties as above. In order to make a choice, one will as a rule take into the account the market prices of the tools, and not bother about their value.

Both objections purport that the concept of value—determined in terms of the subsistence means of labour power—is of no avail for the understanding of a Liberal economic order (or a socialist one, for that matter.) It does not help the entrepreneur or the business man in their calculations (nor the planning administrator in centralized economics), nor does it help the economist to determine (predict, explain) market prices. The statement that values 'underlie' prices, or that prices 'oscillate' around the values is an empty one, a pseudo-proposition, since it cannot be verified (confirmed) or falsified by observation or investigation of economic processes, and permits no predictions. The doctrine of value is a piece of obsolete scientific thinking, of 'metaphysics' (in the sense of Carnap, Reichenbach, Hempel and other 'logical positivists' and empiricists), or perhaps better, 'meta-economics.' These objections—even if valid—do not suffice to make 'value' a *flatus vocis*, a word devoid of meaning in economic contexts.

For even if it be true that we cannot determine the magnitude of the value of goods, we may perfectly well attach a meaning to the proposition that the expenditure of labour power is the source of (economic) value. Indeed, such a proposition appears to make explicit what we take for granted in everyday life (and in this respect Adam Smith's much derided example of archaic barter is adequate). In our society (and most others) the human is considered 'the most important object in the world', to use Kant's expression (in his *Anthropology*). The toil of human beings is therefore regarded with respect, since it is related to the self-preservation and well-being of human beings. Even if man is not sacred to man, we do not treat other human beings on a par with animals, plants or inorganic matter. Now, nearly every benefit existing as an object of possible consumption is a product of human activity, either in the mode of production or transportation, and is valued in this respect. Therefore, the objection that automation shows that the expenditure of labour power is not the only source of value, is not valid. It merely amounts to the statement that in a world where everything we now call work is done by automats, there will be no more creation of economic value.

The notion that prices oscillate around values is vague, but 'vague' is not tantamount to 'meaningless'. Marx says that market competition and the interaction between demand and supply do make it intelligible *that* market prices are established, but not why the prices are established on a determinate level. To be sure, there may be cases where market prices are the results of processes reminding one of poker, bluff, blackmailing, exploitation of momentary urgency. But on the whole, the subsistence of human labour power will tend to determine market prices, for if prices are such that they do not permit the reproduction of labour power, a strictly *in*human situation is arrived at, where theft, rebellion, escape, etc. are resorted to—where, in other words, the Liberal (or centralized) economic order *qua* economic is transcended or has disintegrated. The labour doctrine of value refers to the general conditions of human material existence. The affinity of the labour doctrine value to the Thomist concept of 'just price' (pointed out by Joan Robinson, among others), does not speak against it. On the contrary, it strengthens economics as a science of human existence as a moral science (and not a pseudo-science debasing human beings as one 'factor of production' among others, and whose needs are determined or measured by purchasing power on the market).

Marx and Engels partake of the Liberals' concern with the individual human being and his liberty; theirs is a so-called 'internal critique' of Liberal thought in the sense that the Liberals are taken at their word and then shown to be unable to fulfil their own promises of freedom for all. Hence, Liberal thought is charged with hypocrisy: While speaking on behalf of all human beings, it favours the class of the propertied (and in particular, those in possession of industrial capital). This charge has not only been unanswered, it has also been strengthened through an improved (partly sociological) understanding of how the class structure is reproduced through socialization patterns and otherwise.

Concerning the validity of a general 'materialist conception of History', one should consider the question in relation to both the past and the future.

As an interpretation of the past, it has on many points been gainsaid by well-founded historical knowledge; but it can still uphold claims to validity, especially as regards the development of industrial society.

This must not be taken to mean that the 'materialist conception of history' has succeeded in discovering the laws of human history. For there can be no science of History in the sense of a doctrine which has discerned the 'iron necessity' (or even statistically highest probability) of the direction of historical processes, Human history is, in Bergson's expression, 'creative evolution' and as such essentially unpredictable or free. Instead, the 'materialist conception of history' makes intelligible our past, interpreting it through our 'central cultural values', to use Max Weber's terms. As such, the historico-dialectical interpretation expresses social experience.

As an interpretation of the future, as the science of making history, its criterion of validity is practice. That is to say, if the historico-dialectical conception is to become true, it must be made true ('verified') through human action. Thus, the question whether or not 'class struggle is the motor of History' cannot be answered regardless of what we ourselves intend to do. We may choose to belittle the importance of social classes and their mutual hostility, or deem poor the prospects of raising the oppressed class's consciousness to a level sufficient for concerted action, and so on. But as long as we understand our economy in terms of wage labour, capital and profit, the notion of class conflict is intelligible to us, as is the protension of a society where the Liberals' aspirations are fulfilled, that is, a classless society. For this reason, the Marxian interpretation of our future cannot be discarded, even if it fails to be confirmed by contemporary events.

*

Each in its way, Sociology and Historico-dialectical Thought have shown the insufficiencies of Social statistics, Sociography, and Liberal thought, and have persistently done so for more than a century.

Nevertheless, Social statistics and Liberal political-economic thought still dominate the interpretations of human beings' co-existence, with respect to the attention they receive (especially by the rich and mighty), the number of people trained in these topics, and the means placed at their disposal.

The reason for this is partly a matter of power; Social statistics and Liberal thought suit the ruling classes and strata better than Sociology and Historico-dialectical thought.

But there is also another, epistemological reason: the corrections and attacks implied in the teachings of Sociology and Historico-dialectical thought are in a way pusillanimous.

Thus, Sociology can always tell Social statisticians that their activities presuppose socio-cultural forms, and that their investigations concern social facticity. But since it is of the essence of the distinction between form and facticity not to be clear-cut, it is not feasible to state exactly where statisticians should stop, leaving their topic to interpreters of projects and forms. Hence, statistical institutes can go on pouring out their reports indefinitely. Likewise, Sociology and Historico-dialectical thought may object to the utilitarian and reified conceptions of Liberal economics. And to be sure, this objection will act as a reminder, as a constant uneasiness to the Liberal mind, which senses that a region of being, certain kinds of human relationships and experiences elude it. But on the other hand, this does not hinder Liberal economists in treating any given economic relationship by the mathematical calculus, since it is not possible to show precisely where the validity of economic computations reaches its limit.

Again, when Historico-dialectical thought points to the essential class conflict inherent in any capitalist mode of production, this does not prevent Liberal politico-economic thought from presenting life in the Western world as human mass behaviour in economic and political markets, since the distinction between mass and class is a specification of that between facticity and project, and it therefore is impossible to determine exactly where the limit of massification lies.

It seems therefore, that those who want to supplement or correct Statistical and Liberal thought, are doomed to perpetual opposition, to pointing out shortcomings and presuppositions, to playing second string, to being the bad conscience of the prevailing modes of interpreting human co-existence.

*

The permanent divergencies here laid bare are seldom met straightforwardly, but rather disregarded in various ways: One concentrates upon one's special topic or science, or looks with forebearance or contempt at others, or half-heartedly persuades oneself that, ultimately, the disagreements are not serious and will be overcome in the future.

But exceptions to this general statement are to found among the proponents of synthesis, to which the discussion finally turns.

6. The synthetic attempts
a) Critical theory
To recognize the interminable oppositions and conflicts, ponder them and make them the declared point of departure distinguishes Critical Theory as here described. In particular, the writings of Adorno display an intransigent will not to produce any reconciling palliative that blurs the difficulties.

When Adorno underlines the importance of social research, he pays no mere lip-service.[11]

True, in a non-alienated, liberated world there would be no social research, since the split between meaning and the contingent datum, the spiritual and the material, would have been overcome. But precisely because we do not live in such a world, we need Social statistics and Social research.

As the two extremes of alienated and unalienated consciousness one may consider the Mind in Hegel's *Phenomenology* and Mr. Bloom in Joyce's *Ulysses*. All that happens to the Mind *eo ipso* happens to the World; the awakening and contradictions of the Mind are the awakening and contradictions of the World. Even the alienations of the Mind are those of the World. On the contrary, the thoughts, memories, wishes, desires that constitute Mr. Bloom's consciousness are entirely alienated from the world's structures and processes, as is his humming of operatic arias (*'Là ci darem la mano,* la-la-lalala').

The intention of Critical theory is to remind one of this split, to insist that we live in a world of data that conceal their origin as facts,[12] and that we suffer this world of data. The horrible thing with the kind of social research that Adorno calls 'positivist' is its implicit acceptance of this suffering as something inevitable; its forgetfulness of the hope of a liberated world that does not yet exist or exists only as *ou-topos*. Thus, the datum that most people listen to music as entertainment should never be accepted as true (though correct), but the social conditions of possibility which it mediates should be investigated, to avoid any moral disdain and reproach of the unhappy. Contrary to the original intention of Empiricism, it tends towards conformity and resignation, and for this reason Adorno could state in one of his last discussion contributions: 'To us it is tempting to defend the empirical against empiricism.'[13]

Here, the topic of the Modernist movement—the fragmented,

---

11. Cf. chap. 7 of Jay's book (*op.cit.*), 'The Empirical Work of the Institute in the 1940's'.
12. Hume's conception of consciousness as a container through which passes 'with an inconceivable rapidity' all sorts of impressions, pertains to this caricature of human existence—a caricature truer of most of us than is the Mind of the *Phenomenology,* to the extent that our lives suffer from triviality.
13. Adorno: 'Gesellschaftstheorie und empirische Forschung', in W. Hochkeppel (ed.): *Soziologie zwischen Theorie und Empirie* (1970), p. 82.

exploded totality—is dealt with in full awareness. The only valid position, Adorno contends, is to accept both Sociology, Social Research, and the historico-dialectical conception as bits of a broken whole, as a contradiction not to smoothen, or mitigate, but (as said Hegel) to endure.

One may object that in the long run, such a stance is unsupportable and that one should have the pecuniary and cultural riches of Adorno to persist in this attitude. But the recent research of Bourdieu shows that very fine work can be done in full consciousness of the antinomies inherent in the social sciences. Before commenting on him, however, Habermas's achievement will be considered.

b) Habermas's doctrine of communicative action
Habermas continues the efforts of his teachers to fuse the Marxian heritage, Sociology and Social research. Nevertheless, the direction of his thought has led him ever further away from them, so that it may be more appropriate to consider his 'theory of communicative action' as a rupture with the original 'Critical Theory'. In the first place, the truth claims of Intellect are reaffirmed, That is why Habermas must consider sociology as a misconceived riposte to Liberal thought. Sociology, as seen, opposes Liberal thought by affirming the importance of the affective, the non-intellectual, as when it interprets ritual as the form of action of collectivities as such. Instead, Habermas seeks to enrich Liberal thought, not by limiting, but by extending Intellect and Reason. When unified, the doctrines of Life World and Speech Acts can make Practical Reason the integrative form of human relationships, or the Category of the social realm, This implies turning away from the Frankfurter School's notion of an erotic understanding, beyond the Intellect.

In the second place, Habermas seeks to make milder the Marxian attack on Liberal politics and economics by distinguishing between 'work' and 'interaction', and concomitantly, between 'strategic' and 'communicative' action. He intends to settle the dispute and achieve a new unity through his doctrine of communicative action, imputing a specific mode of social interaction to the various domains of social life. But in this way, he has renounced the intention to persist in an intransigent attitude, and consider as a temptation to be resisted any attempt at reconciliation and unification. In this respect, too, Habermas's endorsement of Durkheim's and Parsons' therapeutic attitude towards social life implies a break with Critical Theory.

The main weaknesses of this reaffirmation of the Intellect seem to be these two: (1) The heavy assaults on the Intellect's claims to truth implicit in Modernist art are simply overlooked or neglected, The doctrine of communication, it seems, gives to Art the same subordinate place it was given within Kantian thought, and is tantamount to a begging of the question (*petitio principii*). (2) Even though by repeacing Tönnies' distinction between *Wesenwille* and *Kürwille* by that between communicative and strategic action, Habermas avoids a non-intellectual notion, his stance will be just as pusillanimous as that of Sociology. Confronted by the spread of the strategic mode of action he can certainly warn against 'colonization of the life world' and make appeal to the importance of some domains where communication reigns, but is, like the Sociologists, doomed to be in the defensive position.

For these reasons, Habermas's synthesis seems to be less advanced than that of his forerunners, a relapse to previous conceptions.

c) Bourdieu's doctrine of socio-cultural fields

Even though Bourdieu presents the contrast between Adorno and Lazarsfeld in order to make it clear that he disagrees with both of them and defends a transcending, third conception, it is no far-fetched interpretation to consider his work as an example of just that kind of activity Adorno recommended (though not fully pursued by himself). His investigations are 'critical' in the sense of the Frankfurter School. As shown, they exploit all kinds of experiences of and about the social field, with the aim of achieving a conceptual construction of this field, starting from, but differing from, one's habits of body and mind. Such a reconstruction entails a painful doubt of what is usually taken for granted, the permanent transformation of the *datum* into a *factum*, a continual passage from the level of appearances to their social conditions of possibility. The difference between Bourdieu and Adorno bears on their ultimate convictions. To Adorno, as to several other thinkers within the Frankfurter School, instrumental knowledge should finally be transcended by an (erotic) reconciliation between Humanity and Nature. Bourdieu, on his side, retains and affirms a confidence in science as a vehicle of ultimate truth.

But as long as this ultimate concern is not approached, the contributions from the two intellectual quarters widely concur.

*

This being so, between Statistics, Liberal politics and economics, on the one hand, and Sociology and the Historico-dialectic (Marxian) conceptions, on the other, the relationship is unstable and uneasy. Yet the relationship cannot simply cease, since the first mode of thinking will always call forth the other, and conversely. Together they constitute a bloc, a delimited field of discourse and action with interminable disagreements. These considerations, it seems, warrant the following conclusion: Given the point of departure—the rise of Statistics and Sociography and of Liberal thought—encompassing conceptions such as those of Adorno or Bourdieu recommend themselves as valid and tenable. It seems impossible to add something essential to them. The understanding of these topics now seems exhaustive and final. As long as Sociology and its affined modes of thought continue to exert their spell, afterthought will lead to these highly demanding conceptions.

But it is possible to question the given point of departure, and, in fact, there have been several attempts, more or less deliberate, to break the spell, to make a shift, begin afresh, to think of human existence in a way that bypasses the old discussions of the State, the Market, the Individual and their opposed notions. What would it be like to think neither as a statistician, nor as a Liberal, nor as a sociologist nor in the historico-dialectical way, but depart from new presuppositions? Attempts to find an answer will be the topic of Part Two.

*

Part Two

8

Neo-Anarchy Conceptions of the Individual I: Sartre

1. Introductory remarks

In all his writings Jean-Paul Sartre treats of human freedom. Asserting this freedom to be unconditional, he at the same time investigated the possibilities of human *un*freedom, in relation to oneself, as well as to others. Even if this point of departure is also that of the Liberals, Sartre always rejected Liberal doctrines. As will be shown, he developed a strikingly original conception of human existence and of Being in general, which deviates considerably from the notions discussed in Part One.

2. Non-thetic consciousness—pure and impure

Initially influenced by Brentano's and Husserl's so-called 'principle of intentionality' (every consciousness is consciousness of something), Sartre soon rejected it as a caricature, propounding his own, extreme version: Consciousness is, literally speaking, nothing but consciousness of something; consciousness is that nothingness by which there is something (par quoi il y a de l'être). The Ego or Self is an object (or more precisely, a quasi-object) to consciousness, which is primordially pre-reflective, or in Sartre's terms: Consciousness is positional or thetic consciousness of an object, and non-positional or non-thetic consciousness (of) itself. Or again, consciousness is not a substance, but a relation to the world, and a pre-reflective relation to this relation.[1]

Now, every consciousness can tend to conceal to itself what

1. This notion of Ego-less consciousness is said to bear a similarity to Buddhist or Taoist teachings.

it essentially is, and pursue the project of being in the mode of objects, being-in-itself. Since consciousness's mode of being is to be for-itself (prereflectively), the project is to be in-itself-for-itself. To pursue this project is the human being's fundamental vice. Virtue consists in not hiding from oneself that one is the nothingness by which the world appears, and being aware that to be in-itself-for-itself is impossible, a contradictory project whose fulfilment would entail the collapse of both the world and consciousness. To be in bad faith is to pursue the project being in-itself-for-itself; the opposite ('authentic') mode of being can be achieved through a conversion or a *katharsis* (purification), accomplished by a purifying reflexion, essentially different from accessory, impure reflexion, striving for all kinds of union between consciousness and the world (from the *unio mystica* to the blissfulness of the oceanic feeling (Rolland) of being swallowed up by a whole greater than oneself, or even adulation of one's own self). When purified by reflexion, the human being will cease this vain pursuit, and affirm himself as that nothingness which makes all Being appear. Through its pre-reflective projects, consciousness reveals the symbolic significance of things and substances. For example, water is the substance symbolizing a purified consciousness, while substances such as honey (intensely sweet and viscous) symbolize a consciousness addicted to bad faith.

Whether the human being is in bad faith or converted to authenticity, the human condition cannot be adequately described in terms of utility and cognate concepts, nor in terms of a knowledge relation. The world and its objects are not means to our ends, nor a topic for our knowing activity, since our fundamental project is neither instrumental nor epistemic, but symbolic.

3. Encountering the Other

The Other as a non-objectal consciousness cannot be apprehended directly, precisely because the Other like me is a Nothingness: he (she) cannot be perceived as such. In my field of perception, the Other is given as an object of a specific kind, that is, a teleological being that acts, plans, smiles, is angry, plays and so on. This behaviour is given objectively, and it is possible to obtain knowledge of it as of other kinds of objects;

in other words, there is or can be a science of human objectity. On condition that the stimulus-response scheme of thought is dropped in favour of the conception of the human being as transcendence and project, Sartre affirms that the behaviourists were right when they rejected consciousness as a subject matter of psychology (even if his work on imagination shows his position to be more complex). I must resist the temptation to 'put myself in the Other's place' and feel, say, his joy or anger. For his feelings are given to me as modes of his bodily appearance, objectively. His body is not a field of expression, if that means that there are feelings existing as objects apart, which express themselves through the body. As modes of a projecting consciousness, the feelings are neantisizing relations to the world which bring out its joyful or frustrating properties—as such, they cannot be known objectively (since they are singular consciousnesses, nothingnesses). Not even 'introspection' can apprehend them. But as bodily phenomena, they are given objectively. Thus, these trembling hands do not express the Other's anger, they are this anger, as a special kind of objectity in the world.

This, Sartre affirms, is the way the Other is given to me. But I am also aware that I am given as an object to the Other. The human condition comprises as one of its dimensions the being-for-the Other (être-pour-Autrui), symbolized by the Other's look. Thus, I undergo the experience of being given as an object to the Other, when, for instance, I feel ashamed. Shame, Sartre says, is the mode (or rather one of several modes)[2] of being-for-Others. It is irreducible to the dimension of being-for-myself. It is not a pure cognitive relation where an object is known with more or less probability. True, it is never more than a probability that an Other actually looks at me, but the look itself, the being-for-the-Other is not itself a probability, but an indubitable ontological dimension on a par with the *cogito*, my self-consciousness.

Such is Sartre's original solution to the puzzle of solipsism (how do I know or how can I prove that there are other consciousnesses in the world so that I am not *solus ipse?*): The

2. In *L'être et le néant* (Being and Nothingness) there are, in fact, two parallel series of descriptions bearing on human encounters; even if Sartre himself presents the second as more concrete, they are equally concrete.

Other's consciousness cannot be proven, nor is it constituted by me transcendentally, nor is it given to me as an object; it is experienced as a shocking, contingent non-objectal *datum*. Even if they are relationships between distinct, separate individuals, these encounters (as will be shown in more detail in the next section) not only defy any utilitarian interpretation of human conduct,[3], they also defy being interpreted as purely intellectual events, as when I (in a Kantian or Neo-Kantian vein) recognize the Other as a thinking or communicative being like myself. The relation to the Other is not basically one of knowledge and epistemology, but of ontology: my being for the Other is a specific feature of my being in general.

Hence, when relationships between human beings are described, one must always reckon with these two dimensions: being (self-) conscious of the Other as an object, and being conscious of being-for-the Other.[4] From this duality Sartre derives the general forms of relationship to Others, both in the mode of bad faith and in the mode of converted, purified consciousness.

4. Encounters as vain passion

In the mode of bad faith, consciousness projects to constitute together with the Other the (impossible) synthesis being-in-itself-for-itself. This means that the goal is to be both a 'naughting' (*néantisant*) and an objectal consciousness in one and the same experience. The specifications of this project are grouped together by Sartre according to whether I choose for my own part to accentuate being-for-myself or being-for-the Other.

If being-for-the Other is chosen as my attitude, my endeavour can be designated by the terms 'love' and 'masochism'.

In love, Sartre says, I constitute myself as an object for the Other, a fascinating object. I want to be 'the whole world for the beloved', whose consciousness is nothing but the apprehension of myself. I try to be that object in the world which

---

3. *L'être et le néant*, Conclusion.
4. One should be warned against one misunderstanding, that to perceive the Other as an object implies a humiliation or a debasement of the Other. For instance, this beautiful child, this benevolent, wise old woman, this charming man are all objects given to me. Their objectity does not as such imply reification in the sense of Lukacs.

constitutes the given limit of the beloved's transcendence of everything else in the world, a limit which the beloved freely shall make his (her) own, that is, choose. If I succeeded in this, the Other's look would be different from the look under which I am ashamed. Then I am an object among many others, but for the Other's loving look I would not be any limited, finite being, but an absolute totality. What I wish to appropriate is the Other's freedom as such, that the Other freely makes my facticity the limit of his world.[5] But this assimilation of the Other's freedom and thereby my being-for-the Other is impossible. The Other's freedom cannot be fixed or captured. Moreover, if both project being loved, they both want to be the ultimate limit of the Other's freedom, which constitutes an irresolvable conflict. Mutual love as a specification of being-in-itself-for-itself is contradictory and impossible.

The distortion of the project of love is the *masochistic* attitude, whereby I project to be, not a limit-object, but on the contrary an object among others. If I could manage to be a sort of object for the Other's freedom, I would have accomplished the synthesis being-in-itself-for-itself. But the masochistic project is also doomed to failure. Thus, among other reasons, the masochist is unable to escape his (her) own transcendence (and freedom), but is obliged to practice his (her) masochism as a project, a fact which especially becomes manifest when he (she) is bound to pay somebody to torment him. For then the Other is used as a means to realize the masochist's project, which is contradictory, since the masochist's urge is to be no project any longer.

If, instead, my chosen attitude is that of being-for-myself, my projects can be specified as sexual desire and sadism.

In sexual desire, the universal project of being-in-itself-for-itself is specified as the attempt to make the Other's freedom be absorbed by the facticity of his body, in order thereby to possess the Other as a pure transcendence and at the same time as a body. To achieve this, the desiring consciousness incarnates itself as flesh in order to impel the Other to realize *for himself*

5. '... that the free upsurge of his being should have his choice of *me* as his unique and absolute end; that is, that he should choose to be for the sake of founding my object-state and my facticity' (*Being and Nothingness,* p. 483) (Hazel E. Barnes' translation).

and *itself his* her own flesh.[6] This project is also in vain, and may lead to its distorted form, sadism. While the desiring incarnates him (herself) to arouse the Other's desire, the sadist projects by no means his own incarnation, but on the contrary wants 'to exist his body' as a centre of action, that is, to transcend its facticity towards goals in the world. It is the Other who shall be forced to 'exist his bodily facticity' as pain. Pain fascinates the reflective consciousness of the suffering, and it results in an incarnation of consciousness on the mode of the obscene. Then the sadistic consciousness is near its goal, to obtain that the Other's consciousness is at the same time flesh, and thus catch the Other's freedom.[7] But this project, too, is in vain: The only freedom the sadist can act upon is the freedom of the Other as object. But it is that of the Other as subject the sadist wants to possess, and that this freedom always eludes him, he discovers when the victim *looks at* the tormentor.

All these relationships are marked by an awareness of the Other which places them outside the domain of instrumental action and notions of utility. There is, however, one attitude towards others which comes close to acting in terms of ends and means, *indifference* towards others, which Sartre terms 'a sort of factual solipsism'. To be indifferent is to ignore that Others can look at me, to regard them as certain kind of objects to look out for or to take advantage of. For the indifferent, to be calculating is the obvious way of dealing with Others.[8] In this mode of consciousness I somehow feel at ease, since I am not at all troubled by embarrassment in the presence of Others. But I am bothered by the ever-present implicit awareness that

6. 'Thus in desire there is an attempt at the incarnation of consciousness (...) in order to realize the incarnation of the Other' (*Ibid.,* p. 508).
7. 'What the sadist thus so tenaciously seeks, what he wants to knead with his hands and bend under his wrists is the Other's freedom' (*Ibid.,* p. 522).
8. 'Those people are functions: the ticket-collector is nothing but the function of collecting tickets; the café waiter is nothing but the function of serving the patrons. In this capacity they will be most useful if I know their *keys* and those "master-words" which can release their mechanism. Hence is derived that "realist" psychology which the seventeenth century in France has given us; hence those treatises of the eighteenth century, *Moyen de parvenir* [How to Succeed] by Beroalde de Verville, *Liaisons dangereuses* [Dangerous Connections] by Laclos, *Traité de l'ambition* [Treatise on Ambitions] by Héreault de Séchelles, all of which give us a *practical* knowledge of the Other and the art of acting upon him.' (*Ibid.,* pp. 495–96).

the Others are there, precisely because I have to choose continually to avoid their look. Worse still, I am even more surrendered
to the Other's look 'since I am seen without being able to
experience the fact that I am seen, and without being able by
means of the same experience to defend myself against "being-
seen"'.

A final possibility is to hate the Other, to pursue his death.
This implies to give up the project of uniting with the Other,
and be content with having got rid of one's being-for-the-Other:
never more being an object for the Other's look, never more
having an outside. But this too will be a failure: 'The Other's
death constitutes me as an irremediable object exactly as my
own death would do.' The being-for-others remains a possibility
of my being which cannot be extinguished.

Hence, whatever attitude I take towards the Other will be a
failure, and if I am driven from one vain project to the next in
a vicious circle, my being-with-Others may take on the hellish
character of Sartre's play *Huis clos*.

5. Encounters purified
This vicious circle is put an end to in the mode of purified
consciousness. Converted from the vain project of being at the
same time both on the mode of consciousness and on the mode
of things, one enjoys being nothing but that which makes the
world appear. Then despair cedes to solidarity with oneself,
since one has come to affirm what one affirms, to will what one
will (instead of tacitly disapproving of what one openly approves of, as one constantly does when in bad faith). This
solidarity with oneself can be transformed into solidarity with
Others.

This conception of being solidary with Others does not signify
a return to sociological (and in particular Durkheimian) notions
of collective existence. The Other remains sharply distinct from
myself, but instead of trying to possess or subdue the Other's
freedom (or conversely, want the Other to possess or subdue
mine), my solidarity with the Other means that I, without inner
contradiction, affirm the Other's freedom as such.

This makes possible love in an authentic sense, which is
briefly outlined by Sartre: To love the Other without being in

bad faith is to affirm the Other in his (her) vulnerability, which means accepting this finitude, this contingency, this fragility.[9]

What is affirmed, is the Other's facticity as such; the Other is not affirmed as pure transcendence and beauty, but as this projecting consciousness transcending precisely this concrete, singular body's facticity, which for this reason becomes 'precious'. This fragility is not only conferred on the Other through me, in addition I make myself 'the guardian of his finitude', and do so in joy: 'I rejoice that the Other becomes through my passion what he is.'

This purified kind of love does not aim at a possession of the Other, nor at a union with him (her) on the mode of being-in-itself-for-itself. The Other's freedom is not the least encroached upon, nor do I give up my own. The relationship is not intellectual (like the Kantian obligation), but 'existential', since it concerns the delicate relation between project and facticity.[10]

Apparently, Sartre never completed this new series of descriptions, though one may easily conceive how they could have been carried on. For instance, one may describe how one may authentically let oneself be loved by the Other, by letting one's own fragility be sheltered by the Other's freedom, and so on.

Sartre's interpretations of love, desire etc. in the subsequent, monumental *L'idiot de la famille* are not as searching as those of the preceding works. They do not deviate, however, from his basic conception defended in the previous works.

6. Experience of 'Us' and illusoriness of 'We'
Throughout his work Sartre rejects the possibility of singular consciousnesses or organisms coalescing into a community. *L'être et le néant* discusses the notion of a 'We' as something essentially different from the 'I', concluding that only the 'Us', not the 'We', is an ontological mode of sociality.

9. 'This vulnerability, this finitude, *that is the body*. The body for the Other. To reveal the Other is his being-in-the-midst-of-the-world, that is to love him in his body', *Cahiers pour une morale*, p. 516 (1983) (My translation).
10. Sartre sums up his indications succinctly: 'This is one original structure of authentic love (we shall have to describe many others): to reveal being-in-the-midst-of-the-world of the Other, to assume this revealing and hence this Being in the absolute; *rejoice* in it without seeking to appropriate it oneself, shelter it in my liberty and transcend it only in the direction of the Other's ends' (*Ibid.,* pp. 523–4) (My translation). This bears a certain resemblance to the 'gift-love' described by C. S. Lewis in *The Four Loves.*

The 'Us' (or 'We as object') is, says Sartre, simply a specification of the being-for-the Other: Two consciousnesses can only experience themsleves as an Us when regarded by a Third consciousness. The *tertius* through looking at *ego* and *alter* transcends their situation, thereby transforming my and the Other's possibilities into 'dead-possibilities'. And if I assume the Other's situation vis-à-vis the Third, he and I constitute an organized whole—the Third looks at Us. This experience is a non-positional consciousness (of) Us, and dissolves before reflection: Then I find myself anew alone before the Others.

The experience of We (as subject) is denied ontological status by Sartre. It is explained away as an illusion ('a purely subjective impression') called forth by structures in our environment. Thus we are surrounded by products made by Others, and by all kinds of signs and sign posts. These are sometimes arranged in such a way that my activity goes on in the presence of and simultaneously with Others', as when, for instance, I walk in the corridors of the underground together with many Others walking in the same direction. Then the impression may easily be that 'we' are walking from one station in order to arrive at another. But this impression of a 'We' dissolves before (pure) reflection.

On the topic of collectivity, Sartre not only disagrees with those who talk of specifically collective experiences, he also tends to disapprove of them morally, as when he speaks of 'gelatinous agglutinations' of human beings. Collectivity in this sense becomes a specification of the Viscous, which to Sartre is the material symbol of moral badness.

7. Scarcity as the origin of the inhuman

Originally, these general propositions on human encounters were presented with a tacit claim to an-historic validity. Subsequently, Sartre according to himself 'discovered History' and became seriously occupied with Marxian thought and the significance of the Communist movement. In the subsequent work, the *Critique of Dialectical Reason* he tried to fill the gap between the seemingly timeless relationships rendered above, and the harsh world of history—starvation, oppression, violence and struggle. In other words, consciousness is now conceived of as historicized, that is, situated in a world marked by (material) scarcity. Scarcity is ultimately contingent, since it can and should be overcome, but has determined the human organism and its relation to the environment as far back in time as we know.[11]

Scarcity means that there is not enough for everybody, which signifies that some of the living human organisms are excessive and must perish. This affects everyone with inhumanity in the sense of a fundamental negation of the human. It makes human beings deadly enemies of each other, and violence a fundamental feature of us all.

Scarcity also involves that territory and space are scarce; therefore, all human organisms are united or totalized by the material environment, since we are bound to the same materiality as the Others. In this material field, human projects appear in the specific mode of work, an activity which is inhuman in so far as it is experienced as fatigue. The possibility of not having to work by forcing others to work instead is inherent in this situation, and grounds such a thing as class oppression.

In this basically hostile world the environment is experienced as a 'practico-inert field', a field already transformed by human praxis of the past, and unceasingly subject to changes through work processes, struggles and their concomitant effects (as, e.g. erosion of the soil). The practico-inert field is essentially alienated, since it constitutes me as a possible excess, as an Other to myself and the Others.

It may seem as if Liberal, utilitarian thought can account adequately for human relations in *l'enfer pratico-inert*, since everybody there treats the Others as means to his (her) own ends. Especially those who take advantage of the situation (through exploitation and otherwise) may tend to justify themselves by individualistic, utilitarian conceptions. But precisely because exploitation and oppression of the human organism seek to deprive *praxis* of its transcendence (reducing it to 'labour force' or the like), exploiters and oppressors tacitly presuppose the recognition of this transcendence. They fear the liberation of the alienated freedom. Hence, the human relation even in the practico-inert field implies the mutual recognition of the

11. This statement has been keenly attacked by some followers of Marx and others. It is, for instance, hardly reconcilable with Sahlin's *Stone Age Economics* (a work appearing after Sartre's *Critique*).

free, transcending objectivating praxis, even if it is negated in actual life: The oppressed or exploited classes suffer from the imposed reification and utilitarianism, while the oppressing and exploiting classes practise the afore-mentioned 'factual solipsism', concealing its untruth to themselves.

8. Serial and group existence

The two general modes of living this alienation of the practico-inert field are, either to affirm it from incapacity to do otherwise, or to combat it, in Sartre's terms, through being in a *serial* existence or in a *group*.

The easiest example of seriality as a mode of human co-existence in the practico-inert field is all kinds of queuing (as an everyday specification of scarcity). Here, everybody has the same end in view, but not a common end; on the contrary, each stands in an external relation to the others to the point that everybody should wish the Others were not there—as it were the zero degree of social life. Seriality makes me an Other like the Others and to myself. Rumours, for instance, have a serial structure; they are spread by everybody in so far as he or she is an Other; their sender is anonymous, and when I transmit this anonymous message, I make myself anonymous and alienated. Again, fashions and fads are serial, as are the reading of best-sellers, the purchase and listening to top hit records or videos, and the acquisition of a classical culture in so far as it is 'classical'. The painful character of seriality is experienced acutely in situations such as panics, where everybody acts to the detriment of himself because of the others—as when everybody by running instead of walking reduces the chances of rescue from the burning theatre, or by behaving as if one's bank is insolvent brings about its bankruptcy,[12] or when wage labourers in a Liberal market lower the price of labour power through their mutual isolation.

Since the reasoning about seriality intends to be a general interpretation of one of Marx's essential thoughts, it is somewhat astonishing that Sartre considers all class existence serial:

---

12. The 'self-fulfilling prophecies' and the unanticipated consequences of social action described and discussed by Merton are special cases of seriality in the practical-inert field. Consider also the serial thought of the neo-Liberal Von Mises: The capitalist is stone-hearted because his clients are stone-hearted, etc.

those belong to the same class who have more or less the same position in the practico-inert field in the essential respects (place in the process of production, property relationship, housing conditions, residential milieu, etc.). Also, what is called the 'objective class spirit' (as, for instance, 'the spirit of capitalism') is said to be thoroughly serial, consisting of gestures, sayings, patterns of feeling and thinking which are internalized and performed by every member of the class in so far as he (she) is an Other (en tant qu'Autre).

Marx's famous distinction between class in itself and class for itself is substituted by class as a mode of seriality, and the group, which is the pure negation of all seriality as such.

Under certain, favourable socio-material conditions power-less, alienated, serialized practical organisms may fuse into a battle group defined in relation to some adversary or menacing object in the practico-inert field. When participating in such a group I am transformed into an *individu commun*. The way in which this happens, is that each participant acts as the Third for the Others. The Third totalizes the Others into a group, being him- (her) self both inside and outside the group. The project of the group is revealed through its activities, where the acts of the Others are experienced as *my* acts, and the Other's freedom and transcendence of the situation as *my* freedom and transcendence.

Being-in-group expands my being in the sense that it makes me act at several places at the same time.[13] The actions of group members who fight together with me are experienced as my actions. This 'We' is not a substance, but a common praxis. Here the group members is neither another than, nor externally identical with, myself (as in sociality), but *the same* as myself. Being-in the group entails a multiplication of myself, not the fusion of individuals.

This battle group, called forth by urgency, is no 'We'; the *individu commun* is no 'collective consciousness' in the sense of Durkheim. Being in the group, it is rather the 'great I' that is experienced. The notion of group is meant to replace the various collectivity conceptions of Sociology.

---

13. 'It is not that I am myself in the Other: it is that *in praxis* there is no *Other*, there are only several *myselves.' Critique of Dialectical Reason,* p. 394–95.

On the other hand, Sartre warns explicitly against a utilitarian interpretation of the group fusion, to the effect that everybody participates in the group in order to raise his (her) 'life chances' (in Weber's sense). This presupposes that the individual experiences himself as distinct from the group as a group, making more or less deliberate calculations on behalf of himself. Instead, the urgent situation is experienced as the group's, and it is as a group member that the individual commits himself through his acts, 'producing his own possibility of being killed or imprisoned as a specification of the common danger'.[14]

In order to preserve itself, the battle group may infect itself with inhumanity and inertia. This happens when the members, tacitly or explicitly, swear to remain in the group. This oath, like any other oath, means a decision to remain the same, to resist change. It also, in the limiting case, means to support this commitment by invoking death. To swear not to leave the group, is to demand that I be killed if I do so. The sworn group becomes integrated through mutual obligations to kill or be killed in case of desertion.

This is the foundation of all other, diluted forms of obligatory groups.

9. Possibility of classless abundancy

Scarcity being a contingent feature of the human condition, its abolition is possible. Of such a world we cannot yet have any very determinate conception, since the end of scarcity will signify the end of the human as we know it; to use Marx's expression, it would mark the end of Humanity's pre-history, inaugurating a new era where human existence is free and rich. The protensions of this future world tend to indicate a 'communist' existence in the sense that all human beings somehow participate in a community. Sartre's ontology, on the contrary, indicates a profoundly 'anarchic' co-existence of human beings.

For not only does a world freed from the yoke of scarcity make possible the disappearance of classes and all other forms of seriality, since the others will no longer indicate myself as being superfluous (*de trop*). The end of scarcity's reign will also

---

14. *Ibid.,* p. 368.

involve the disappearance of all kind of group structures. For, as noted above, any group derives ultimately from battle groups, and any struggle is ultimately an attempt to negate scarcity. When there is no longer scarcity, the material world will no longer be experienced as a practico-inert field against the alienation impact of which groups emerge. Materiality will no longer threaten us as mediator of the other's and our own previous actions; which means that materiality will become just that facticity which is the necessary correlate to any project. If, according to Sartre, human beings unite from urgency provoked by the practico-inert field and its seriality, the reason for the upsurge and maintenance of groups disappears in a world of abundance.

Therefore, classless abundancy will not imply the emergence of Society in the strict sociological sense as an affirmative fusion of singular human beings into some collectivity. Rather, Sartre's ontology indicates a possible future world where a multitude of human beings co-exist—or, perhaps more precisely, of situated projects, since the concept of human being may disappear, too[15]—where everyone at last exists according to the possibilities described in *L'être et le néant:* transcending oneself towards the world, revealing its qualities, and revealing being in general. The fundamental relationship to Others may be one of affirming them as situated projects, that is, affirming their freedom, whether it be in the mode of co-operation, playing together, caring and loving, or just leaving the Others as they are in the mode of recognition. This would, of course, be a world without any kind of domination, hence an anarchy, but quite divergent from the prospects of the last centuries' great anarchy thinkers.

10. Concluding comments

Sartre's ontology of encounters between conscious beings can easily be stated as an attempt to bypass Conservative and Liberal thought like (French) *sociologie* and (English) *political economy.*[16]

15. 'In fact, in a humanity which was a true totality, men would be *men through each Other;* which means that the concept of man would disappear'. *Ibid.,* p. 752.
16. 'Thus, it seems as if we have the choice between the abstract and analytical myth of the individual and the concrete myth of society ... The problem must be considered anew'. *Cahiers pour une morale,* p. 117 (My translation).

On the one hand, he rejects the notion of the positive, mutually affirmative social whole, whether it be in the form of a society, a nation, a corporation, a primary group and so on, in so far as this notion somehow implies the existence of a We, a fusion of individual consciousnesses, as for instance Durkheim's 'collective consciousness' or 'collective representations'. All consciousness, Sartre asserts, is consciousness of one, singular (pre-reflective) Self.

On the other hand, he rejects the notion of mutually external, independent individuals, whose fundamental reciprocal relationship is either one of utility or of mutual intellectual recognition.

Or to put it in slightly different terms: On the one hand, Sartre disposes of the Liberal individual pursuing his 'self-interest' or 'self-respect'; on the other he disposes of the Social as a false totality concept, produced in bad faith, and disappearing when our experience of Others is cleansed by purifying reflection.

Thereupon, he works out his own conception of human encounters as strictly individual, non-intellectual[17] and non-utilitarian, and the corollaries of this conception for the understanding of the various kinds of human multitudes. Ultimately, his descriptions point to a kind of anarchy as the truth of human co-existence.

---

17. But not for this reason vital, in the sense of biology.

9

Neo-Anarchy Conceptions of the Individual II: Foucault, Deleuze & Guattari

The Surrealist movement sought to break with the alleged realism of everyday life and art through an unfettered exploitation of imagination and its phantasms. This implied the rejection of dominant notions of sanity and insanity, the normal and abnormal, and a corresponding urge to contribute to the upheaval of a society strongly marked by the quest for, or even obsession with, the useful, efficient and instrumental. A certain co-operation and even conjunction with the revolutionary Communist movement took place, but this alliance proved unstable and short-lived, since one of the partners emphasized discipline in thought and action, while the other was fundamentally opposed to all sorts of authority, displaying a strong leaning towards anarchy.

Two recent contributions that both owe much to the Surrealist movement will now be considered. First, the attempts of Michel Foucault to escape from the general notions discussed in Part One and arrive at a different understanding of human beings and their relation to each other; next, the even more daring explorations of Gilles Deleuze and Felix Guattari.

A. Foucault's Archeologies of Recent Conceptions of the Human

1. Introduction

Michel Foucault wrote extensively on the beginnings or 'archeologies' of several institutions, the psychiatric institution, the medical institution, the correctionary institution, the institution of sexuality. These writings were not simply contributions to the history of ideas, they aimed at profound changes of the Western modes of conceiving of human existence. In addition to being strongly attached to the Surrealist movement, Foucault was also influenced by those French scholars who, like Koyré, accentuate the discontinuity of the history of science.

2. Archeology of the sciences of man—first attempt

Les Mots et les Choses[1] presents the thought that 'man' in our time is constituted in terms of the concepts of biology, political economy and linguistics. The 'man' of our time is a being who lives, labours and speaks. The sciences of man—or *anthropology*—are reflexes, surface effects—of the great transformation of natural history into biology, the doctrine of wealth into political economy, and universal grammar into linguistics.

The human sciences are not really sciences, they are not on the level of *episteme*, and should better be termed 'discourses'. Their main notions are meaning *(sens)* and system (taken or derived from linguistics), conflict and rule (derived from political economy), and norm and function (from biology). *Culturology*—the 'study of literature and myths' etc.—is primarily constituted by the reign of the forms and laws of language, and consists mainly in a play of representations of these forms and laws. *Psychology* as a 'region' is constituted by the representation of the living being's functions.

As to *sociology*, its basic concepts are derived from political economy's preoccupation with production and consumption. These economic concerns are transformed into representations about a totality or encompassing context, a 'society' ordering and sustaining economic activity through laws and norms, rites and beliefs.[2] The topic of social integration and conflict is mainly a derivation of that of economic integration, but also stems from biology and linguistics. Generally, all three 'sciences' or discourses apply notions basic to the two others.

Thus, sociology is fundamentally a study of man in terms of

---

1. Published in 1966, English translation: *The Order of Things.*
2. '... the labouring, producing and consuming individual "who" offers himself a representation of the society where this activity occurs, of the groups and individuals among which it is divided, the imperatives, rites, festivities and beliefs by which it is sustained and regulated', *Op. cit.,* p. 355.

rules and conflicts, in the terminology of Foucault. He mentions Marx and Comte, Durkheim and Mauss.

According to Foucault, the history of the *sciences humaines* was first dominated by the biological notions (thus, the prevalence of organicist 'models' in sociology), then by economic notions (thus, the sociological preoccupation with struggle), and finally by 'the rule of the philological model' (presumably the sociological interpretation of myths and symbols). This change has been accompanied by another: The first terms of the pairs have lost their predominance, and made the second terms dominant. Instead of function, conflict and signification, the notions of norm, rule and system have imposed themselves. For sociology, Foucault describes the following consequence: As long as the notion of function dominated, one had to distinguish between normal functionings and those that were not; thus there was in Durkheim a pathology of societies. But when the norm came to dominate together with rule and system, each whole 'had its own coherence and validity'.

As one of the *sciences humaines*, sociology's existence as a mode of discourse is conditioned by that of biology, political economy and philology. If they vanish, so will sociology. Foucault foretells that 'man' is going to disappear. His reason for doing so is that recent philosophy and literature are so preoccupied by language as such.[3]

According to the conclusion of Part One, sociology and historico-dialectic thought are conditioned by Liberal politics and economics, and will not disappear until they crumble. Foucault's conception is discrepant in so far as he discerns Liberal economics as one among three conditions of sociology (including Marxian thought) and other sciences of man; moreover, when he predicts their disappearance, he does not refer to any great change within economic thought, but to a new mode of linguistic concern.

It may be hard to find out how to meet this discrepant interpretation. On the other hand, one might spare onself the

3. 'Since man was constituted at a time when language was doomed to dispersion, will he not be dispersed when language regains its unity?' Foucault suggests: 'Ought we not to admit that since language is here once more, man will return to that serene non-existence in which he was formerly maintained by the imperious unity of Discourse?', *Ibid.*, p. 386.

task, since Foucault himself some years later left this line of thought, working out a wholly different 'archeology' of the sciences of man.

3. Archeology of the sciences of man—second attempt

Later, Foucault confronts the very notion of the individual in the Liberal sense—a human being that is essentially free, but is often oppressed and to be liberated by others or itself. Foucault ventures to show how this notion is at least partly constituted through a series of measures on the part of those in power.

The point of departure of the examination is the transition in all European States from punishment by inflicting bodily pain and mutilations, to sentencing to imprisonment for shorter or longer periods of time. Durkheim[4] gave an interpretation of this change that did not involve reference to mild, tender-minded humaneness. (Such a reference, he said, rather ruined itself upon reflection.) Instead, he understood the transition as an aspect of the general differentiation process (presented in Part One). In evolutionary superior forms of society, he states, each human being is treated with more deference and respect, whence the transformation of penalties. (This evolutionary tendency is sometimes counteracted by another 'law', that centralized societies punish more severely than less centralized ones. Thus, the ancient Hebrew society was less centralized but also less evolved than the Roman Empire, the net result being that punishment was milder among the Hebrews.)

Foucault rejects this interpretation. While limiting himself to the investigation of the period 1650–1850 (approximately), he considers the abolition of cruel bodily penalties to be a response to demographic and economic changes calling for new, more efficient social controls. While 'the spectacle of the scaffold' represented the Prince's terrifying and awe-inspiring power over his subjects, torture in public became out-dated in a society where detailed supervision was required to secure property and political authority. Anyway, Foucault restates Weber's assertion about the general spreading of *discipline*, underpinning it through detailed descriptions of the factory, the army, the hospital, the school as disciplinary institutions. He seeks to make

4. Durkheim: *Deux lois de l'évolution pénale* (1900).

convincing the statement that the prison as an instrument of correction should be understood as part of a structure of discipline.[5]

Discipline is a way of exercising power which endeavours to shape and mould those exposed to it. Thus, the so-called disciplinary punishment consists in forcing those who have committed an error to perform the correct act over and over again, as a compulsory learning process. The relation between those who maintain discpline and those who are subject to it is therefore much closer than when the mighty are satisfied by mere outward signs of obedience from time to time, or collect and extort use values or money (as tithe or taxes). Discipline involves inspection, detailed control and supervision of the body and behaviour of those to be disciplined.

Now, Foucault assumes that the more those who are exposed to disciplinary devices stand out as individuals, the more efficient or easier the discipline will be. The increasing differentiation therefore expresses or reinforces disciplinary power.

For instance, we may consider Foucault's account of military discipline in the seventeenth and eighteenth centuries and the changing conception of a good soldier. In the seventeenth century, the soldier was trained to behave in a rather stiff way, and the battle division was constituted as a massive block, where the most habile and experienced formed as it were the surface, and the rest the ponderous mass. Then, the manual exercises were changed in order to be more 'natural' and 'organic', and each soldier was seen as distinct from the others. Something akin to a shift from Durkheimian 'mechanical' to 'organic' solidarity took place, since an undifferentiated mass of human beings was sought to be turned into a differentiated whole. But Foucault does not interpret this as a change for the better, as Spencer and Cooley (if not Durkheim) would have done. On the contrary, he considers this organic individual just as much, or even more, the result of disciplinary power, as the mechanically trained.

Generally, Foucault conceives the trend from generality

5. Foucault does not quote Weber, but the whole section on Discipline in Foucault's book is sketched in *Wirtschaft und Gesellschaft*. Since Weber's conception of struggle and power is affined to Nietzsche's, Foucault's continuation of this Weberian text accords well with his affinity to Nietzsche.

towards specification and specificity as a feature of the ever-increasing control exercised over human beings subject to domination. Hence, to stand out as an individual with a distinct individuality is an effect of the exercise of power, in so far as the human beings in question are enclosed by a disciplinary apparatus or the target of disciplinary devices. Therefore, one should not think that individuals are always repressed by power structures, since disciplinary power also produces (disciplinary) individuals and (disciplinary) individuality.[6]

The relationship between the individuals and such a power apparatus as the French State since the 1600–1700 should therefore neither be conceived of as one of protection nor of oppression solely. It is also—and perhaps above all—a relationship of production: the Liberal as well as the Absolutist State produces its citizens through disciplinary means. Liberal political thought affirms the independence of the individual, and by so doing overlooks that the Liberal individual is conditioned by discipline.[7]

The sciences of man, Foucault now states, were originated by the police, since they were the first to gather knowledge about the citizens and store it in archives. Even if the sciences of man may aim at liberation, their very constitution makes them part of a normalizing power apparatus. Foucault presents a striking historical development: While the rulers formerly were those of whom one wrote chronicles and poems of praise, the ruled being over-looked, today it is almost the other way around: The deviants are those who are subject to all kinds of psychological observation and tests; their childhood is perused, their social network evaluated by social workers. The rulers are spared such inquiries. Hence, those of whom there exists the fullest complete knowledge are the deviant, abnormal and dominated; they are individualized against their will.

Do not ask me who I am, he wrote, for such a question

6. Here, Foucault joins the reification doctrine of Lukacs and his followers. In addition to the usual sciences of man, Foucault also deals with medicine. The clinic and the physicians' 'medical gaze' is internally related to the possibility of getting sick people to expose their bodies to medical examination as objects. At the 'birth of the clinic', such an exposure is the poor people's payment for treatment.
7. This holds in the case of Locke, for instance, though when giving educational advice he is surely aware of the importance of discipline.

belongs to the sphere of police inquiries.[8] He repudiates the cult of the (unique, individualized) individual, since that involves establishing norms and normalizing practices, a notion of what human beings ought to be, and corresponding notions of the abnormal, of those who fall short of normative expectations, for instance, those with a 'weak ego'.

Seemingly, Foucault continues the thought of Husserl, who insisted that the human being is not an object of knowledge. But instead of the distinction between *objectity* and *existence* which several of his followers introduced and worked out, Foucault's protension points in another direction.

The preponderance of discipline as a form of power means that prescriptions rather than prohibitions are addressed to the citizens, the Norm rather than the Law. In our time the old severe forms of discipline have mostly given way to what Foucault terms *normalization*. Pedagogy, criminology and 'all the sciences with the prefix "psycho" ' are normalizing professions and discourses. This kind of knowledge serves normalizing purposes and is itself obtained from, and ambiguously produces, the objects of which it is knowledge. Knowledge is not only a means to power, but obtained through constituting a power relation between knower and known.

Through this consideration, Foucault connects to Nietzsche's thinking in *Beyond Good and Evil* and *The Genealogy of Morality*, where Nietzsche claims that not only does morality spring from the struggle between strong and weak, the victor deciding what is morally good and bad; even our fundamental concepts of knowledge do not transcend the struggle for power: Truth cannot be appealed to as to an impartial instance above the fighting parts.

From this Foucault seems to infer that in so far as all relationships between human beings are permeated with domination of one kind or another, all claims to knowledge and truth must be opposed or at least regarded with suspicion. To distinguish between the normal and the deviant (the pathological, the perverse, the insane, etc.) is a way of exercising power. The sick, the mad are constituted as such through the domination of others. The abnormal is established through definitions, dis-

8. Foucault: *L'Archéologie du savoir* (1969).

courses, and patterns of behaviour towards those who deviate from the normal. Abnormality is not just forbidden, frowned upon or repressed, but also called forth, produced through the power exercise of the normal.

4. Archeology of sexuality

Foucault's volumes on *The History of Sexuality*, which describe several modes of activity and understanding (discourse) related to the sex organs, can be read as a corroboration of this statement. In ancient Greece, parts of the male ruling class used sex organs in order to obtain a kind of pleasure called *aphrodisia*, and which entered into a life style in combination with food and drink, sleep, gymnastics and the like. Their concern with the proper use of these pleasures was guided by the notion of *enkrateia* or self-control, the balance between micro- and macro-cosmos, etc. The strain of desire was not dominant in *aphrodisia*, which therefore differed markedly from the Christian Church Fathers' notion of (sinful) carnal lust. During the age of Hellenism, the life-style of which *aphrodisia* was an integrated part, changed. Worries about the sexual act became more outspoken, the writers more inclined to recommend continence. But this change should be seen in a broader context, according to Foucault, as 'the development of an art of existence dominated by the concern with one-self.'[9] That is, the change does not, he claims, stem from more accentuated prohibitions than in earlier times, but from concern with the self as such, *le souci de soi*. And this engenders a style of sexual behaviour that differs both from that of the ethics of *aphrodisia* and that of coming Christianity. The self of the Christian differs as to its mode, and so does his or her sex. Finally, Foucault determines 'sexuality' in the strict sense as a topic constituted by a discourse about four normal figures and their corresponding deviants: the Mother, who gives birth to fine, healthy children, and whose body is saturated with sexuality—the deviant being the hysterical, frigid woman; the Child, on the borderline between sexual and a-sexual existence—the deviant being the masturbating child; the married Couple—the deviant being the childless, Malthusian couple; and the human beings with a normal Sexual

9. *Histoire de la sexualité*, vol. III, Conclusion (1984).

Instinct—the deviant being the sexually abnormal, the Perverse.[10]

To Foucault, sexuality is a discourse and an apparatus—a *dispositif*—which exerts a normalizing power in the double sense of correcting sexual behaviour and creating sexuality. The sexual power apparatus should therefore be disassembled. The relationship between sexual desire, and sexual morality and its guardians is similar to that between the citizen and the (Absolutist or Liberal) State. More important than sexual morality's repression of our desires, is the sexual discourse imposing disciplinary notions and devices of normal sexuality. One should not—like Reich above all—fight to liberate sexuality, but on the contrary, liberate oneself from it. What one should strive for, is simply 'the body and its pleasures'.

5. Comment: a neo-anarchy stance

Thus, Foucault, like the Sociologists, denies the opposition between the individual and the State as fundamental. But unlike them, he does not affirm the social as the encompassing or fundamental level of being. As noticed, he rejects the mechanical, undifferentiated and the organic, differentiated form of sociality as well. He suggests a state of affairs where there are neither individuals nor society in the sense of Sociology. What remains? Foucault speaks of bodies that are no longer subject to objectification. They need not be distinguished from each other; they may coalesce without for that reason constituting a 'collective consciousness'. Foucault suspends the very conception of a unitary, synthesizing consciousness—be it individual or collective. The scattered and accidental is not feared, nor anomie and social disintegration. Foucault strives to get away from all such notions as totality, unity, expressive individuality, reconciliation of subject and object. The masquerade and the carnival—ambiguous, subversive feasts where all identities are played with—are events that accord with the thought of Fou-

10. *Ibid.,* vol. I. I have not succeeded in seeing the difference between this conception and that of Marcuse and Brown. They envisaged a 'polymorphous eros' that may come into being through the possible transcendence of the instrumental and the sexual, a human body in a loving and reconciled relation to its surroundings. This conception carries on a deep protension within Romanticist thought, which, through the mediation of the Surrealist movement, may also be at the origin of Foucault's.

cault, as is the concert of rock music (commented upon by Foucault in a conversation with Boulez).

The doctrine of Kropotkin and other proponents of anarchy took as its point of departure that the human being is inherently good, friendly and helpful, and that therefore, there is no need for any social organization other than that which evolves spontaneously in the intercourse between independent and free members of society. This spontaneous organization will of its essence be without any use of power and force; there will be no 'military' and 'police' apparatus, no public authority. The human individuals will develop their capacities and enjoy life together in peaceful co-existence, characterized by solidarity and mutual aid.[11]

The contributions of Foucault partake of the basic intention of this traditional anarchy doctrine, since he, too, attacks all forms of power in human relationships. However, his attack aims at more profound changes, through, as it were, twisting Nietzsche's thought. Foucault shares Nietzsche's urge to transcend the cult of the human individual, of Humanism. However, whilst Nietzsche looked forward to the coming of Superman, Foucault seems to anticipate a world where the human being's character is almost effaced. And while Nietzsche has been understood, at least by most readers, as hostile towards the vast majority of human beings, Foucault takes the opposite direction. He attempts to think not from the standpoint of such celebrated, highly individualized figures as Goethe and Schiller, but from the standpoint of the *plèbe*, that is, all those who do not count as decent, respectable, neat—the mob.

B. Deleuze and Guattari on Socius and Desire

1. Introductory remarks

Deleuze and Guattari[12] offer a reinterpretation of Marxian Historico-dialectical thought on the basis of a specific conception of desire, a conception which mainly stems from the Surrealist

11. 'But it is not love and not even sympathy upon which society is based in mankind. It is the conscience — be it only at the stage of an instinct — of human solidarity'. Kropotkin: *Mutual Aid* (1904), the introduction.
12. Deleuze, a philosopher by profession, is the author of a great treatise of metaphysics: *Différence et répétition;* Guattari is a practising psychiatrist.

movement, but, presumably also owes much to Bergson. Connecting this interpretation to a certain practice and experience of psychiatry, they outline a schizoanalysis (in opposition to Freudian psychoanalysis), the aim of which is understanding the forms of desire and destroying desire's self-distortions.

To Deleuze and Guittara, as to Reich, The Frankfurter School and many others, the Fascist movement looms large, and calls for penetrating understanding on the level of unconscious desire as well as on the level of institutions—an undertaking which leads them to invent an astounding series of concepts to replace those widely current today.

2. Desire as constitutive of the social field

The notion of desire should, of course, not be taken in any narrow sexual, but rather in the widest possible sense, perhaps assimilated to the *élan* of Bergson (with whose thought Deleuze is thoroughly acquainted): a flow of joyful creation.

Therefore, they state, desire should not be thought of as some kind of acquisition, nor as a *lack* of some object. Desire is not sustained by the needs. Desire does not project or long for the phantasmagoric; it is close to existence's real conditions, and produces what is real. Desire is inherent in production as desiring production. The lack and its phantasms spring from a distortion of social production, from anti-production. In order to make clear that desire is no urge to fill some lack, to consume with the purpose of satisfying, the expression 'desiring machine' is used. Desire is a *flux* with no determinate goal, and differs from lacking, which is organized.[13]

Desire is not connected to utility.[14] Its ultimate aim is to have or be a 'body without organs'. This strange expression (taken from the actor and writer Antonin Artaud) does not convey the wish to be an undifferentiated body, but rather not to be an organism where each organ is co-ordinated in order to serve as means to an end.

True, those who experience the body without organs nearly always do that in sick and painful ways, such as those who

---

13. *Anti-Oedipe,* p. 409. In the following, all references are to the two volumes of the work *Schizophrénie et capitalisme,* Vol. I, *Anti-Oedipe* (1972), and Vol. II, *Mille plateaux* (1980).
14. 'Seul le désir vit d'être sans but.' (I, p. 441).

enjoy having pains inflicted on them. But this can be explained by the obstacles that confront the desiring flow. To break through the wall is a terrifying experience, which often leads to partial retreats. The schizophrenics are those who have got a glimpse of the body without organs, but do not succeed in their protension, and fall back into a numb state called 'catatony'.

If the suffering, sick mode of de-territorialization is schizophrenia, the corresponding mode of re-territorialization is paranoia.

Prevalent Freudo-Marxist doctrines combine psychology and economics in order to show how the *libido* is suppressed, channelled or sublimated through confronting the socio-economic order. Deleuze and Guattari consider this rather barren, since the two realms are conceived as relatively external to each other. Instead, they pose the identity of the social and desire, in the sense that the social is a mode of desire.[15] This permits them to raise anew the question of desire's self-repression or desire's desiring of repression. As their forerunner they refer to Reich, since he tried to understand how the German wage-labour class somehow desired their own repression through the National Socialists. But they estimate that Reich's thought should be continued more relentlessly than he himself was capable of doing.

Desire does not confront external institutions which inhibit it, desire inhibits itself, through its self-made institutions. Therefore, Schizoanalysis moves freely back and forth from the unconscious to the institutional, as one great domain.

3. Socius, de- and re-territorialization

Socius denotes the forms of Power. It is a social machine, or a social organization. In *socius* there is desire of repression. The purpose of *socius* is to *code* the flows of desire in order to control them. Albeit in shifting modes, desire has at all ages been thwarted and moulded by a *socius*.

The earliest forms of *socius* is that of the Territory, which is *inscripteur*, and marks human beings in order to make them belong to a determinate territory.

---

15. '... la production sociale est uniquement la production désirante elle-même dans des conditions déterminées ... Il n'y a que du désir et du social, et rien d'autre.' (I, p. 36).

Desire responds to territorialization by attempts to fly and escape, by de-territorialization. As such, it is desire's way towards the body without organs.

Generally, *socius*'s activities of coding, or even overcoding, are met with de-coding (in the sense of desire's uncontrolled flow), and so the struggle between desire and *socius* goes on. This liberating movement is then met by re-territorialization. While previous modes of social organization obviously were power forms that tried to repress desire and hold the human beings in a firm grip, the *socius* of our time, the capitalist mode of production, is peculiar. It is itself a flow[16]—of products, commodities, of money, of mobile wage-labour power—and to this extent comes near to being a desiring machine. But its desiring movement is interrupted, and therefore the capitalist mode of production acquires schizoid traits. Its internal split being deep, it is partly sane, partly insane, partly real, partly phantasmagoric. For this reason, it becomes important to understand that the suffering known as schizophrenia is essential to capitalism. For the great schizophrenics (like Artaud) aim at de-territorialization.[17]

Attached to Capital as *socius* is the Family in its recent, conjugal form, the spouses and their children. It distorts desire into sexuality as a 'dirty, little secret' (D. H. Lawrence) even if it is made public, dealt with by medical science, sexologists, etc.[18] This sexuality, especially when interpreted by Freudian psychology with its Oedipus complex, is an effort to re-territorialize. Freudian liberation of desire is half-hearted. While foisting upon everybody a sexual *cathexis* to one's parents, the flow of desire is fettered.[19]

Fascist movements are paranoic.[20] They assert themselves

16. 'Le capitalisme se forme quand le flux de richesse non qualifié rencontre le flux de travail non qualifié, et se conjugue avec lui.' (... *axiomatique générale de flux dicodés* ...)(II, p. 565).
17. Deleuze and Guittara comment upon the hatred the schizoid writers Kleist and Lenz aroused in Hegel and in Goethe, the latter a 'veritable Statesman' of literature, as the first of philosophy.
18. Here, the unanimity with Foucault is seen at once.
19. Therefore, Artaud's denunciation of the Oedipus complex is approvingly cited: 'Ja na crois pas en papa et maman.'
20. The figure of Salvador Dali should become disquieting and intriguing according to this conception: He professed a 'critical paranoia', but also showed a leaning towards Fascism in the 1930s.

through designating menacing enemies everywhere (the Jews, the Bolshevists, the yellow race) and desire the repression of desire. They affirm the territory, codes and controls, the rites of sacrifice and self-abnegation, the voluntary serfdom.

Revolutionary movements, too, may be subordinated to a *socius*. In that case, they are pre-conscious, (slightly) paranoiac, and make a *groupe assujetti*; they are revolutionary on the *molar* level, but not on the level of the *molecule* where they are Fascist.[21]

Then they do not really desire revolution, as does the group-subject.[22] If their revolution succeeds, they will afterwards establish a new *socius*.

4. Nomadic and sedentary existence—war machine and State

The opposition between de- and re-territorialization is further described as that between *nomadic* and *sedentary* existence. Desire is essentially nomadic,[23] it is a flow, and its space of the smooth kind—the ocean, the desert or the steppe. The State is sedentary by essence, and attempts to assign to its citizens a position in geometrical ('striped') space, and to fix them in their place.[24]

The nomad produces the war machine, directed against the State. Its activity consists in emitting 'quanta of de-territorialization', directed against the State. The war machine does not necessarily aim at triggering war;[25] on the contrary, warfare is essentially a State activity. It comes to war when the State has taken hold of a war machine. In particular, a Fascist State is a State which has implemented a war machine at every point and on all levels.

The distinction between the nomad and the State is also connected to that between two kinds of numbers—the number-

---

21. '... c'est trop facile, d'être anti-fasciste au niveau molaire ...' (II, p. 262).
22. '... révolution par désir, non par devoir' (I, p. 452). In the group subject, 'les investissements sont eux-mêmes revolutionaires'. Here, there is an explicit reference to the Sartrian concept of group, cf. the preceding chapter.
23. The nomade is 'le Déterritorialisé par excellence'. (II, p. 479), 'Le désir est un exil'. (I, p. 452).
24. II, p. 479 Once more, they concur with Foucault, cf. his account in *Surveiller et punir*.
25. One might conceive of a war machine 'qui n'a justement pas la querre pour object' ete. (II, p. 523).

ing and numbered number. The nomads' groupings are constituted by dint of the numbering number, a creative number
deploying itself as 'subject' in the smooth space, and which does
not measure, but directs the war machine, and the aim of which
is to displace. The numbered number constitutes and belongs
to the State, with its large numbers of men, forced to make an
army, and with its masses of citizens, treated as arithmetic
magnitudes.[26]

Likewise, Deleuze and Guittara try to pinpoint a difference
between the nomads and the State with respect to their general
form of thought as such.

The State thinks through universal concepts, and supports
and gets support from those who think universally. Thus Kant,
an official in Prussia, conceived of 'a republic of free spirits, the
prince being the supreme Being'. Likewise, Hegel is a State
thinker (as Durkheim wanted to be the thinker of the French
Third Republic).

Nomadic thought proceeds otherwise; it is the relation between a singular tribe and its environment.[27] This may seem
dangerously close to Fascist thought, with its cult of the superior
race and its specific mode of thought (thinking with the blood
etc.). But, Deleuze and Guattari meet their own objection by
affirming that there never exists a superior race; any race is
inferior and oppressed, is a minority. Nomadic thought is the
thought of the oppressed in the process of de-territorialization.

5. The individual and the crowd

Deleuze and Guattari, too, face the unpleasant choice between
the individual and the social whole, the collective, and sketch a
third conception, through a discussion of Romanticism in the
musical field. The Romantic movement, as noted already in
preceding chapters, is concerned with the understanding of
wholes, and often thinks of the singular human being as expressive of a larger (social, rational) whole. But neither undifferentiated nor differentiated collectivity will do; Deleuze and Guattari

26. 'Bien plus, l'usage du nombre comme numéro, comme élément statistique,
appartient au nombre nombré d'Etat, non pas au nombre nombrant' (II, p.
486).
27. 'Une tribu dans le désert, au lieu d'un sujet universel sous l'horizon de
l'Etre englobant.' (II, p. 470).

seek for something else. They contend that in Wagner's operatic work, for instance, the voice and the orchestra stand in the relation of the soul, the One-Alone and the One-Whole of the earth. This music is territorializing. The relation between orchestration and the vocal is not external, they affirm, and in the case of Wagner, the orchestra imposes upon the voice its roles. The singer acts as subject, as subjectivated individual with sentiments, while the orchestra arouses effects that are not subjectivated. The orchestration consists in a group of powers, expressive of the universal or collective. Against this musical collectivism Deleuze and Guittara set a music of the One-Crowd (l'Un-Foule), where the orchestration obtains a group individuation which brings forth a new relation, which is called the *Dividual* (to avoid the usual associations with or connotations to the Liberal's individual). Here, they refer to Debussy, who said that the people in *Die Meistersinger* were really an organized German army, and not a crowd. The relations of the crowd is of the dividual kind, neither a universal entity nor a collection of contiguous, externally related human beings (individuals).[28]

Similarly, the unity of nomads is sought to be expressed without resorting to concepts of the Whole and the individual 'subject'.[29] Their collectivity is vague, fluent, their *esprit de corps* not that of a military army or any other battle unit founded upon the State's power.

Again, they refer to the opposition between the sociology of Durkheim and that of Tarde, siding with the latter. His infinitesimal limitations, they say, are related, not to the individual, but to waves, flows of beliefs and desire. Tarde indicates how to transcend the opposition between the social and the individual, since one avoids the concepts of collective and individual representations; on the molecular level described by Tarde, it becomes no longer meaningful to separate the social from the individual.

28. 'Debussy posait bien le problème de l'Un-Foule lorsqu'il reprochait à Wagner de ne pas savoir "faire" une foule ou un peuple: il faut qu'une foule soit pleinement individuée, mais par des individuations de groupe, qui ne se réduisent pas à l'individualité des sujets qui la composent. Le peuple doit s'individualiser, non pas d'après les personnes, mais d'après les affects qu'il éprouve simultanement et successivement.' (II, p. 421.)
29. II, p. 469.

Yet another attempt is to substitute for the notion of the One and the Manifold that of a multiplicity: Desiring production is pure (Bergsonian) multiplicity, that is, an affirmation irreducible to a unity. Desire is neither a collective nor an individual entity or process, it is multiplicity, crowd, war machine.

6. Brief comment

These two thinkers do not set Society or the social against the relationship State/Individual. Nor do they conceive of Society as a whole of which each individual member is an expressive part. Instead they invent the notion of the Dividual and its crowd, which shall be understood as a fluent, diffuse multiplicity.

Nomadic warfare against Fascistic re-territorialization, against State, Capital and Family and all forms of sedentary existence—this is what Schizoanalysis leads up to.

They also go well beyond the domain of Statistics through the preoccupation with the numbering number (nombre nombrant), which cannot be submitted to mathematical treatment.

Finally, while sharing the main tenets of Marx, they are, like Reich, keenly aware of the authoritarian features of actual Communist movements, and propose wholly different politics on the mode of de-territorialization

Even, though all this sounds strange, its protension points unmistakably towards a hitherto unknown kind of anarchy.

10

Beyond Economics: Touraine's Doctrine of the Historic Subject

1. Introduction

Educated as an historian, Alain Touraine's main concern has been history as a contemporary process. The impact of Marx upon his thinking seems pervasive in the sense that the ultimate question he poses is how human beings can make their own history through engaging in productive conflicts. He starts with the historico-dialectical conceptions framed by Marx, and tries to find new solutions. In so far as Marx's doctrine presented itself as a 'science of making History' Touraine is certainly a follower of Marx. However, the influence of more recent, anti-Positivist thinking on his mind clearly separates him from the prevalent interpretations of Marx.

Especially, the influence of Sartre is both declared and notable. With Sartre he insists on the essential free and creative character of human action. This entails both that the human being himself must confer meaning on his actions, create his own morals, and that human action is not caused, determined, by something other than the human agent himself (which excludes, for instance, its determination by the 'economic factor'). Published five years after Sartre's *Critique de la raison dialectique*, Touraine's first major book shows several similarities. But by and large, Touraine's doctrine, as it has been elaborated over the decades, is unique. It revolves around the formation and struggles of social movements as participants in the historical process, or, to use his expression, as historic subjects. Beginning as a sociologist of labour (doing research on the Renault plant, or on workers with an agricultural background), proceeding to the topic of class consciousness, the scope of his investigations has widened and bears on the fundamental traits of society and the social sciences.

2. From the meta-social to the social

Touraine asserts that during the last centuries there took place a cultural change involving the shift from 'meta-social' to 'social' guarantees and justifications of human action. That is to say, instead of an appeal to God, to Development, Evolution, History, and so on, human action is interpreted in terms of itself. *Homo mensura:* Human action is judged and understood in the light of values created by human action. As the human being according to Kant is his own legislator, similarly humanity (at least in the West) becomes conscious that it produces its own world, its values and goals. This, again, comes very close to Kant's interpretation of the meaning of Enlightenment. When the consciousness is attained that what happens in social life can ultimately be imputed to human action, the threshold of the social and of sociology is passed: The urge is raised to understand the foundation and direction of social life as a product of social action. It becomes clear that Evolution or History are not transcendent forces in relation to social life, since the human actors decide about the direction of evolution, and (in Marx's famous expression) 'create their own History'. This marks the birth of sociology as the science of social action, which, as will be shown, also signifies the science of how men make their own history. Touraine also rejects every appeal to 'nature' (including 'human nature') as a ground for the understanding of society. Thus, when the ecological movement refers to the disturbed equilibrium between humanity and its natural environment, caused by industrial society's over-exploitation and production, Touraine cannot agree that the aim must be to restore the natural equilibrium, since that implies making Nature a meta-social entity.

3. The concept of action

Touraine's concept of action is a fusion of Parsons' and Sartre's. As noted above, both these thinkers arrived at the conception of the situated action, involving choice, and did so because they could not accept either that human activity is entirely conditioned by external impact, or that it is an emanation of (free) spirit. Touraine continues the attack on what he terms 'naturalism', that is the notion that the human being is part of nature and as such externally conditioned. With Parsons, he affirms the normative orientation of every action. With Sartre he affirms that every action is a project that is a temporalized movement towards the future, and hence, a historic event. While Parsons tends to emphasize the actor's choice between already existing value patterns and interprets this as a kind of compliance, Touraine conceives of action as a movement that creates something new, that changes the environment. In other words, social action is conceived of as historic. When taking over from Parsons the concept of action systems, he therefore adds the historic aspect and speaks of historic action systems as his specific subject matter. Action is, in this sense, both social and historic. In this respect, Touraine follows quite closely Marx's doctrine of human praxis, with the signal difference pointed out above, that Touraine will do without Marx's allegedly meta-social notion of inevitable historical progress.

The alienation concept is essential to Touraine's doctrine of social action. To be excluded, debarred, sidetracked from participating in historically productive action is to him the gravest privation *(steresis)* that members of society can experience. On the one hand, there is historic action, collective participation, and control over a production process, on the other there is isolation, powerlessness, alienation in relation to this process. This is the fundamental or *class* opposition within a system of social action. Once more, this accords perfectly with Marxian teachings. (The discrepancy appears, however, when it comes to the interpretation of the direction of historical change and the question of the determining primacy of the mode of economic production.)

In order to make his own position clear to others, Touraine often comments on intellectual approaches that differ from his own. Thus, in the *Production of Society*, he discusses those strands of thought that concentrate on the concepts of function, control and decision, respectively.

The first he associates with what in this book has been described as the science of social integration, and in particular, with the structural-functional approach of Parsons. This thinking is concerned with the conditions and reproduction of order in society, which Touraine considers to be an important topic, though he also contends that the functional approach often decays into a Conservative defence of traditional ruling classes by praising conformity with prevailing values and norms. When this transgression is avoided, Touraine appears to grant the research into the reproduction of society a complementary position relative to that of the production of society.

The second he associates with those who seek to unmask the language of values, norms, functions and roles as really a way of obtaining or maintaining control over the members of society, by trying to get them to interpret their opposition as deviance, their tendency towards rebellion as a subject matter for the therapist etc. Critical Theory, as it has been expounded in the present book, clearly belongs to this sociology of control, as Touraine terms it. Though he approves of its exposures, he thinks it is prone to commit the same mistake as those it attacks, that is, to underestimate the actors' capability to act on their society instead of merely being shaped by it (through internalization of norms etc.).

The third he associates with Liberal and neo-Liberal conceptions of social life, which have been referred to several times in the present work. To interpret the members of society as actors who decide about their course of action (instead of merely expressing the values and norms that have been inculcated into them) is certainly valid in many domains of society, especially within the political apparatus. But when generalized to cover all kinds of social relationships, presenting them as strategic games of decisions, this approach is erroneous. In particular, the interpretation in terms of decisions tends to take the point of view of the dominant class.[1]

This decision approach and Touraine's own concept of his-

---

1. 'La sociologie des décisions ... réintroduit le système en l'identifiant aux intérêts de l'élite ...' '... comment en même temps ne pas prendre position contre une sociologie des décisions ou du "planning" qui n'est pas seulement un ensemble de travaux souvent remarquables, mais qui est avant tout l'arme idéologique de la nouvelle classe dirigeante?' *Production de la société* (1973), pp. 60–1.

toric action are, he says, 'intimate enemies', since both refer to creativity, control and change by the human beings themselves. The first tends to identify the ruling class, while the second, insisting on the class conflict, is oriented towards the challenge of class dominance.[2]

4. The interpretation of industrial civilization
Work is a kind of action, denoting an activity which tries to control and change a resisting material environment, and producing works, that is, tools and other objects of use. When work is given paramount importance, the industrial era begins: There goes on—in the form of capital accumulation—a transformation of the environment and the social relations through ever more vast projects of co-operative work processes, which are continuously subjected to improvements to achieve more effectivity. In the industrial era, religious and juridical meta-social entities have lost their sway to a considerable extent, but two meta-social notions still exert influence, the economic notion of the market, and the notion that the economic institution determines the historical development. Partly, this is the dominating class's interpretation of the situation, referring to economic laws govering all activities. Partly, it is a true account of early stages of industrial civilization, where the alienation of work is glaring. During the Liberal (capitalist) time span what is called 'the economy' is in fact out of control, and appears as the 'alien, hostile force' of which Marx and Engels wrote. At this stage, their 'historical materialism' corresponded fairly well with the given situation, since the economy had a markedly independent existence. The class conflict between Labour and Capital is the essential conflict here: the workers struggle against debasing toil and capital's uncontrolled expansions (and recessions), and the various forms of workers' movements arise. This movement did not spring from misery, nor was it animated by those who (in the words of the *Communist Manifesto*) 'have nothing to lose but their chains'. On the contrary, those who challenged the capital owners' leadership were the most highly

2. George Gurvitch defined sociology as 'the science of freedom'. While the relationship between Gurvitch and the younger Touraine was one of mutual disapproval, in this statement they might have concurred.

trained professional groups, who acted from pride in their own works.[3]

5. Social movements in general—'Touraine's triad'
The workers' movement is considered by Touraine to have acted historically in the past, but in our time he thinks it has begun to lose in importance as a historic subject. Now, the worker's movement is understood as a social movement among others, and can be described on a more general level. Here, Touraine distinguishes four main kinds of social movement: protest movements, idea movements, movements of demand, and critical or reform movements. Their *differentia specifica* pertains to their relation to what may be termed 'Touraine's triad'. Any action may or may not involve taking a stand towards a social whole or totality (T), towards opposing social forces or groups (O), and towards the actors' own identity (I).

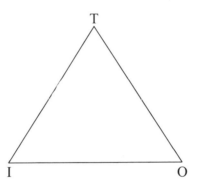

A protest movement is constituted merely by its opposition to others; it neither affirms its own identity nor makes claims on behalf of society as a whole. An idea movement, too, is one-sided: It defines itself exclusively by reference to the universally recognized values of society as a whole, but does not designate any adversary, nor present itself as a collective actor with a singular identity. As such, it fails in posing definite goals and runs the risk of being vague and harmless (what all men and women of good will must endorse etc.) Demand movements are

3. Cf. *La sociologie de l'action* (1965), the section on 'Misère et revolution'.

collective action groups that at the same time know who they are and whom or what they fight, while the reference to totality is left out. So-called 'interest groups' often fit this description well: eager to obtain some advantage or better their own lot, they do not try to defend their claims by appeal to the morality of society as a whole (or if they do, such appeals are more or less hypocritical or in bad faith).

Only a full-fledged social movement, constituted both by relations of identity, opposition and totality, can be a historic subject in the strong sense. A historic subject must launch a project that claims validity for the social whole; it must challenge and oppose other collective groups (reproaching them, for instance, for not being concerned with universally valid values), and it must be capable of presenting itself both to the participants and the environment as a distinct action group.

6. Historicity and class conflict

Touraine speaks of historicity in a specific sense; the term denotes the mode of society's self-production.[4] He thinks of it as a unity of three components, a mode of accumulation, a mode of knowledge, and a cultural mode or model.[5]

The modes of accumulation differ historically, from storage of crops to investment in education. The mode of knowledge is a society's general conceptions of the world and the place of human beings in it, while the cultural model expresses society's conception of its creative capacity. These components are distinguished for the sake of convenience, and should not be thought of as independent 'factors'. On this issue, Touraine disavows the historico-materialistic doctrine of Marx and Engels; not because he gives priority to the spiritual or cultural, but because he finds meaningless the quest for some determining 'factor'.[6]

The specific historicity of a society denotes what the social

4. 'Nommons historicité ce travail, ce travail sur le travail, de transformation de la société par elle-même. *Pour la sociologie* (1974).
5. Cf. for instance *L'après-socialisme* (1980).
6. 'En réalité, la question de savoir qu'elle est la catégorie de faits sociaux, quel est le 'facteur' qui a un rôle dominant me semble absolument étrangère à la sociologie.' *Production de la sociologie,* p. 128.

relationships—the unifications and conflicts—are about, what are their topics or concerns.

This notion of historicity may seem not so different from, say, Sorokin's or Parsons' classifications in terms of paramount cultural values. However, Touraine attaches crucial importance to the thought that any historicity is a field of conflict, while those who speak of society's values, overtly or tacitly presume a fundamental consensus. By contrast, Touraine asserts that historicity and its correspondent historic action system are dominated by a class of rulers, a group that has taken charge of the accumulation and the cultural model, and that there is, on the other side, an opposing social movement that claims the right to interpret and develop society according to this cultural model. In other words, because historicity is never handed over to a group of leaders by a unanimous population, but is on the contrary subject to disputes as to who shall control it, historicity and class conflict are inseparable.

It will be seen that a full-fledged social movement, as described above, is the same as a class that opposes dominance and claims to be in charge of the cultural model.

According to Touraine, the workers' movement at its best has participated in this basic conflict over the control of the cultural model. For it has been committed to industrial civilization and its development just as have the industrial capitalists who have dominated this development. On behalf of society as a whole the workers' movements have claimed to be better suited to direct industrial civilization in a way that expresses reason and justice. Social classes, as conceived by Touraine, are not at all to be confounded with statistical aggregates of people who possess certain traits in common. They are collective actors, constituted by the relation to the opposing class in a field of historicity, and, consequently, constituted by their historic orientation.[7]

---

7. 'Pour la sociologie, l'analyse ne peut partir que des rapports de classes et non de chaque acteur particulier, consideré dans ses attributs ou ses intentions... Les classes doivent être conçues comme des adversaires luttant pout le contrôle du systeme d'action historique.' *Production de la société*, p. 206. 'Les rapports de classes ne sont pas séparables de l'historicité parce que l'opposition des classes est l'agent de la distance que la société prend à l'égard d'êlle-même et de l'action qu'elle excerce sur elle-même.' *Pour la sociologie*, p. 66.

7. From industrial to programmed society

Touraine assumes that the cultural model and its carrier, the historical subject, is changing before our eyes. The industrial society's project is conceived as unceasing progress through the investments of labour's products. Hence, the basic or class conflict is about production relations and forces, the opposition between industrial capital and wage labour. But gradually it has come to be seen that what determines accumulation and progress is the very insight into these processes. There exists a knowledge of the conditions of growth and expansion, and this knowledge is itself highly conducive to accumulation and expansion. In other words, there has been a shift in the level of reflexivity. In the industrial era, society was produced by the work of its participants, who changed themselves through changing the environment. This is the historic dialectic of which especially Marx wrote. In our time, however, there has been a growing awareness of this dialectic to the extent that it has become the new cultural model. Our society is not just one that produces itself through its productive activities, but that knows this and plans its production accordingly. The self-conscious productive society is termed the programmed society, where information and communication have taken the place formerly occupied by work. The production programs of contemporary society take into account not only economic relations (which no longer have an independent existence)[8] but also political and cultural relations, where scientific knowledge is particularly important.

A consequence of this transition to the programmed society is that the conflict between wage labour and capital is no longer essential. Certainly, there are still all sorts of oppositions between the two adversaries, and the wage-labour class is still exposed to hardships, sufferings and injustice. But it can to a dwindling degree pose as a historic subject, since work no longer has the same importance as being productive of history. In so far as its identity is internally linked to notions of work, it cannot claim the right to take charge of the new cultural model that orients society's production and self-production. Depri-

---

8. 'J'avoue que je ne sais pas ce qu'est, cet économique définissable indépendamment des acteurs sociaux et politiques.' *Désir de l'histoire* (1977), p. 88.

vations and frustrations, even misery, may be the lot of the wage-labour class, without for that reason making it a 'rising historic class', in Marx's words, or, in Touraine's, 'a coming historic subject'.

The workers' movement is concerned with industrial development, towards which it is favourable, provided it is for the benefit of all. Industrial leaders and wage labourers have in common this conviction that industry is a good thing. Their opposition and conflict stem from the relations of production which the workers' movement wants to change.

Touraine discards the Marxian distinction between class in itself and class for itself, saying that there is no working class without class consciousness. This consciousness is triadic in the above-mentioned sense, and directs, supports and is itself reinforced by the workers' movement. As such, it is neither narrowly economic, political or professional in its claims and orientations. Its project is above all to develop and control industrial society as a whole, and the way is class conflict.

Now, this unitary class consciousness shows signs of dissolving, and so does the workers' movement. To be sure, there still exists a working-class culture and consciousness sustained by large numbers. But the tendency is for the workers' movement to renounce this total project and fall back upon more limited and less universal goals. Thus, a large bulk of the wage-labour class confines itself to questions of wages and money only, preoccupied with defending or improving their financial position or standard of living. Other strata of the wage-labour class withdraw into what is termed corporatism, whereby they seek to obtain or preserve advantages for their own specific job groups (for instance hindering access by imposing qualifications of all kinds). Again, the leading strata of the workers' movement, those who design the specific, actual issues over which to fight, feel it ever more difficult to act in terms of class consciousness. Instead, they are inclined to share the conceptions of the dominant groups within the State and the great corporations, since the important topics put on the agenda do not easily lend themselves to an interpretation in terms of class conflict. The syndical leaders tend to become politicians, while the rest of the movement tend to dissolve into a multitude of pressure groups.

The original unity (which attained its maximum in the era of Taylor and Ford) cannot be restored, in the judgment of Touraine. The decomposition of the workers' movement goes on inexorably, albeit slowly, and should be understood as a feature of the transformation of industrial society itself.

From this and similar investigations Touraine concludes that the basic social conflict in our society is no longer class struggle in the Marxian sense, or if one wants to preserve the notion of class, that new class conflicts have arisen, or are in the making. The basic opposition in post-industrial society he assumes to be that between what is called 'technocracy' and the rest of the population: between those who have usurped the right to participate and decide, exert control and display creativity, and are prone to think of other citizens as 'objects' of benevolent planning and programming.[9] The neo-Liberal conceptions of decision-making and strategic action that have come into fashion during the last decades are seen by Touraine as expressive of such an arrogant ruling class of technocrats, who do not feel themselves at all threatened or even challenged by any other social class or movement with regard to domination over the cultural model and the corresponding historic action system. This new class domination implies very serious alienations on the part of the dominated, so long as they fail to initiate important social movements which strive towards control over the cultural model. This indicates a task for the social investigator: to help get such movements started by clarifying the situation of the dominated. Touraine himself, together with collaborators, has practised what he calls the 'intervention method' in several cases: Discussion groups composed of militant members of social movements are established with the sociologists as leaders and catalysts, the purpose being to find out whether or not the group succeeds in presenting their identity, opposition, and totality references in such a way that the social movement in question can with good reason challenge the ruling class and

9. While Touraine does not doubt that the present ruling class is the technocracy, he has, as he mentions himself been characterized as a supporter of the technocracy. One reason for this may be that Saint-Simon, the first technocrat, made 'production' the basic concept of his doctrine, and so does Touraine. But while Saint-Simon looked forward to a society administered by technical experts, Touraine is concerned with the opposition to such leadership.

pretend to be a historic subject. In addition to the workers' movement, Touraine and associates have engaged themselves in the student movement and the anti-nuclear movement, following the intervention method or way.

8. *In search of the new historic subject*

Touraine has devoted much attention to the French students' movement, both at its fulminant moment in spring 1968 and in later years of less spectacular events. For centuries, students have been recruits to dominant positions of society. The student organizations, however, pose as representing an oppressed social group. What kind of social movement, then, is or can the student movement be? Can it take a place in the new programmed society similar to that of the workers' movement in industrial society? Touraine and his collaborators are inclined to disbelieve that; at most, they confer upon it a heraldic role, announcing a great future social movement.

One may discern, as it were, two wings of the student movement, one striving to get the students to throw in their lot with the workers in their struggle against capitalism; the other rejecting vigorously the paramount cultural values and life styles in favour of hitherto unknown sensuous enjoyment and unhampered self-expression.[10] But neither wing nor those who stand in the middle of the road can give a significance to their activities that enables the student movement to assume the task of a historic subject. Thus, the dismissal of everything the university transmits as 'bourgeois ideology' or the like, without opposing any other kind of knowledge as a substitute deprives it of an affirmative content. Further, to perceive the adversary as the capitalist mode of production makes it backward looking. Finally, since the students' fusion with the workers has failed, their identity is very uncertain.[11]

The women's movement—as distinct from Feminism—is also considered by Touraine in its relation to historicity. In this case, it is at once clear that in so far as this movement designates the other sex as the adversary, it cannot assume the central conflict

10. One may interpret this as the resurrection of the opposition between the Communist and Surrealist movement in the interwar period.
11. 'Les étudiants ne savent ni qui ils sont ni qui ils représentent. *La lutte étudiante* (1978), p. 368.

of our society. This is because its reference to totality is lacking. However, the women's movement is partly occupied not merely with obtaining the same rights for women as for men, but also with more far-reaching (qualitative) changes of human relationships.[12] If this becomes its main concern, it may turn into the social movement that expresses the basic conflict of the post-industrial era. The same lack of universally valid claims and goals is notable in the various regional movements that have emerged in Europe during the last decades, as, for instance, the Occitania movement investigated by Touraine and his associates.[13]

The most promising movement subject to sociological intervention has until now been the movement struggling against the implementation of nuclear power stations in France. To be sure, the participants in the various militant groups represent highly divergent conceptions of what they combat. Some reject nuclear energy as part of science in general, advocating a return to simpler ways of thinking. Others connect the anti-nuclear campaign with a defence of nature and its equilibrium, affirming that mankind is part of nature. Others again react to the arrogance of the State and fear that to rely on nuclear energy will augment the State's control over the citizens, while still others oppose the construction of atomic power stations because they are deemed too dangerous.

Now, Touraine thinks it is warranted to state that the dispositions towards seclusion, withdrawal or one-sided refusal are overshadowed by attempts to challenge the governmental authorities on their own ground and project a better exploitation of science and technology, with a reference to society or even humankind as a whole. Then the anti-nuclear struggle may develop into a full-fledged social movement in conflict with the technocracy, driven by an urge for participation and control over one's life. And the movement will not be directed by a wish to obtain an ecological equilibrium by finding a suitable niche for the human species, but by insisting that the human

12. 'Le mouvement des femmes, comme celui de toute catégorie dominée, va jusqu'au bout de lui-même quand il lutte pour recréer des relations là où la domination avait instauré l'ordre.' *L'aprés-socialisme,* p. 151.
13. *Le pays contre l'Etat.*

capacity for change and creation be given full opportunity for all, instead of being usurped by a few, as now.

The later development of the anti-nuclear movement may have disappointed Touraine in many ways, without for that reason making him give up his basic assumption: that only a social movement different from, but with the same scope as, the workers' movement can render full significance to our social lives.[14]

9. Concluding comments

After this sketch of the doctrine of the historic subject its fundamental assumptions can be discussed. To what extent can it be said that Touraine offers a new approach?

The most striking feature of his doctrine (relative, of course, to the main issues dealt with throughout the present work) is the way Touraine bypasses Liberal economics and its subject-matter, the market and the capitalist mode of production. These entities, in his judgement, have long since ceased to exist as such. They have merged into a new whole together with political and cultural topics. This new whole is a historic action system oriented towards accumulation, development. But these aims cannot be conceived in a narrow economic sense. What is at stake, is the self-production and change of society, not the economy. Therefore, the basic or class conflict will no longer be about the exploitation of labour power and the usurpation of surplus value, ultimately a matter of economic calculation. What is at stake is the management of change, the direction of the historic process, where knowledge, commitment and communication are so essential to the production process that economics' notions of allocation of scarce means and the like no more apply. If not work, but programmed action is at the core of the production of society, Liberal economics no longer has any topic, since it has fused into another (ontic) object, the historic action system of programmed civilization.

---

14. It is easy to object that Touraine's interventions cannot really teach him anything new, since he knows beforehand what the future social movement should look like. This may be admitted as regards the social movement's most general traits. But still only fresh experience and a social action can discover and create the content of the movement in all its details, and reveal who will be its participants.

Similarly, Touraine attempts to transcend both Liberal politics and its Marxian riposte. By asserting that social movements and classes do not consist of individual participants, but of collective actors struggling for control over society's production of itself, he tries to avoid the Liberal starting point, the individual citizen. And since he states that these collective entities are not, not even basically or primarily, economic, he attempts to go beyond Marx. In other words: to the extent that the Marxian doctrine is internally related to Liberal 'political economy' as its 'critique', it has become obsolete. Instead of the Marxian 'science of the mode of productions', Touraine attempts a participatory investigation of historical action systems and their essential ('class') conflicts. It seems, therefore, that Touraine's conception has not been developed as a response to the concepts that have emerged around the State, the Market and the Individual, nor as a complement to the doctrine of utility. His doctrine is not, it seems, from the beginning the Other in relation to the One, the internal negation of what already poses for itself, a reaction to an action. The actionalist approach appears to be independent of the modes of thought that gave rise to Sociology as a science of social integration.

True, doubts may creep in at this point. Thus, the relation to what Touraine calls the sociology of decisions could turn out to be one resembling, say, that of *Gemeinschaft* to *Gesellschaft*, or dialectical to instrumental action. For Touraine grants the theory of strategic action and games a certain field of validity, and one may therefore ask: what will happen to the doctrine of the historic subject if this field is steadily expanded, to the effect that a historically oriented social movement becames nothing but a receding—or even only longed-for—entity? It remains to be seen whether such doubts are justified or groundless.

11

Beyond Sociology: Luhmann's Doctrine of Communicative Systems

1. Introduction

After having worked as a civil servant and published contributions to the sociology of law, Niklas Luhmann turned his attention to a wide range of topics, the essence of which he has presented in a general treatise titled 'Social Systems—Outline of a General Theory'.[1]

A former pupil of Parsons, Luhmann, purposes to supersede Parsons in the same way as Parsons tried to supersede Durkheim and Weber. While they investigated cultural and social integration on the basis of their European experience, Parsons endeavoured to interpret the socio-cultural integration obtained in the USA as the more general experience. For instance, in the US 'national solidarity' was transformed into a 'supra-national consensus', and the Protestant ethics into a more generalized value pattern founding the 'societal community'. Luhmann, in turn, aims at the understanding of world society through the elaboration of still more general conceptions than those offered by Parsons.

He also attempts to ground social interaction in a way different from that of Parsons' 'theory of action', which he considers unsatisfactory. To improve upon it, he finds it necessary to adopt the basic concepts of 'General Systems Theory' and their epistemological derivations or presuppositions. Thus, Cassirer's *Substance and Function* is helpful, but even more so Whitehead and the Pragmatist movement, owing to their preoccupation with Becoming.

1. *Soziale Systeme—Grundriss einer allgemeinen Theorie* (1984). In the following, all translations are mine.

2. Adherence to 'General Systems Theory'

Luhmann then interprets social life in terms of what is known as 'general systems theory', a conception initiated in the 1930's by the biologist L. von Bertalanffy and developed further by an array of thinkers and researchers. It differs from the system concept inherited from Antiquity and its concern with wholes and parts, through being based upon the difference between *system* and *environment*.[2] This relation is one of degrees of complexity. The environment is more complex than the system, and the system endeavours to reduce its complex relation to the environment and to transform it from *un*determined to determined complexity. This comes about through selections among indefinitely many possibilities. The relation between system and environment is fundamentally *contingent*, since other selections are always possible.

This is one main reason why Luhmann has couched his doctrine in terms of general systems theory. Another bears on what he calls the second 'paradigma shift' within this way of thinking, that is, the transition to concern with such systems as have a relation to themselves, that is, are *self-referential* and self-producing (*autopoetic*) in the strong sense of referring to its own reproducing activity. This is a more complex topic than the former topic of open and closed systems, since it permits notions like self-description, self-observation, self-simplification, etc. Such relationships make untenable the subject-object epistemology, and for that reason, also, the notion of self-referential system recommends itself, since social relations and social life very often involve reflection upon itself.

Luhmann, of course, is aware that what is called transcendental and dialectical thought deals with self-reflection and the internal relation between subject and object. Nevertheless, he opts for another direction of thought, presumably because he will not participate in the search for the unity of all things but affirms their ultimate *difference* and *plurality*. The task is not to grasp society as a totality that unifies all contradictions, but

---

2. The biologist von Uexküll developed the conception that each species has its specific environment (Umwelt) to which it responds and adapts, and which consists of the selections performed by each species (the bee and the dog have different environments, since they perceive and react to different 'stimuli'). The distinction between system and environment generalizes this insight.

as a differentiated, complex system which of necessity can be interpreted in many different ways, as basically contingent and nevertheless continually reproducing itself.

Self-referential systems are said to have *temporality* (in the sense of Husserl and his followers), thereby adapting to the irreversibility of time. When such a system reproduces itself, this should not be understood as a return to or restoration of a stable position of rest (the equilibrium of neo-classical economics and Parsons' first doctrine), but as an unceasing innovation.[3]

Temporalized complex systems do not find themselves in a state of integration; on the contrary, they disintegrate all the time. Therefore, they must be 'rapid' or 'hot'.

Self-referential, complex systems are constituted through relationships of *meaning*, which is described as surplus of possibilities. This necessitates selection among possibles, and thereby connects meaning to complexity and contingency. Every intention of meaning is self-referential. Moreover, the environment of meaning systems confronts them in the form of meaning, and their limits are meaning limits.

3. The notion of communication

Communication to Luhmann is a synthesis of *information, conveyance* (Mitteilung) and *understanding* (of the message). The *difference* between information and conveyance is essential, and shows clearly the contingency and selectivity of communication. But selection is active both at the level of information, conveyance and understanding. Communication implies double contingency, and self-reference, reflexivity in both Ego and Alter, the participants. Communication, Luhmann, asserts, is only possible as self-referential process. It is not just mutual tuning in as, for instance, in dancing. It must also contain a reference to the Other and to oneself, and to the differences referred to above.

Coding unifies information and conveyance. Non-coded events are experienced as *noise*. Communication controls and tests preceding communications, and is therefore a temporal process, that is a synthesis of past, present and future. (The

---

3. 'Reproduction does not simply mean repetition of the production of the same, but reflexive production out of products.' *Soziale Systeme*, p. 79.

self-reference of basic communication should be distinguished from reflexive communication in the sense of communication about communication).

On each level—that of information, conveyance and expected understanding—success is improbable, Luhmann asserts. The evolutionary products that serve to transform this improbability into probability, he calls *media*—and mentions language, media of expansion (writing, printing and broadcasting) and generalized symbolic media (the term borrowed from Parsons), that is media that channel the most important and successful communications—examples given are truth, love, property/money, power/law, 'basic values'.

Parsons linked communication and value consensus as the basis of socio-cultural integration. Luhmann takes the opposite position, contending that if communication produced exclusively consensus, that would be self-destructive, undermining the social system's own foundations. The reason given is that mere consensus increases the risk of making errors and thereby threatens the system with decay. Consensus means redundancy, but difference is also needed.[4]

Communication is described as a state of enduring self-reproducing stimulation, but also as stimulated from outside. Communication makes sensible all kinds of disturbances and noise. It imposes the form of meaning upon disturbances, as for instance, when something is recognized as a misprint. This state of sensibility exposed the system to evolution.

The usual conception, Luhmann observes, is that talking together, oral dialogue, is the best or true form of communication. But he states that writing and printing are more communicative forms of communication, since they accentuate the difference between information and conveyance. The reason for this statement is that, to Luhmann, to communicate is to experience that one does *not* share the other's experience, but selects parts of his (her) conveyance, which in turn is selected from the (selected) information.[5]

4. *Ibid.*, p. 238.
5. The opposition to Habermas is telling: While Habermas presents himself as a UNESCO thinker, contributing to Humanity's unification through the prospect of a universal *consensus*, Luhmann affirms that communication goes on and on, breaks down and starts afresh without ever reaching, or necessarily striving for *consensus*.

A limiting case of communication is *intimacy*. A relationship is intimate in so far as more and more traits of each of the participants become important to the Other, and next to nothing is concealed. Such mutually open and near relationships are often considered as the highest or purest mode of communication, but Luhmann does not think so. On the contrary, he states that search for intimacy tends to make communication break down, since this pursuit implies the wish to annihilate the difference between those who are intimate with each other, even though this difference is essential to communication. If the striving for intimacy succeeds, it confronts what cannot be communicated. Moreover, he who seeks intimacy, will discover that the Other is unfathomable, is infinitely complex, and therefore impossible to know exhaustively.

As the clearest case of communication as conceived by Luhmann one should rather think, it seems, of what goes on in a State department, a big corporation or some research institute. Here, the flow of communication is the opposite of intimate, the messages often have no definite human being as 'sender' or 'receiver', and are transmitted through documents or other printed matter. Such organizations are constantly aware of the difference between information and conveyance, and of the fact that the members and participants only contribute to the organization's functioning by a narrowly selected part of themselves and their activity as a whole. Precisely for this reason, the organization should not be thought of as a 'machine', since it has to reflect all the time upon itself, its self-reflection being necessary to its perpetuation (staff-meetings, evaluations, discussions in the internal journal, etc.).

4. Social systems' self-reference

The general conception of a social system proffered by Luhmann goes like this: A system of communication is constituted through some code, which structures what goes on in terms of the opposition between meaning and the meaningless. Within the realm of the meaningful there are as a rule a host of possible choices and combinations, between which selections are made, and have to be made, lest the system shall dissolve. Contrary to Parsons' assumption, Luhmann denies that a communicative system has inertia: being no substance, but a process, it must continue itself through continual activity.

Moreover, this activity is self-referential, in the sense that it entails a reference to the difference between the system and its environment. This kind of reflexivity acts in a variety of ways, as self-observation, self-description and so on. Evolutionarily, the invention of writing and printing has made possible a permanent self-commenting activity of a social system. Observing and acting have been differentiated to an unprecedented extent. This self-reference also implies the recognition of the self-reference of social systems in the system's environment—which is to say that reflexivity is no accidental trait of the social system, but essential to it.

One consequence of self-reference is the tendency to proliferation of new possibilities of selecting, that is, of alternative actions which will serve as well or better than those which tend to be performed as present. In other words, the unceasing search for *functional substitutes* is inherent in a self-referential system's evolution.

Another consequence of reflexivity is that all planning within a social system is insufficient because it can be observed by the system itself and be counteracted. This leads to planning of planning, to reflexive planning, to 'hyper-games' and 'meta-games' between planners and those who are included in the plans.[6]

Conflicts are immensely frequent in social systems, and in most cases short-lived and unimportant ('bagatelles'). To interpret conflict as a possible outcome of deviant behaviour or as an essential source of evolutionary change, is therefore misplaced. Instead, Luhmann thinks of conflicts and contradictions as an 'immunity system': They contribute to reproducing a sufficient number and variety of social systems, corresponding to society's level of evolution. When this is not achieved on the basis of expectation structures, conflicts arise instead.

5. A-centric world

Luhmann's doctrine offers itself as an interpretation of a social life where nothing is unconditional ('absolute'); there are no

6. 'In hyper-complex societies the exposition of the system in the system will be experienced as contingent,' (*Ibid.,* p. 638).

ultimate values, norms, truths, adherences, allegiances. There are always functional equivalents. The world is wide; outside Verona there are other cities with other customs and mores, other beliefs and convictions. Everything is contingent upon something else, and hence every social system floats in air, so to speak, without having its roots deep in the ground, without any anchorage. Luhmann wants to show that we can do without such metaphors, so dear to the Conservatives and Sociologists. The world is a-centric, and there is no point of view on all the points of view, no ultra-perspective from which it can be described in a true way. There can be no univocal localization and imputation of any item in the world, since everything that appears, is always at the same time belonging to one system and to the environment of other systems.[7] This is the basic relativity of perspectives.

In this sense, Luhmann's doctrine is contrary to Einstein's. Einstein through his general theory found a solution to the question of how an absolute description could be given of what appeared as relative; his solution is an 'invariance' theory. Luhmann, however, conceives of an absolutely relativity of the social world.

The task is to show how, by sufficient generality, world society and all other social systems can be understood, in spite of, or (of course) rather because of, this contingency and relativity, which comprises at least features of what Luhmann terms 'modernity' or 'modern society'.

Society is world society.[8] As such it is never threatened by disintegration, since it somehow always reproduces itself. World society tends towards ever more complexity, and thereby its relation to the infinitely complex environment becomes more complex: Society tries to transform ever more undetermined complexity into determined complexity. Reduction of complexity and increasing complexity are accompanying processes.

To understand world society means to renounce the conception of Reason and Rationality inherited from the time of Descartes and Locke; society cannot be 'rational' in the sense of reflecting upon the unity of difference, or reinternalizing its

---

7. *Ibid.*, p. 243.
8. *Ibid.*, p. 585.

effect upon its environment, since that would lead to insuperable difficulties.[9] On the other hand, society does not have to solve this impossible task in order to survive; evolution suffices. (Here, the Pragmatist leaning of Luhmann is especially visible.) To understand that this rationality is nothing but a system's most extreme pretension is to be truly rational. This entails that sociology's pretension to be an encompassing conception of society as a whole cannot be upheld. On the contrary, sociology is itself a social system in society, as such it is self-referential, and as a 'sub-system of a sub-system of a sub-system of society', of trifling importance for society as a whole. The dream of the Sociologist King should be shelved.

6. Tendency of social evolution: from the stratified to the functional

There is one great evolutionary tendency: that towards ever greater complexity and corresponding *differentiation*. This takes the form of a process from *stratification* to *functional* differentiation. 'Functional' refers not merely to that which solves or accomplishes a task, but also and above all to that which has an *alternative*. The 'functional method is ultimately a comparative method ...'[10] A functional society abounds with alternatives, functional equivalents.[11] This abundance is a specification of 'the general systems theory''s notion of redundancy. Every message must have both sufficient redundancy and noise. Hence, every society must produce itself by both innovations and redundancies, a multitude of equivalent solutions and means. A functional orientation engenders redundancy, and thus security.[12]

Stratified societies interpret themselves in terms of 'substances' and 'subjects', while functionally differentiated societies interpret themselves in terms of processes and events. There do

9. 'Above all is missing a societal sub-system which perceives the environmental inter-dependances. Such a thing cannot exist, in a society of functional differentiation, since that would mean that society appears once more in society. Modern society's principle of differentiation makes the question of rationality more pressing—and at the same time more unsolvable.' *Ibid.*, p. 645.
10. *Ibid.*, p. 85.
11. While Kolakowski wrote of 'Man without an Alternative', Luhmann affirms the opposite: In modern society, there are always alternatives, the 'semantic of alternative' is part of the modern code.
12. *Ibid.*, p. 406.

not exist 'elements' in any external relation to the systems to which they belong. System and element are given at one stroke.

In stratified societies there is a consecutive reference to something *alien (Fremdreferenz)* to Nature, God, etc.; in functionally differentiated societies it becomes necessary to substitute for it a consecutive *self*-reference.

Within the economic this goes on through communicative use of *money*. The elementary autopoetic process is payment, which as such is nothing else than making possible another payment. Through payments the economic system is a closed—self-referential—system, but at the same time open. 'A fully monetarised economy is an outstanding example of a system that is at once closed and open.'[13]

In the political system *power* cannot act in a strictly similar way, since use of power is not in itself a political event. The unity of the system comes about through a self-description, in order to obtain a reference point. The concept of the State fulfils this function. 'The State is the self-description of the political system.' It makes possible the closed self-reference that in the economy is assured by money.

In the educational system it is still more difficult to arrive at a generalized medium of communication. This is because education aims not only at communication, but also at changing those who are educated. In this case, self-reference arises through the fact that learning very often is also learning to learn. The consecutive self-reference of education is expressed through the concept of *cultivation (Bildung)*.

In German attempts were undertaken to unite these three self-descriptive concepts through the concept of the *Kulturstaat* (Fichte, Humboldt, List, etc.), but these efforts failed. Functional differentiation was already a fact. The consequence is that there is no longer a point of view from which the State or society, the whole, can be looked at in a correct way. This corroborates an earlier proposition, according to which the world is a-centric.

7. *Against the primacy of utility and the economic*

Luhmann rejects the primacy of utility in communication systems on two grounds: In the first place, because social systems

13. *Ibid.,* p. 626f.

do not come into being for reasons of utility; in the second place, because of the social world's differentiation and a-centricity.

a) The first tenet is dealt with by scrutinizing Parsons' account of how a social system emerges. Taking as the point of departure the undertermined relation between Ego and Alter, both of which are contingent upon each other, Parsons asks how this relationship can be given a direction instead of remaining an empty circle. The answer given is that this comes about through the existing of a value consensus and a shared symbolic system (or 'code' in Luhmann's language). Luhmann objects that this answer begs the question, since it refers to an already established social order ('tradition') which has been internalized during infancy; the constitution of sociality is displaced towards the past and therefore remains as unintelligible as before.

Luhmann proposes a different solution which exploits temporality: The first participant makes a tentative advance towards the Other, and waits to see if the Other accepts the suggested definition of situation. If an acceptance takes place, a step-by-step construction of a communication system is feasible whereby uncertainty and contingency are reduced.[14]

Ab origo, two 'black boxes', i.e. two psychic systems, confront each other. Since they are not transparent to each other, they cannot predict and control each other, and precisely this conditions the emergency of the social system. The two black boxes, both self-referential systems, observe each other and attempt to influence each other, in order to reduce uncertainty and complexity, while presupposing that the other is doing the same as oneself.

While a social system according to Parsons is constituted by a fundamental unity of the members of the system, by fundamental consensus and reciprocal role-expectations, Luhmann affirms the opposite: a social system is constituted by the mutual uncertainty and unpredictability of its 'elements'. It gives no basic trust; it only reduces each participant's own uncertainty through the structuring of expectations about others and the environment. In this way, a relative transparency is obtained, but haunted by the experience of its contingency—it could have been otherwise.

14. 'In the light of this beginning, every step that follows is an act with contingency-reducing, determining effect.' (*Ibid.*, p. 150).

Pure double contingency means a completely undetermined situation which, since experienced as such, acts as *auto-catalysis*: The undeterminacy and its unrest stimulates the constitution of sociality. The tautological structure of pure double contingency acts as a drive to *de*-tautologize the situation, make it more determinate. When both Ego and Alter experience that the Other experiences this situation as unstable and even unbearable, they become ready to constitute an emergent social system, to overcome the 'anxiety threshold'.[15]

During this process of constitution, Luhmann states, the pursuit of one's own utility cannot be basic or initial for the participants. When a social system is in the making, selfishness comes next to the preoccupation with whether one's activity will be useful or harmful to one's communication *partner*.[16] In other words, one is primarily eager to contribute to the emergence of a communication system, to reduce the impossibility of communication. Questions as to whether I gain or lose from participating in the communication system can only come to mind afterwards; they are derived questions, and are not posed in the nascent state of communicating.

b) The second tenet is defended in a more implicit way by Luhmann. He speaks of 'calculation of costs'[17] as a code, or a 'semantic' which functions like an 'immunity system'. The notion of cost warns against certain undertakings, and Luhmann remarks that the Liberal belief that cost calculation suffices to integrate society implies an overestimation of the function of society's immunity system. This means that (Liberal) economics are denied prime importance.

He also touches upon the 'semantic of competition', and points out that the notion of competition presupposes a differential relation, not only to exchange, but also to cooperation and communication (the competitors do not have to communicate with each other). Interpreting competition (and non-competition, respectively) in terms of its immunity function, Luhmann asserts that it does not have prime significance for society. His reason is that the semantic of competition presupposes 'a semantic of unity', more precisely, the unity of an autopoetic

15. *Ibid.,* p. 179.
16. *Ibid.,* p. 169.
17. *Ibid.,* pp. 519–20.

system, which, for its part, does *not* depend upon competition for its self-reproduction to continue.[18]

There is also another reason for denying the economy primacy (albeit not mentioned explicitly by Luhmann)—the world's a-centricity. If the world has no centre, no institution can be primary in relation to any other, since any rank-order must presuppose a hierarchy of goals and values common to all participants and systems of society. But hierarchy pertains to stratified society, not to modern, functional society.

8. Against the primacy of the Individual and the Collective
Perhaps the most decisive proposition within Luhmann's doctrine is that the individual human being is not part of any social system, but belongs to his environment. This has far-reaching consequences, since it excludes all notions of the individual as expressive of his (her) society, or society as somehow constituted by individuals as the 'substance' of society. Instead, the relation between (wo)man and society is designated as one of interpenetration, which means that both kinds of system place their complexity at the disposal of the other's self-construction. This concept purports to replace not only the doctrines of Natural Right, but also sociological doctrines of roles, needs and socialization. The Aristotelian notion of *zoon politikon* or *animal sociale* can be dispensed with in the attempts to understand how the human being is linked to a social order. Instead, *meaning* is pointed to as that which makes possible the interpretation of physical and social systems while at the same time their autopoiesis is preserved.[19]

This stance is meant to transcend both (individualist) Liberal thought and (collectivist) Sociology. On the one hand, the individual agent has no ontological or epistemological primacy, in the sense that social events and relations can be ultimately reduced, traced back to, singular human acts. Moreover, human acts can never be imputed solely to individual agents. Most

18. 'But an immunity system can at least develop forms wherein the *unity* of the system as *self-reproduction* continues, and it can do so even if future and competition, utility and consensus remain unattainable as communication.' *Ibid.*, p. 524.
19. 'Meaning makes possible consciousness's understanding and production of itself during communication about (auf) the participants' consciousness. The concept of meaning, thus, replaces the concept of *animal sociale.' Ibid.*, p. 297.

often, acts are understandable and predictable by reference to their social contexts. Nevertheless, in everyday life acts are imputed to individuals, and this fact should be accounted for. Luhmann offers the following explanation:

Communication cannot be observed directly, but only inferred; in order to be observed or subject to self-observation. a communication system must be interpreted as an action system. This is Luhmann's answer to the question of how individuals' actions are related to social systems: Acts can never be imputed solely to individual agents, Acts are mostly understandable and predictable from understanding of the social context. When actions in everyday life nevertheless are imputed to individuals, this can be interpreted as expressive of the need for reduction of complexity. To reduce communication to action facilitates the temporal a-symmetricalization, that is, the giving of a direction in time to the communication flow.

Thus, social systems are constituted by a temporal flow of communication, and not by actions. But the imputation of actions to agents is the social system's simplest form of self-description.

On the other hand, this also, as Luhmann says, bids farewell to all the 'mythologies of Gemeinschaft', if this latter term is taken to mean partial fusion of psychical and social system.

For that would contradict the very concept of interpenetration, which expresses their difference. Likewise, Durkheim's conception of solidarity is re-interpreted by the concepts of inclusion and exclusion: Especially when human beings participate in a social system through co-operation, they must distinguish themselves, in order to know who contributes what. Their inclusion in the social systems entails mutual exclusion, and this is achieved through the process called 'individualization'.[20]

To drop the notion of the individual agent as a substance is very hard, and it is equally difficult to drop the notion of the social whole as collectivity *sui generis* in the substantial sense. But modern society is functional in the above-mentioned double

---

20. 'Therefore, it is in principle wrong to suppose that individuals are better or at any rate more directly observable than social systems.' *Ibid.,* p. 347, and: 'The social can never be entirely reduced to individual consciousness.' (*Ibid.,* p. 594).

sense. Therefore, Luhmann seems to carry on the efforts of Simmel to understand modernity. Modern individuals, he said, are fragmented, owing to the multitude of disconnected contexts within which they appear.

9. Concluding comments

To show where and how Luhmann breaks with the conceptions discussed in Part One may be superfluous, since he has himself been at pains to point to all the ruptures.

At the risk of being repetitious, I shall nevertheless resume his basic contentions: The Liberal notion of the Individual as an irreducible ontological entity (a 'substance') is discarded. Individual experience is not the stuff social life is made of; social systems *qua* self-referential communication constitute an ontological realm of their own, where the social and the psychic mutually penetrate each other while maintaining their difference.

The Liberal notion of utility is also discarded as fundamental for the understanding of social systems. Communication seeks first and foremost to keep itself going on, to produce meaning out of the meaningless, which implies that considerations of utility must take second place. The emergence of a specific economic system is contingent upon its relation to other non-economic subsystems, and cannot claim to be primary or fundamental.

Sapping the foundations of Liberal thought, Luhmann at the same time invalidates the doctrines of social integration and historico-dialectical thought. In so far as their essence is to be a riposte to Liberal thought, they lose their raison d'être when he deprives them of their adversary. He invites us, as it were, to convert to a new conception of the world where all social systems are aware that they are part of each other's environment, that their experience of the world is partial and different from the others, that the only universal truth is that there is no universal truth to be attained through increasing consensus, and that our experience of other human beings must of necessity be selective. Perhaps this is another neo-anarchy doctrine; perhaps it leads to the opposite or to complete indifference, perhaps his doctrine is nothing more than an intellectual game—for me, at least, it is too early to pass judgement.

Postscript

These, to my knowledge, are the main attempts to get beyond or elude the tenets and tensions described and discussed in Part One. Being *avant garde*, that is, unguarded and undefended by authority or common sense, they may seem risky, odd or conspicuous. And surely, they cannot all be right; they may even all be wrong, but since all of them are so little tried out and worked out, one cannot yet know. Confronting such unusual thoughts, it is difficult to give good reasons for the attitude one takes towards them; one's stance will to a great extent be the outcome of arbitrary decision. For my part, I am especially attracted by two of the resumed conceptions:

In the first place, Touraine's research on social movements, and his general conception of a social movement able to act as a historic subject, easily arouse the attention of one who is deeply attached to Historico-dialectic thought. For even though the last decade's development has shown beyond doubt that we in the West are still living under a capitalist mode of production, the weakness and decay of the traditional wage-labour class and its movements make the prospects suggested by Touraine look very sensible and promising.

In the second place, the possibilities of Sartrean (or other Husserlian) phenomenology seem to me not at all exhausted. As an indication, I shall comment on the following occurrence: Recently, a sudden feud developed concerning an interview-based inquiry, posing to the Norwegian population the question: 'Are you lonely?' Some sociologists found this rather laughable, but their ridicule provoked the anger of people committed to Social research: To deride such a 'survey', they exhorted, implied rejecting the possibility of well-founded knowledge of the social world. The prohibition of laughter seldom assures one of the truth of the prohibiter's conception. Reflecting on the disagreement, the core seems to be this: To ask whether somebody is lonely, involves a tacit promise to help or love the person asked, if the answer turns out to be in the affirmative. That is why such a question is 'intimate', and why it is tactless for a stranger to pose it. Now, we cannot help or love an indefinite number of human beings, and therefore we cannot in the full sense of the act pose the question about loneliness to an infinite number of people. On the other hand, those who receive this question in the context of Social research will usually be aware that the one who asks, is not prepared to help or love if the respondent declares him (her)self to be lonely. The meaning of the answer does not imply that the respondent expects any intent to help or love on the part of those who pose the question. This implies, at the very least, that the meaning of a proposition such as 'x % of the Norwegian population are lonely' is uncertain.

Generally, it is far from clarified what it means to know something about a manifold of human beings; in some cases, such knowledge is easy, in others, it is doubtful or even impossible. In this realm, delusions abound; to expose them and depose of them is a task which is far from complete, and for which reflection of the kind performed by Sartre, seems very appropriate.

Detailed Table of Contents

Index of Names